REGIONAL STRUCTURE, PROCESSES AND PATTERNS OF DEVELOPMENT

Regional Structure, Processes and Patterns of Development

A case study of the Chota Nagpur Region

Savita Sinha

CONCEPT PUBLISHING COMPANY, NEW DELHI

The Indian Council of Social Science Research gave the financial support towards the publication of this work. However, the responsibility for the contents of the bookfacts, opinions, conclusions, etc.are entirely that of the author and not of the ICSSR.

First Published 1988

Savita **Sinha** (*b.* 1949)

Published by
Naurang Rai
Concept Publishing Company
H-13, Bali Nagar
NEW DELHI-110015 (India)

Printed at
New Gian Offset Printers
495, Shahzada Bagh
NEW DELHI-110035 (India)

Preface

It is rather astonishing to find that the region of Chota Nagpur despite its vast mineral and forest wealth and huge investments in industries has not developed to the extent it should have. The development is rather imbalanced and sporadic. Consequently, I got interested in investigating inherent weaknesses underlying the restricted development of the region. Although there has been a considerable amount of work on different facets of the region, one is struck by the paucity of a comprehensive micro-level study of the region to provide insights into the problems of development.

The research aims at analysing different processes and patterns of development in the region of Chota Nagpur at the District as well as Block levels. The book is divided into six chapters. Chapter One introduces the theoretical and methodological dimension. Chapter Two examines the regional structure in terms of physical landscape, landuse and cropping patterns, forest, mineral and water resources as also demographic characteristics of the human resource. Processes and patterns of industrialisation and urbanisation are analysed in Chapters Three and Four respectively, against the background of regional structure, bringing out the factors responsible for the polarised growth. In Chapter Five, the processes and patterns of functional organisation of settlements have been discussed. Large rural and urban settlements have been treated as parts of a system of settlements arranged in a hierarchical order with a view to give an adequate focus on an integrated approach to planning process. The analysis reveals a weak spatial relation among the nodal centres which accentuates the polarisation of development. On the basis of the aforesaid analysis, a ninefold typology of development of the 152 Development Blocks of the region have been identified. Chapter Six summarises the findings and synthesises the emerging patterns and process of development/underdevelopment. It is hoped that the book will help in enriching knowledge about the region and provide a framework for future planning and development.

I wish to express my sincere thanks to Prof. L.S. Bhat, Indian Statistical Institute and Prof. Anil Kumar, Bhagalpur University for their invaluable comments.

I gratefully acknowledge the financial support received from the NCERT for the cartographic work and the ICSSR for the publication of this work.

New Delhi
31 January, 1987

Savita Sinha

Contents

List of Tables

List of Figures

ONE

Introduction

REGIONAL DEVELOPMENT - A SPATIAL VIEW

Regional Development is relatively a new field in geographical research. It is concerned mainly with spatial aspects of development, which otherwise has a sectoral and temporal dimensions as in a national plan. While recognising the relevance and importance of the spatial dimension, the regional analysts have also used a system of sub-national area units as regions. A region is not an arbitrarily demarcated area, rather it is defined on the basis of its distinguishing characters. Regionalisation or the method of delineating regions would depend on the objective of the study. In regional development studies, regions are identified from the development planning purposes as such the resource potential of the region, the degree of their utilisation and associated problems form the basis for their identification. Usually politico-administrative units provide the multi-regional framework for national development programmes, the choice of such units again depends on the purpose and the spatial nature of the attributes involved.

Development is a difficult word to be defined in a true sense because it means expansion in material as well as nonmaterial things. Measurement of nonmaterial things is impossible so it has been left out in our scientific studies. By development, we refer to economic and social aspects of human life only which could be measured in some way (Isard, 1975, pp. 373-374).

'Development', 'Growth' and 'Progress' are usually used as synonyms and mean increase or expansion, but in economic development literature, these are used as different concepts. Boudeville (1966, pp. 168-169) defines growth as "set of increases in qualities produced"; development as "growth plus a favourable change in production technique and in consumer behaviour" and progress as "development plus a diminution of social tension between groups within a society". Development is thus a qualitative change together with the quantitative expansion.

The social aspects of development has often been ignored in the literature of economic development, but these two aspects of development are interrelated and interdependent. Barkin (1972, p. 84) defines development as "... a dual process of enrichment and structural change..." and recognises "... its counterpart in the human level ... which also involves enrichment and structural change".

Thus development could be explained as economic and social growth tied up with "introduction and diffusion of successive waves of innovations ... in geographical space" (Hermansen, 1972 p. 6) bringing about a 'structural transformation of the social systems' (Friedmann, 1969). On the basis of the various definitions put forward, it can be stated that development is a complex process having four main components - economic, social, cultural and politico - administrative (Chandrashekhar and Sundaram, 1969). Though the pattern and pace of development is greatly influenced by the laws of economics and practical politics, these systems "operate within an environmental and demographic framework which they do not themselves create" (Hoyle, 1974, pp. 19-20). Resources - natural as well as human - and technical knowhow for their exploitation are distributed over space unevenly. Human effort is to allocate these resources efficiently among alternative uses through an economic system which involves basically three activities, i.e. production, consumption and exchange. These economic activities are regulated by the demand and supply, which too have a spatial component. For any given goods there will generally be a spatial variation between the places at which it is demanded and the points of supply. Thus an economic system has a spatial dimension and, therefore, it is significant in regional development studies. It is this view point which distinguishes a geographer's approach to regional analysis from an economist's. Variations in the level of development are observed not only in space but through passage of time also. Friedmann (1966) has argued that regional development takes place in an orderly fashion during which spatial sub-systems change their boundaries and rearrange themselves from relatively isolated regional enclaves to well integrated and functionally inter-dependent system of cities. Development patterns can, therefore, be explained within a spatio-temporal framework. Here the principles of spatial organisation state vividly that the development process takes place around a system of nodal centres and their tributary areas and as the tempo of development increases the system of nodal centres and their tributary areas becomes increasingly complex. This is a sign of regional specialisation and emergence of economic regions.

Regional variations in the level of development has been a growing concern for the people all over the world, who are interested in removing disparities between the regions or at least minimising it for improvement of the living conditions of the society. It was felt that development being a complex process involves many issues which cannot be understood properly without a multi-disciplinary approach. This brought about a change in the trend of the research work being undertaken in traditional social sciences and hence regional science emerged as a seperate branch of social sciences. It is an integrated (multi-disciplinary) analysis of the various factors (political, social, economical, cultural and psychological) affecting the development of a meaningful region or system of regions and provides a "systematic study of the time-space patterns of systems and the ways in which social problems associated with these patterns can be effectively attacked and resolved" (Isard, 1975, p. 5) through methods of urban and regional analysis. Regional science has influenced considerably the conceptual framework and methods of geographical research particularly in economic geography. It is a common feeling that regional science has "stimulated, prodded and pushed methodological development in geography" (Berry and Hankins, 1963, p. 15) and has "encouraged economic geographers to be more interested in theories of location and economic growth and in their application" (Britton, 1967, p. 2).

APPROACHES TO REGIONAL ANALYSIS

Various concepts and theories have been put forward to examine the anatomy of regions in order to understand the structure and process of regional development. These theories may be grouped under two heads: non-spatial economic theories and theories of spatial development. Studies are being conducted to analyse inter-regional and intra-regional variations.

An inter-regional approach seeks to explain the differences between the regions, taking regions as a whole. This approach is concerned mainly with growth and change and depends heavily on economic concepts. Development of regional accounts presents a comprehensive picture of the regional economic structure. It provides a detailed picture of the inter-relationships of the major sectors of the regional economy and also provides an insight into regional variations and the underlying factors responsible for them. In recent years, inter-industry relationships in the form of an input-output table, has grown into one of the most widely accepted methods of describing the industrial structure of an economy and linked with other techniques, of predicting changes in that structure. However, regional input-output table presents a comprehensive and ordered picture of the regional economy in a limited way and because of its highly aggregated nature of the activities it becomes difficult to relate the intersectoral relationship to the spatial interaction of activities.

Economic structure of the region is basically responsible for the variations in the level of development between regions. Regional accounts and the input-output tables provide a descriptive framework of this structure assuming regions to be static which in fact are not. Over the years, economic models have developed which are concerned with the analysis of the regional economy as a whole. There are a series of economic theories collectively known as the regional multiplier theories which seek to explain these changes in the economic structure stressing the inter-relationships among sectors within the regional economy. These take into consideration the spread of impulses originating in any one sector to all other sectors either directly or indirectly. The economic base theory is the most simple and therefore looks attractive. It relates changes in total regional employment to changes in basic employment. But the theory has several conceptual and technical problems especially the problem of identifying the basic/non-basic components. Inter-regional trade multipliers are more complex. This multiplier, calculated in money terms, introduces relevant import, savings and taxation factors and throws interesting light on large-scale regional multiplier variation. It is also an aggregated approach abstracting from specific industries and inter-industry linkages. The input-output table can also be used for predictive purposes besides its descriptive role, but a number of procedures and basic assumptions are involved. An early and well-known study is on the impact of the establishment of an Iron and Steel Mill in the Greater New York - Philadelphia industrial region (Isard and Kuenne, 1953, pp. 289-301). Data problems are formidable and yet it is one of the most valuable methods of regional analysis.

Short-run changes are less marked and almost all regions experience it. But the long-run growth rate of regions usually measured in terms of output and/or income varies widely. It is generally accepted that regional growth may result from either endogenous or exogenous determinants or a combination of both. Important internal determinants are the factors of production such as land, labour and capital while the major external determinant is the level of demand for region's commodities from areas outside the region. The complexity of this variety of factors, makes the formulation of a single, generally accepted and comprehensive regional growth theory very difficult. Sector theory is the simplest regional growth theory which states that a rise in per capita income in different areas at different times is accompanied by a resource reallocation with a decline in the proportion of labour force from primary to secondary and to tertiary sectors. This specialisation provides main dynamism to regional growth. The main criticism of the theory is to the rigid sequence of primary-secondary-tertiary shift. A more recent approach to regional growth explanation is via the use of macro-economic models which are highly aggregated. These theories emphasise on the internal productive capacity of a region and the factors like capital, labour, natural resources and technical progress which influence them. But regional growth is also influenced by external demand factors in the form of the flows of trade and information. The export base theory, the inter-regional resource allocation models, and national economic growth models have been adopted in an explanation of the external determinants of regional growth. Export base theory is an application of the short-run static economic base model to long-run dynamic growth situations. The inter-regional resource allocation models assume that factors of production especially labour and capital will flow from low rewarding regions to high rewarding regions. National economic growth models explain rates of growth in terms of exogenous demand factors like investment and exports. All these theories are limited by one-sided approach and high level of aggregation. In this situation, the industrial structure analysis (Leser, 1951; Perloff, et.al. 1960; Hemming, 1963; Brown, 1968; Stilwell, 1969) has enjoyed popularity. Although not a growth theory, it does complement the other more formal theories emphasising the relationship between industrial structure and regional growth, and separating out the internal and external elements of that growth. Inspite of its weakness, this approach is of considerable practical value in examining variations in regional growth. The centre-periphery theories (Hirschman, 1958; Myrdal, 1957; Friedmann, 1966) with their emphasis on cumulative causation and divergent regional growth provide a valuable insight into the growth process bringing together many of the elements of the other theories. This concept of cumulative causation suggests that inter-regional differences widen as the process is cumulative and the prosperous regions will be more prosperous by attracting more goods, capital and skilled labour.

Thus inter-regional approach tells us a great deal about the inks between regions in the national economy. But it does not say anything about what happens within regions. Moreover, implicit in this is the assumption that regions are homogeneous, a necessary assumption if we wish to treat the parameters of inter-regional multiplier and trade models as having stable and constant values.

Yet the most obvious feature of the space economy is its non-homogeneity and there are agglomerations in economic activity and in population distribution at given locations. Acceptance of the lack of uniformity in the space economy and its economic significance leads us to the concept of nodes. Region is composed of heterogeneous units (e.g. human population is distributed in cities, towns, villages and hamlets which form a hierarchy of settlements), but these are closely interrelated with each other functionally as is revealed in the flow phenomena. These flows do not occur evenly over space. The heaviest flows tend to polarise towards and from the dominant nodes. The functional linkages within regions can be traced from many sources: the distribution channels of retail and wholesale goods; intra-regional commodity flows; migration flows; labour catchment areas and journey-to-work patterns. The intensity of functional interaction varies directly with the size or attraction of nodes and tends to decrease with increasing distance from the higher order settlements.

Intra-regional approach helps to explain the unevenness of economic activity over space and development of hierarchy of settlements even within the regions.

Industrial location theories (Weber, 1909; Hoover, 1948; Losch, 1940; Isard, 1956; Greenhut, 1956; Smith, 1966) provide valuable insight into the economic structure of regions. The key elements in location theory - transport, labour, agglomeration and market factors set the basic parameters and thus influence the location decision no doubt; but behavioural and institutional factors also pay important roles in such decisions. There are three approaches to industrial location theory - the least cost approach, market area analysis and the profit maximisation approach. Each has something to contribute to the general body of theory, but no theory can be accepted as a single general theory for a wide variety of industries and firms. Besides, these are basically theories of the location of firms and cannot properly explain the spatial structure of regions.

Central place theory is probably the most researched and well known model of regional and spatial structure, it is also the most criticised. The notion of this theory is linked with Walter Christaller and his work on the central places of Southern Germany (1933). However, many others have worked on this concept - Dickinson (1934), Losch (1940), Berry and Garrison (1958a), Dacey (1966) and Berry (1967). The theory seeks to relate central places to their hinterlands and defines a central place as a settlement providing services for the population of its hinterland. It is purely deductive theory of a highly simplified and abstract nature and developed on the basis of very idealised assumptions. The theory relates only to the service element of regional structure, failing to explain distortions in the hierarchy caused by the location of primary and manufacturing industries which tend to group into clusters or agglomerations due to resource localisation. It is also static in its approach as it explains the existence of regional spatial structure but fails to explain how that structure has evolved and how it might change over time. Despite the theory's numerous weaknesses and criticisms, empirical studies (Smails, 1944; Brush and Bracey, 1955; Berry and Garrison, 1958b; Smails and Hartley, 1961; Carruthers, 1962; Thorpe and Rhodes, 1966; Smith, 1968) lend support to the central place hierarchies. Thus the theory provides a framework for understanding the regional spatial structure and in regional planning a hierarchical system of centres avoids duplication and waste. The application of the theory in the regional planning of some of the developing countries like Ghana (Grover and Huszar, 1964) and Israel (Jackson, 1970) has proved to be useful.

In many regions, the regular central place spatial structure tends to be rather distorted by agglomeration. Growth pole theory has been adopted not only to explain such distortions but also a policy tool in regional planning. The basic concepts and subsequent refinements and developments are to be found in the 'core' literature of Perroux (1955); Myrdal (1957); Hirschmann (1958); Boudeville (1966); Hansen (1967) and Allen and Hermansen (1968).

The basic idea of the theory is that economic activity within a region tends to agglomerate around a small number of focal points. Polarisation flows will gravitate within a region towards these focal points with a gradual reduction in the flow density by distance. With the help of minimum critical level of flow densities, a boundary may be demarcated around a focal point which can be described as the growth point. On this interpretation the spatial distribution of population can be regarded as being organised into hierarchical system of nodes and functional linkages. Stronger the nodal characteristics of the regions higher their growth rates and their levels of economic and social development are likely to be. Regional plans will be more successful if they effectively reinforce the natural nodal characteristics already in evidence in a region.

Owing to their versatility, the theory of growth poles and central places enjoyed a great popularity. But a vast confusion of terminology appears in the literature like growth poles, growth points, growth centres, and deployment poles, central places, service centres, and so on. It is, therefore, necessary to keep the distinction clear between the important terminology. The term 'growth pole' can be taken to refer to the original concept of Perroux (1955) which focusses on the development of growth poles in economic space without any specific geographical dimension, while the term 'growth centre' or 'growth point' refers to a spatial location. Some writers distinguish them on the scale basis - growth pole relating to the national scale and growth centres to the regional scale (Kuklinski, 1970).

Various writings on growth poles and growth centres suggest three economic concepts and their geographical developments:

(a) The concept of leading industries states that at the centre of growth poles are large propulsive firms which dominate other economic units. The original geographical location of such industries at certain focal points may be due to several factors - localisation of natural resources, man-made advantages (communications or existing service-based central places with infrastructure facilities) or just chance.

(b) The concept of polarisation states that rapid growth of the leading industries will lead to agglomeration economics and other economic units will be brought into the pole of growth. The economic polarisation will lead to geographical polarisation with the flow of resources and the concentration of economic activity at a limited number of centres within a region.

(c) The concept of spread-effects states that in time the dynamic propulsive qualities of growth pole radiate outwards into the surrounding space which has been termed as 'trickling down'or 'spread' effects.

These concepts taken together provide a valuable complement to central place theory in an explanation of the regional structure and spatial process of development. It is in this context that the process of regional development should be viewed as a process in functional organisation of formal spaces and system of nodes and their tributary areas would constitute the basis of development at different scales of areas and activities.

GEOGRAPHER'S APPROACH TO REGIONAL DEVELOPMENT STUDIES

The foregoing discussion on the methods of regional analysis reveals that the two approaches to regional analysis i.e. inter-regional and intra-regional analyses derive their concepts from economics and geography respectively. It is true that a substantial body of economic theories concerning the problem of development exists. But the element of space and the physical environment have been overlooked by them, whereas we know that physical space is all around us and that all developmental problems arise because of the discrepancies in the spatial distribution of various resources, activities, population and organization. Thus problem of location and space are worthy of analysis in their own right and the geographer is well equipped to delve into the locational, regional and spatial problems. Through the study of agricultural systems and industrial locations, the changing patterns of development in spatial terms could be of much help in regional planning. The geographer could apply his skill into his investigation in a more overt fashion especially through explicit formulation of hypotheses and their testing, if possible, in quantitative fashion.

REGIONAL DEVELOPMENT STUDIES IN INDIA

Regional Development study in its present form is a comparatively new area of research in India as in other parts of the world. But regions were studied by geographers much earlier. Regionalisation were based on natural factors. Besides, these studies mostly used qualitative analysis. Recent trends show that methodology has advanced rapidly and there has been a growing interest in the applicability of theories and skills for the solution of real developmental problems.

Indian studies related to aspects of regional development may be grouped under the following heads - regional surveys, regionalisation and topical studies.

Regional surveys for planning purposes have been conducted at various levels by individuals, groups of people or Government research workers for a particular region or state as units (Learmonth and Bhat, 1961; National Council of Applied Economic Research, 1962; Bhat, 1962; Joint Committee for Diagnostic Survey of the Damodar Valley Region, 1968; Planning Commission, 1969; Town and Country Planning Organisation, 1970.)

Several studies have been conducted on the regionalisation of the country and the criteria used differ from one another. Earlier studies used natural factors like physiography, soil, climate and vegetation for regionalisation as the purpose was to identify natural regions for studying regional geography (Bhat and Learmonth, 1958). Since 1940, there has been a change in the very objective of regionalisation and it has been directed towards planning (Chatterjee, 1940). Various schemes of planning regions have been suggested for specific regions or the country as a whole keeping in view the physical resource-structure of the region/regions and problems of development (Deshpande, 1948; Rao and Bhat, 1960; Planning Commission, 1965). In order to make the region more meaningful, the country has also been delineated into economic regions on the basis of production specialisation (Sengupta and Sdasyuk, 1968), economic viability and ecological balance (Town and Country Planning Organisation, 1968). A hierarchical regionalisation on the basis of inter-state migration flow presented well-defined regions displaying several aspects of inter-relationships among states (Slater, 1977).

Identification of areas having different levels of economic development is an important aspect of regional development studies. Studies have been conducted in this area using district and state level data for different parts of the country and India (Pal, 1963; Mitra, 1965; Pal and Subramaniam, 1965). Regions have also been identified on the basis of their functional linkages revealed by the commodity flow (Berry, 1966).

Topical studies include works dealing with some of the aspects of development individually or in combination with others and policies and framework for urban and regional planning.

Industrialisation is closely associated with high economic development. Location of industries is, therefore, an important factor in the process of industrialisation. Location of specific industries like cement and (Bhat and Mathur, 1967), Iron and Steel (Gidadhubli, 1966, 1967, 1968a, 1968b) in relation to national and regional development perspectives have been analysed. The trend in general has been to review the present industrial structure, problems of growth and prospects for different regions mostly in a qualitative manner.

Agriculture is another aspect of development which has been studied in terms of broad land-use and cropping pattern at different area levels.

Urban surveys have been conducted at various levels for tackling problems of development through identification of least urbanised areas and regional imbalances in urban infrastructure (Rao, 1964a; Rao, 1964b; Rao, 1969). While planning new townships, regional surveys have been conducted for an integrated development of town and its surrounding rural areas. Integrated rural-urban development approach has been followed in a number of studies (Patankar, 1968; Wanmali, 1970; Johnson,

1972; Deshpande, et. al., 1979; Mishra, et. al. 1980) because urban centres and rural communities both play crucial roles in the development process. The whole spectrum of human settlements - villages, market towns, intermediate cities and metropolises - must be strengthened and integrated into well-articulated spatial system performing specialised and diversified production, distribution, consumption and exchange functions. Location of physical and social amenities and productive activities in rural centres forms the basis of development strategy aimed at providing basic human needs to the people living in an area and also to develop the resources of the region. It is thus helpful in reinforcing a network of development centres which can counter-balance the pull of urban centres. Through these centres it is possible to transform the subsistence agricultural and rural sector into employment and income-generating elements of national economy.

In this context, multi-level planning approach has been adopted by the Government of India and plans will be prepared at national, state, district, block and village levels. Mishra and Sundaram (1980) have elaborated concepts, methods and operational procedures of multi-level planning in the Indian context.

Planning at and below district level is termed micro-level planning and these may be the first ladder of the development plans. Bhat et. al. (1976) in their study on Karnal District have emphasised on the spatial integration of human settlements and land-use and recommended for providing a three-tier pattern of central places from among the rural places. Roy and Patil (1977) formulated a manual for block-level planning for identifying rural growth centres.

Besides these studies, concepts, policies and other aspects of urban and regional planning have also found place in various publications (Mishra, 1969; Sundaram, 1977; Mishra, et. al. 1978).

Some of the important works on the Chota Nagpur region which might be relevant in the context of present study cover urban, industrial, transport and settlement aspects (Pandeya, 1970; Sinha, 1969; Singh, 1964; Prasad, 1969; Sinha, 1973). Pandeya (1970) studied the impact of industrialisation on urban growth of the Chota Nagpur region. He identified five important factors - the mining activity, forest resources, river valley projects, communication lines, and manufacturing industries which have stimulated urban growth in the region. He further opined that towns have grown rapidly attracting large rural population but they lack basic amenities. On the basis of 19 indices like education, health, electricity, drinking water and other civic amenities, he has tried to present an urban hierarchy for the region which is different from tho traditional status of towns in the census. This study may be referred to as the starting point for the urban development study of the Chota Nagpur region. Sinha (1969) in his work on industrial landscape of the highlands of Chota Nagpur discussed the industrial growth of the region and analysed the locations of different industries. Singh (1964) studied the transport pattern of the whole of South Bihar including the Chota Nagpur region. Prasad (1969) centred his work on the nature and distribution of rural settlements in the Chota Nagpur region but Sinha (1973) expanded his area of work and included both rural and urban settlements of the region. He examined the physical, economic and cultural processes for explaining settlement change. The hierarchy of urban settlements was attempted and tested against the postulates of Christaller's central place model.

As is apparent, all these studies have been oriented to different aspects of development separately and present partial picture of the region. The study by the Town and Country Planning Organisation (TCPO, 1970) on the South East Resource Region also covers the region in question and analyses the resource potential. For planning purposes, it forms the benchmark for the regional analysis. All these studies have used district level data and are thus useful for macro-regional plans but planning starts from the village and block level of the administrative divisions. We find variations in development at all levels and a study of the region from the regional angle is, therefore, stressed for the developmental studies. Keeping in view this broad objective the present study has been designed.

The study area - Chota Nagpur region - is a classic example of a geographical region which stands out as a less developed subregion of the State of Bihar. It also emerges as a less-developed part of the larger South-East Resource Region comprising parts of Bihar, Madhya Pradesh, Orissa and West Bengal. The region has marked contrast in the regional structure and processes of development. The dichotomy between markedly rural and tribal population with limited agriculture on the one hand and the locations of basic and heavy industries which are by and large the only centres of economic importance at the national level, on the other hand, is quite apparent. The spatial processes of development have thus a marked discontinuity leading to low levels of development inspite of heavy inputs on major industries. The space relations are relatively weak among the nodal settlements within while the region's external relationship through the major industrial centres is quite strong. It is against this background that salient features of selected concepts and theories related to regional development are reviewed in the foregoing pages. What follows in the study of Chota Nagpur region is an attempt to portray the spatial processes that are at work within the region, which serve to bring out the causes for underdevelopment of this region.

THE STUDY AREA

The present study relates to a part of the Bihar-Bengal industrial belt lying entirely in Bihar and forming its one of the administrative divisions known as the Chota Nagpur (Fig. 1). The Chota Nagpur region as defined for this study comprises of six districts - Hazaribagh, Giridih, Dhanbad, Ranchi, Palamau and Singhbhum and spreads over an area of 65,509 sq. kms.

Structurally, the region is a part of the Peninsular India consisting of various rock systems ranging from Pre-Cambrian to Cainozoic era. Hard crystalline archaean rocks form the base and are exposed to surface in most parts. Other rock systems are the Dharwars and the Gondwanas. Being a part of the oldest landmass on the earth, the region has passed through various phases of landscape evolution such as erosion, deposition, uplifting, faulting, and volcanic eruption. The region, therefore, displays a variety of landscapes e.g. hills and plateaus of different heights and intermontane valleys of varying width and size. Broadly speaking, the physiography of the region may be explained in terms of a series of four plateaus descending towards north, east and south from the highest 'Pat' region of the north-western Ranchi and southern Palamau, which is a continuation of the hilly tract of Madhya Pradesh. The main drainage lines follow the general slope of the region and they flow to the north, east and south. Important river basins are that of North Koel, Damodar, South Koel and Sankh.

Although, Chota Nagpur has a tropical location because of higher elevation in most parts, climate is sub-tropical. Temperature is high during mid-April to May. Region is characterised by medium rainfall and is confined to four months of the year i.e. June to September. Because of the rolling topography with impervious surface, the run-off is rapid and the soil suffers from deficiency of moisture during a greater part of the year. Soils of the region belong to Red soil group and are produced **in situ** weathering of the parent rocks like gneisses, schists and granite in most of the places. Regional variations do occur in response to physiography and parent rocks. Soils of the 'Pat' region are mainly laterites which has high bauxite content but has little productivity. Because of less moisture content in the soil and steep slope, soil erosion is very fast wherever vegeta-

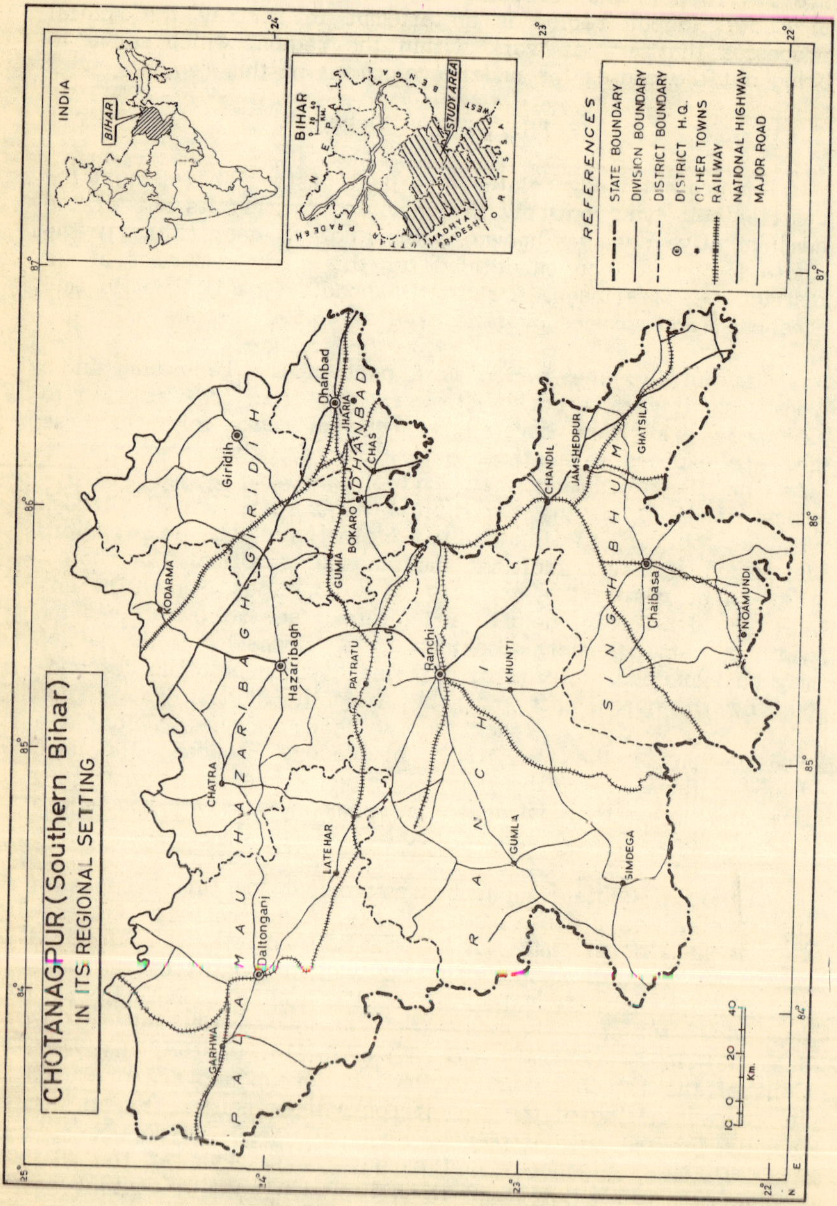
CHOTANAGPUR (Southern Bihar)
IN ITS REGIONAL SETTING
INDIA
BIHAR
BIHAR
STUDY AREA
NEPAL
WEST BENGAL
ORISSA
MADHYA PRADESH
UTTAR PRADESH
REFERENCES
STATE BOUNDARY
DIVISION BOUNDARY
DISTRICT BOUNDARY
DISTRICT H.Q.
OTHER TOWNS
RAILWAY
NATIONAL HIGHWAY
MAJOR ROAD
PALAMAU
HAZARIBAGH
GIRIDIH
DHANBAD
RANCHI
SINGHBHUM
Giridih
Dhanbad
JHARIA
CHAS
BOKARO
GUMIA
KODARMA
Hazaribagh
CHATRA
PATRATU
Ranchi
KHUNTI
LATEHAR
Daltonganj
GARHWA
GUMLA
SIMDEGA
CHANDIL
JAMSHEDPUR
GHATSILA
Chaibasa
NOAMUNDI
Km.

Fig. 1

tion cover has been destroyed.

Much dissected topography and poor quality lateritic soil have made agriculture difficult in the uplands. River valleys and plains with loamy soil are better suited for agriculture and productivity in these parts can be enhanced with scientific management.

The region is a treasury of valuable minerals like coal, iron-ore, manganese, limestone, bauxite and mica. Availability of all essential minerals for heavy industries has favoured the start of a number of large-scale public and private sector enterprises. Still the region exports majority of its mineral produce to other parts of the country. Besides minerals, forests are the other important resources of the Chota Nagpur. Spreading over the large parts of Ranchi, Singhbhum, Palamau and Hazaribagh, they contribute a maior part of the timber and lac production of the State.

Density of population is low compared to Bihar plains. According to 1971 census, the region had 11 million population with a density of 168 persons per sq. km. compared to 324 persons per sq. km. for Bihar. Of the total population, 9 million (82%) live in 18,901 rural settlements while 2 million (18%) live in 85 towns. The small rural settlements with a population of less than 2000 persons dominate the region which is obvious from the fact that more than 96 per cent of settlements are in this category and they contain more than 81 per cent of population. On the other hand, about 41 per cent of urban population is concentrated only in 7 large urban centres in the size-range of more than 50,000 population.

On the basis of structure, physiography, climate, soil, resource base and their development patterns, it can be said that the Chota Nagpur has altogether different land form, soil type, ecological condition, economic potentiality and population characteristics which make it a distinct areal unit.

But an intra-regional analysis reveals marked differences in the industrial, urban and economic growth. Dhanbad and Palamau districts present two extremes within the region. With an area of 2994 sq. km. Dhanbad is the smallest district in size in the region but has the highest number of towns (26 out of the total number of 85 towns) and the highest density of population i.e. 490 persons per sq. km. which is higher than the state average too. This is the only district in the region as well as the State which is highly urbanised with approximately 44% of urban population engaged in nonagricultural activities. Per Capita income is also the highest in the region (Rs. 882). Palamau, on the other hand, with an area of 12,677 sq. kms. has the lowest density of population (119 persons per sq. km.) in the region. Only 5 per cent of its total population is urban distributed in five towns. Per Capita income is also the lowest in the region with Rs. 140/-. These are the paradoxes in a situation of extensive underdevelopment both vertically and horizontally.

Region's salient features and patterns of economic development are similar to those of its neighbouring districts in Madhya Pradesh, West Bengal, and Orissa. On this basis, it forms a part of the South-East Resource Region as conceived by the Town and Country Planning Organisation, Government of India for the regional planning purposes which includes 9 districts of Madhya Pradesh, 6 districts of Bihar (all six districts of the Chota Nagpur division), 9 districts of Orissa and 2 districts of West Bengal.

Within this framework, the Chota Nagpur region has been selected for a detailed study of the intra-regional variations in development patterns and the spatial organisation of settlements so that the finding could be used in the planning for a balanced development of the region.

DESIGN OF THE STUDY

The study is attempted at two area levels, i.e. at the district and block levels. The district level study includes the analysis of the resource base - natural and human, industrial and urban growth, spatial patterns of settlements, functions and the hierarchic nature of the space relations, for settlements of more than 2000 population. It provides the framework of regional study at the macro-level and helps to identify the broad patterns of region's resources and development. Block-level study supplements to this knowledge further details at the micro-level and thus helps to assess the intricate nature of development taking place within the region.

The physical landscape and its spatial variations, land-use patterns, cropping patterns, crop yields, forest resources, mineral resources, water resources, demographic characteristics of the human resources provide some clues to the variations in the land-use structure, productivity, development of nodal centres within the region at the district and block levels. Process and patterns of industrial development have been analysed with references to (a) growth and change of manufacturing industry during pre and post-independence period; (b) location pattern of major industry groups on the basis of distribution of industrial units by type and size and their employment; and (c) agglomeration of economy and nodality. An attempt has been made to analyse the scale and pace of urbanisation through the decennial changes in population of size ranges of towns beginning from 1901. Spatial patterns of settlements have been analysed at the block level and the hierarchic nature of the space relations for settlements of more than 2000 population has been worked out on the basis of demographic, economic and social characteristics. These studies together help in synthesising the spatial development pattern at and below district level in the region and evolving strategies for planning.

Data on economic, demographic and social characteristics of the region at the district, block, and settlement level were tabulated, mapped and analysed before arriving at meaningful conclusions. Statistical techniques involved mainly ratios, location quotients, coefficient of spatial variation, application of rank-size rule to measure hierarchy of urban settlements and ranking the settlements and blocks of the region on the basis of composite scores.*

---

* **Statistical Sources**

As indicated above, wherever possible, quantitative data have been used for introducing precision into the analysis. Data collection for a study of this magnitude was naturally not an easy task and it involved extensive field work. Most of the statistics used have been collected from Government offices and publications, as for example, Directorate of Industries, Bihar; Town and Country Planning Department, Bihar; Geological Survey of India, Patna; Department of Geology and Mines; Bihar Electricity Board; Directorate General of Technical Development, New Delhi; Fertiliser Association of India, New Delhi and Census Publications.

TWO

Regional Structure

Regional structure explained in terms of physical landscape, resource base - natural and human, economic activities and distribution of human settlements and amenities provide a basis not only to understand the spatial variations in them but in understanding the pattern of association among them which contribute to the variations in the processes of development. Hence analysis has been made in this chapter of only those aspects of the regional structure which have a bearing on the spatial organisation of the economy.

PHYSICAL LANDSCAPE

The Chota Nagpur region being a part of the Indian peninsula is a landmass of hard archaean rocks and is higher than the Bihar plains. To the west it continues as the highlands of Madhya Pradesh and descends towards east, north and south in four steps. These steps or erosion surfaces have been recognised as (a) the 'Pat' region, (b) Ranchi and Hazaribagh Plateaus, (c) Lower Chota Nagpur Plateau and (d) Outer Fringe (Ahmad, 1965). Geologists believe that the Chota Nagpur plateau since Pre-Cambrian time has remained above sea-level. The present surface is the outcome of numerous cycles of erosion which reduced its initial surface to a peneplain (Dunn, 1942). During Pleistocene and Tertiary periods this peneplain was subjected to three successive uplifts as a side effect of the Himalyan Orogeny. As a result three levels of plateau surface, i.e. 950, 600 and 300 meters of height may be observed in the region. Each of these three plateau surfaces descend to the next lower plateau by steep slopes known as scarps (Ahmad, 1965) though the intensity of scarps varies from one part to another. This feature has affected the drainage system and most of the rivers flowing in broad shallow channels over plateau descend through waterfalls.(Fig. 2)

The 'Pat' Region

The 'Pat' Region with an elevation of more than 900 meters

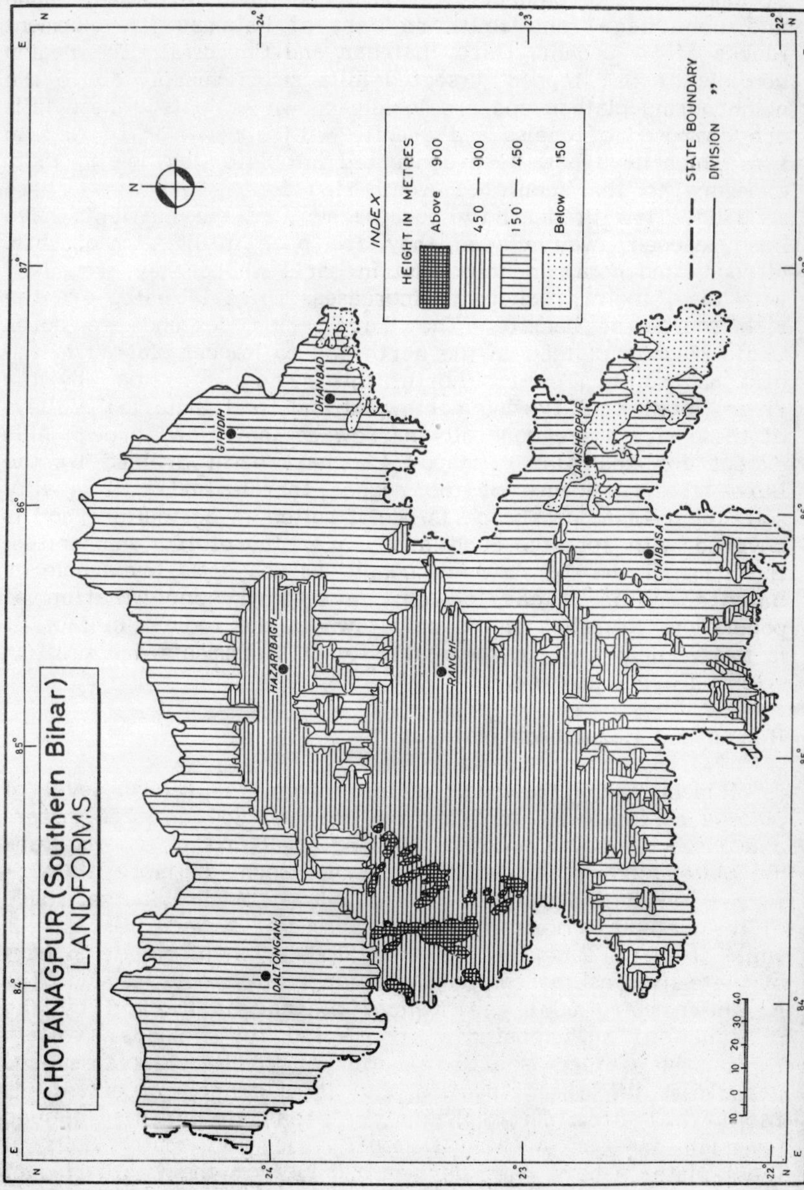
CHOTANAGPUR (Southern Bihar)
LANDFORMS
INDEX
HEIGHT IN METRES
Above 900
450 — 900
150 — 450
Below 150
STATE BOUNDARY
DIVISION ,,
DALTONGANJ
HAZARIBAGH
RANCHI
GIRIDIH
DHANBAD
JAMSHEDPUR
CHAIBASA
N
E
84°
85°
86°
87°
24°
23°
22°
10 0 10 20 30 40

Fig. 2

above sea level is the highest surface. It is located in the western central part of the Chota Nagpur division. It includes north western part of Ranchi (Development Blocks of Dumri, Bishunpur, Kisko, Chainpur, Ghaghra and parts of Gumla, Senha and Lohardaga) and southern part of Palamau (Development Blocks of Mahuadanr, Garu, Latehar and Chandwa). The region consists of flat topped dissected hills rising sharply above the neighbouring plateau and are locally known as 'pats'. These hills are composed of gneiss and granite with a covering of Deccan lava which have now been converted into laterites due to their exposure to the agents of weathering for a long time. These soils have low productivity because most of the nutrients have been leached away and so they are poor in lime, magnesium, nitrogen and potash content. But in parts where they are mixed with clay, their productivity increases. These laterites are the rich source of bauxite. The 'Pat' region descends to outer Chota Nagpur plateau in the north and to Ranchi plateau in the east and south. Towards north, this region is drained by the river North Koel flowing northward and its tributaries. Valleys of these rivers are generally narrow as they flow through hills except for the saucer shaped Chechari basin drained by the Burha river. Because of the rugged terrain and poor quality soil, the region in most parts is not suited to agriculture and is covered with forests. Such areas are, therefore, uninhabited. But some of the 'pats' where conditions are little favourable or bauxite mining is carried on, have small concentration of population. Netarhat is the only town in the region. In fact, it is the smallest town in the state. Rural settlements are small in size and are scattered.

Ranchi and Hazaribagh Plateaus

Ranchi and Hazaribagh plateaus form the second level of plateau surface with an elevation between 600 and 750 meters above sea level and are separated by the Damodar trough. Ranchi plateau covers the major part of Ranchi district. It's surface is undulating marked by few hills at places. Southern side of the plateau is more rugged and dissected towards Dalma hills while it is more gentle towards Simdega plain. Northern part of plateau faces the southern side of the Damodar trough. The northern margin of the Ranchi plateau is marked by the presence of an imposing scarp facing the Damodar valley. Hazaribagh plateau is a continuation of the Ranchi plateau and has almost the same elevation, but it is smaller in extent. It faces the outer Chota Nagpur plateau in north, Dhanbad peneplain in east and the Damodar trough in south. Soils of these plateaus have been derived mainly from the weathering of granite and gneiss. Over the undulating plateau productivity of soil increases or decreases in proportion to gravel-sand proportion and dryness of the soil. Productivity increases from uplands to lowland areas where surface seepage of ground water makes it best suited for wet crops like paddy. Forests cover large part of the Hazaribagh plateau whereas on the Ranchi plateau, they are found only in the scarp regions. Important forest products are bamboo, timber and lac. This region has only small reserves of few minerals like beryl. Rural settlements are comparatively larger in size and more in number than the 'Pat' region. A number of towns have developed on the base of the scarplines or at the margins of the forests as break of bulk towns or collecting centres for forest products.

Lower Chota Nagpur Plateau

Lower Chota Nagpur Plateau with an elevation of about 300-450 meters above sea level is the third plateau surface extending over a wide area and covering large part of Palamau, Hazaribagh, Giridih and Singhbhum districts. There are level plains and broad expanses of cultivable lands too but even these are intermingled with isolated hills and irregular ranges of rocks. Some of the important river basins in this part are the North Koel, the South Koel, the Barakar and the Subarnrekha. Soils in major part of the region have been derived from the gneiss and granite like Ranchi and Hazaribagh plateaus but in few areas in Singhbhum districts they have been formed from quartzites and schists. Like Ranchi and Hazaribagh plateaus cultivable lands may be divided broadly into 'Tanr' lands and 'Don' lands - the former representing the uplands where cultivation is difficult without irrigation and the latter consisting of the lowlands mostly on the banks of rivers. Whereas maize dominates the 'tanr' lands, paddy is the chief crop of the 'don' lands. Though soils in general are deficient in lime, phosphoric acid and nitrogen, use of fertilisers can increase the productivity of these lands tremendously. This region, particularly Singhbhum district is rich in minerals like iron, copper and manganese and Palamau district has reserves of coal,limestone, fire clay, iron ore, graphite etc. Because of better conditions for agriculture and mining activities, population concentration is generally high and a number of mining towns have come up in the region.

The Outer Fringe

The fourth level, the outer fringe is represented by plains, river-valleys and marginal areas of the outer plateau with an elevation of 150-300 meters above sea level. Though the soils of the region like rest of the Chota Nagpur have been derived from granite and gneiss, the clay content is generally high which makes it favourable for agriculture. One of the important minerals of the region is mica which has been associated with the lower parts of the outer plateau in Hazaribagh and Giridih districts. The mica belt runs through northern parts of Hazaribagh and Giridih and extends into Gaya and Munger districts. The Damodar valley, an important unit of this region is an elongated trough between the plateaus of Ranchi and Hazaribagh and the whole of Dhanbad district. It contains the most valuable coal reserves of the country and many other associated minerals like fire clay and china clay. The Subarnrekha valley is yet another unit of the region with huge mineral reserves in iron ore, kyanite, manganese and copper in its vicinity. Besides the Damodar and the Subarnrekha valleys, the other river valleys are that of the North Koel, the Sankh, the South Koel which provide relatively plain areas for cultivation as well as sites for industrial establishments. Due to availability of various minerals and good agricultural land, the region has a dense population and several towns. In many places these towns are so nearby that they have formed clusters and are known as urban agglomerations.

CLIMATE AND RAINFALL

The climate of the Chota Nagpur in general is dry and bracing because of the height. December and January are the coldest months with lowest minimum temperature of 3° - 6° celcius, while May and June record the maximum temperature of the year varying between 40° and 45° celcius. The hot wind of the plains during the summer is absent here which makes it less uncomfortable. Yearly fluctuations in rainfall is a notable feature. The region receives a greater share of annual rainfall from the south-west monsoon during the months of June to Septermber. The 'Pat' region receives the heaviest showers because of its height. Rainfall decreases towards the rainshadow belt of the 'Pat' region in Palamau district. Annual rainfall (in mm) in the Chota Nagpur during four subsequent years reveals the uncertainty of the monsoon (Table 2.1).

Though amount of rainfall is adequate, it is not much beneficial to the agriculture on account of its seasonal character, yearly fluctuations in the onset of monsoon, the sloping terrain permitting quick runoff of the rainwater and impervious nature of rocks in most parts disallowing storage of water underground.

PHYSICAL CONSTRAINTS ON THE ECONOMY OF THE REGION

The rugged terrain of the Chota Nagpur region as a

whole and much dissected 'pat' region in particular have restricted the spatial organisation of economic activity of the region.

TABLE 2.1

Chota Nagpur : Annual Rainfall

(in mm)

Districts	1973-74	1974-75	1975-76	1976-77
Hazaribagh	1135.1	985.0	1274.4	1256.8
Giridih	1323.5	1022.7	1391.2	981.5
Dhanbad	1453.9	1172.8	1994.1	944.0
Ranchi	1497.6	1154.5	1470.3	1456.4
Palamau	1067.5	918.6	1140.6	1287.0
Singhbhum	1312.5	1111.2	1357.8	1110.0

Source: Bihar Statistical Hand Book, 1978, Government of Bihar.

(a) Agriculture is the worst affected sector of economy because of the unfavourable topography in terms of steep slope, poor quality soil having high content of gravels on the uplands and less moisture because the surface run-off is rapid and underlying rocks are impervious.

(b) The gradient of slope has not only initiated soil erosion but has hindered the construction of transport lines in the region which generally follow the easier relief e.g. the Grand Chord line of railway which passes through the Damodar and the North Koel valleys. avoiding escarpments.

Rivers of the Chota Nagpur region have narrow steep sided valleys in their upper parts. They are associated with falls and rapids and hence not fit for navigation. These streams are mainly seasonal and underground storage is also not possible on account of impervious crystalline rock structure. In the plateau region, therefore, these rivers are sudden torrential flows of water during the rains which otherwise become disconnected pools of stagnant water rest of the year. Because of these uncertainties most of the rivers cannot be used for navigaton, irrigation and power generation.

Deforestation leading to rapid soil erosion is not only responsible for deterioration of agricultural land but also creates silting problem in the rivers and riverines making their maintenance costlier and their lives shorter.

RESOURCE-BASE OF THE CHOTA NAGPUR

Agricultural land, forests, minerals and water are some of the natural resources which are used by mankind for various purposes e.g. fulfilment of basic needs and creation of wealth. But resources of a particular area acquire significance only when human effort transforms them into valuable products. As such natural resources and human resources both combined together help in the developmental process.

Land Resources

The physical characteristics and economic factors are equally significant in deciding the pattern of land-use in the region (Fig 3). Thus the land-use patterns show variations not only spatial but also temporal.

An analysis of the land-use pattern (Table 2.2) reveals that agricultural land is very limited in the region due to rugged hilly terrain and poor soil in most parts. It should have, therefore, accounted for a large share under barren and culturable wastes. But it is not so, because a major portion of such land is under forest cover and is, therefore, under some productive use. In fact, forest is the most dominant user of land covering about 32 per cent of the total area which is just double the state average. Barren and culturable waste land taken together account for only 8.5 per cent of land. Net area sown (30 per cent) in the region is less than the state average (44 per cent).

Within the region, there is marked variation in the land-use pattern at the district and block levels and the topographical influence is clearly visualised in the land-use maps of the region (Figs 4,5,6 and 7). Districts and blocks having more of plain lands and valleys rather than hills and escarpments naturally have more agricultural land. Ranchi has an undulating topography with relatively better soil in lowlands and smaller area under forests (23.3 per cent). As such more land could be brought under cultivation here and among all the districts of the region, the net area sown (42 per cent) is the highest. Hazaribagh district on the other hand, with 45.7 per cent of land under forest and 10 per cent of barren land has the minimum percentage (20 per cent) of net sown area. Dhanbad district has about 32 per cent of net sown area which normally should have been more because it is situated in the Damodar

TABLE 2.2

Chota Nagpur : Land Use Patterns (1958-59: 1978-79)

(Figures in Percentage to total Area)

LAND USE CATEGORY	HAZARIBAGH		GIRIDIH		DHANBAD		RANCHI		PALAMAU		SINGHBHUM		CHOTA NAGPUR		BIHAR	
	58-59	78-79	58-59*	78-79	58-59	78-79	58-59	78-79	58-59	78-79	58-59	78-79	58-59	78-79	58-59	78-79
(1)	(2)	(3)	(4)	(5)	(6)	(7)	(8)	(9)	(10)	(11)	(12)	(13)	(14)	(15)	(16)	(17)
Total Area	100	100		100	100	100	100	100	100	100	100	100	100	100	100	100
Forests	49.6	45.7		34.0	15.1	8.4	28.2	23.3	49.1	43.8	47.2	24.2	-	31.6	21.8	16.3
Barren Land	5.1	9.6		8.0	10.2	11.4	5.0	5.9	6.8	6.5	5.1	8.3	-	7.7	5.0	6.0
Non-Agricultural use	4.2	4.8		6.3	19.9	20.1	4.2	5.2	2.2	3.1	6.5	8.8	-	6.2	7.9	9.5
Permanent Pasture	2.3	1.7		1.9	0.9	1.0	0.7	0.2	0.6	0.6	1.1	0.7	-	0.8	1.2	0.9
Miscellaneous uses and culturable waste	6.3	3.1		6.2	12.1	8.3	5.2	4.6	4.5	2.4	7.3	7.6	-	4.9	5.2	4.0
Other Fallow	6.4	5.9		8.3	8.7	9.4	11.3	9.3	8.9	7.5	6.6	9.4	-	10.2	4.9	5.2
Current Fallow	6.8	9.5		8.7	9.9	10.0	10.7	9.4	5.8	11.6	6.8	11.2	-	8.3	8.0	9.2
Net Sown	19.3	19.7		26.6	23.2	31.8	34.7	42.1	22.1	24.5	19.4	29.8	-	30.2	46.0	48.9

* Giridih was a part of Hazaribagh District.

Source: Directorate of Statistics & Evaluation, Bihar.

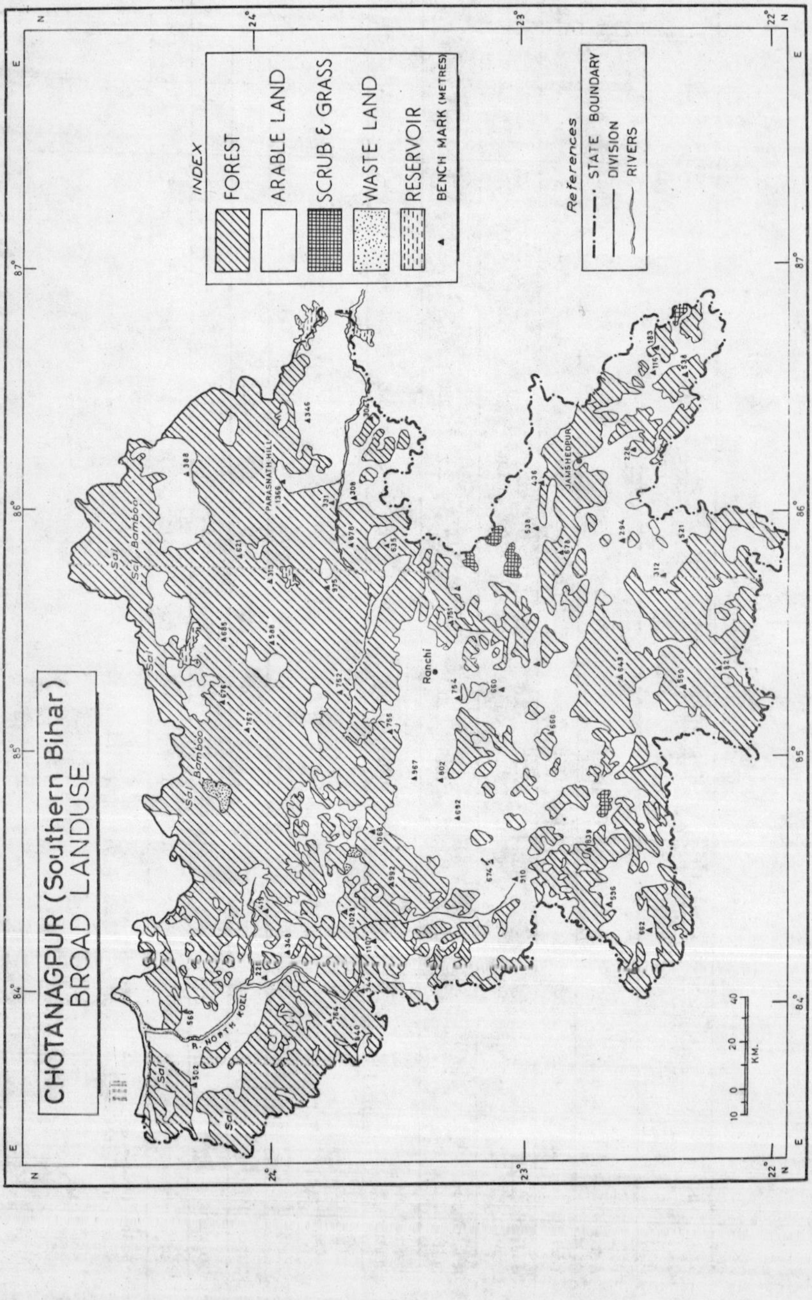
CHOTANAGPUR (Southern Bihar)
BROAD LANDUSE
INDEX
FOREST
ARABLE LAND
SCRUB & GRASS
WASTE LAND
RESERVOIR
BENCH MARK (METRES)
References
STATE BOUNDARY
DIVISION
RIVERS
Ranchi
JAMSHEDPUR
PARASNATH HILL 1366
NORTH KOEL
KM.

Fig. 2

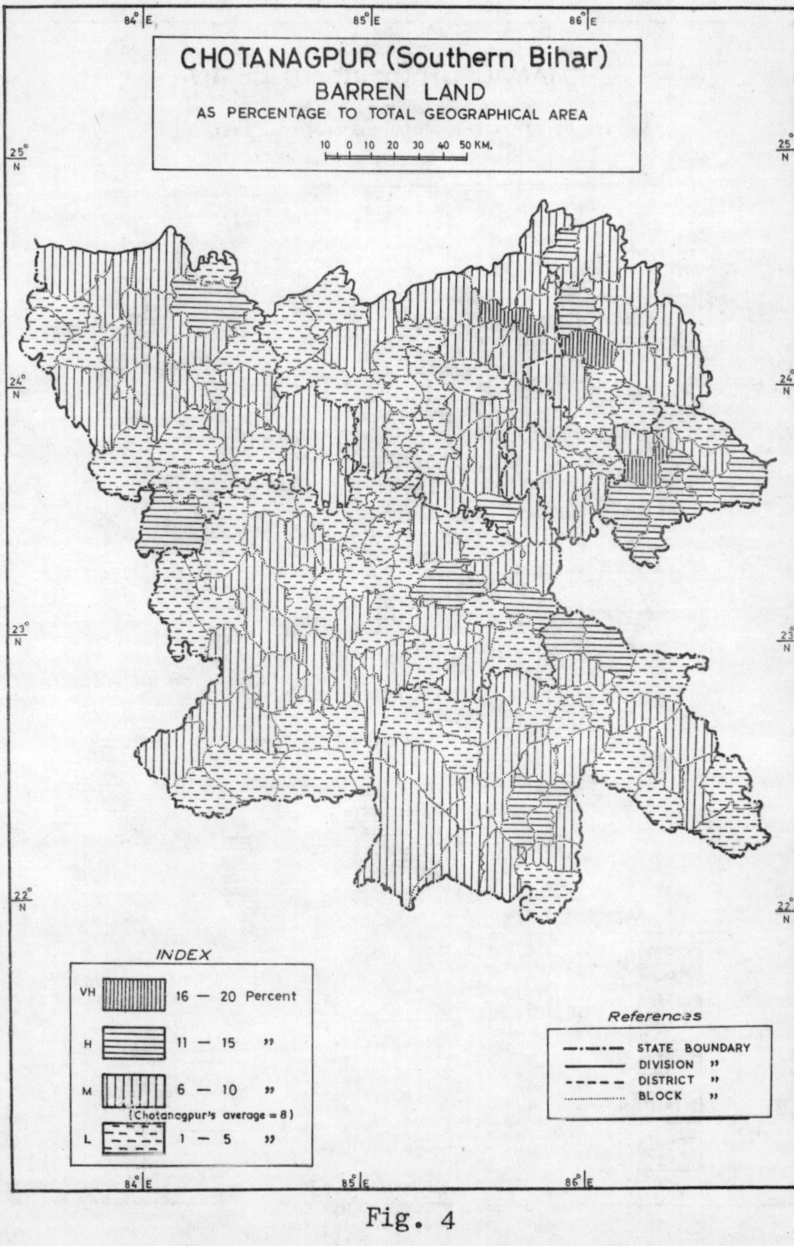

CHOTANAGPUR (Southern Bihar)
BARREN LAND
AS PERCENTAGE TO TOTAL GEOGRAPHICAL AREA
10 0 10 20 30 40 50 KM.
84° E
85° E
86° E
25° N
24° N
23° N
22° N
INDEX
VH 16 — 20 Percent
H 11 — 15 "
M 6 — 10 "
(Chotanagpur's average = 8)
L 1 — 5 "
References
STATE BOUNDARY
DIVISION "
DISTRICT "
BLOCK "

Fig. 4

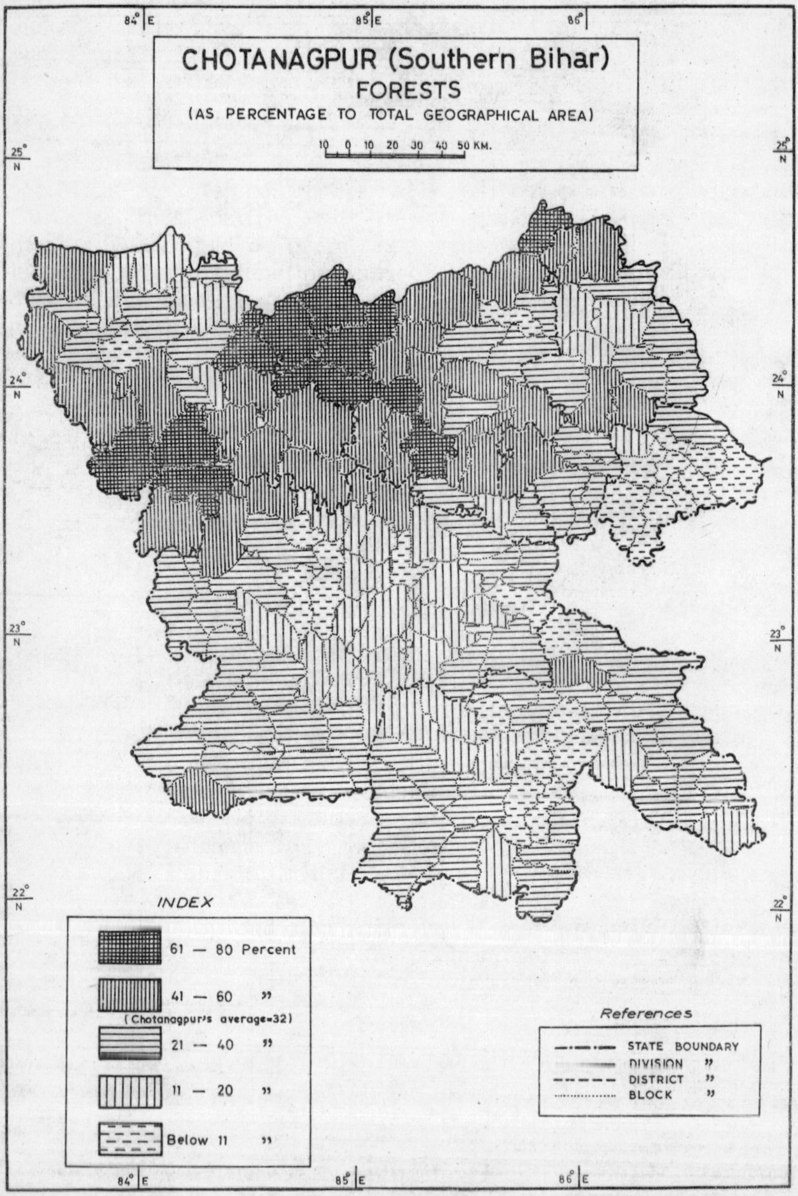

CHOTANAGPUR (Southern Bihar)
FORESTS
(AS PERCENTAGE TO TOTAL GEOGRAPHICAL AREA)
10 0 10 20 30 40 50 KM.
84° E
85° E
86°
25° N
24° N
23° N
22° N
INDEX
61 — 80 Percent
41 — 60 "
(Chotanagpur's average=32)
21 — 40 "
11 — 20 "
Below 11 "
References
STATE BOUNDARY
DIVISION "
DISTRICT "
BLOCK "

Fig. 5

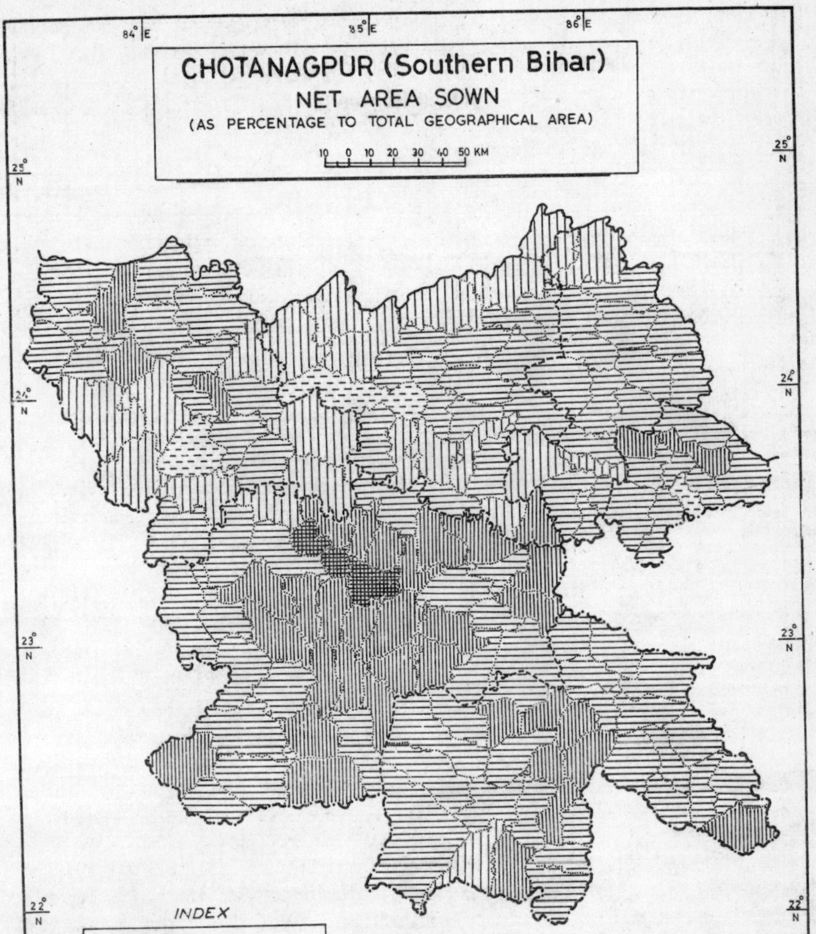

CHOTANAGPUR (Southern Bihar)
NET AREA SOWN
(AS PERCENTAGE TO TOTAL GEOGRAPHICAL AREA)
10 0 10 20 30 40 50 KM
84° E
85° E
86° E
25° N
24° N
23° N
22° N
INDEX
61 — 80 Percent
41 — 60 "
21 — 40 "
(Chotanagpurs average = 30)
11 — 20 "
Below 11 "
References
STATE BOUNDARY
DIVISION BOUNDARY
DISTRICT BOUNDARY
BLOCK BOUNDARY

Fig. 6

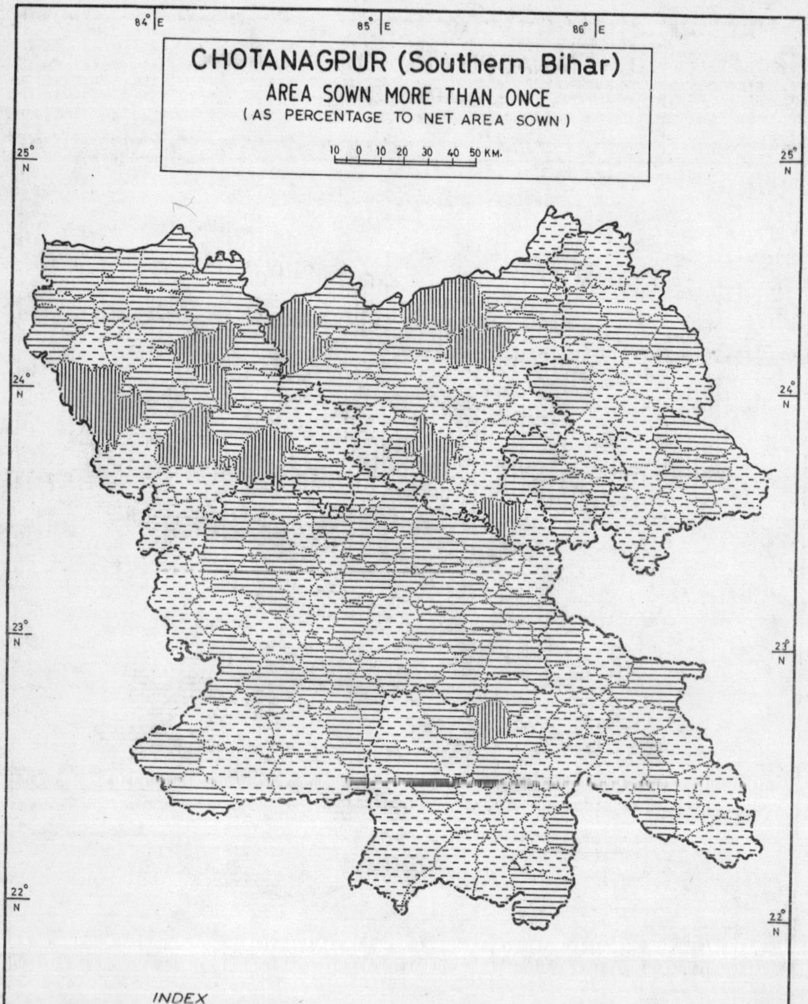
CHOTANAGPUR (Southern Bihar)
AREA SOWN MORE THAN ONCE
(AS PERCENTAGE TO NET AREA SOWN)
10 0 10 20 30 40 50 KM.
84° E
85° E
86° E
25° N
24° N
23° N
22° N
INDEX
31 — 50 Percent
(Chotanagpur's average = 13·3)
11 — 30 "
Below 11 "
References
STATE BOUNDARY
DIVISION "
DISTRICT "
BLOCK "

Fig. 7

basin. But availability of several minerals particularly coal has attracted a number of industries in the region. As a result, as high as 20 per cent land is put to non-agricultural uses by way of factories, mines and settlements. Coal mines have converted large areas into barren land which occupy about 11.4 per cent of total land in Dhanbad district. Singhbhum with 24.2 per cent of its land under forests has about 30 per cent of land as net sown. Next to Dhanbad, non-agricultural use of the land is high in this district again due to its mineral resources and manufacturing activities.

A comparison of the land-use pattern in the region at two points of time i.e. 1958-59 and 1978-79 after a gap of two decades shows the temporal variations (Table 2.2). It reveals that the region like the State has lost its forest areas on the one hand and has gained in all other categories. There has been an impressive increase in the net sown area particularly in two districts, i.e. Dhanbad and Singhbhum but at the cost of forests. Pressure on cultivable lands have increased because of the fast growing population which have been attracted due to rapidly expanding manufacturing activities. But overall pattern of land use has been almost static since 1958-59 in the sense that even during that time Hazaribagh and Palamau districts had higher percentage of land under forests than the net sown area which is true even now. Similarly, Dhanbad and Ranchi districts have higher percentage of net area sown than the forests, revealing the same pattern as that of 1958-59. Only change is noticed in Singhbhum where deforestation has been so rapid that the forest cover has been reduced to nearly half of the area recorded during 1958-59.

Intra-district variations in the landuse pattern are still more striking. In general, forests and cultivated area tend to be mutually exclusive (Figs 5 and 6). There is an elongated forest belt in the northern part of the region running in an east-west direction covering nearly 40 development blocks where more than 40 per cent of land is forested. Within this belt, two distinct patches with thick forest cover (more than 60 per cent of land under forests) are observed in south-western and northern parts and they include 4 development blocks of Palamau and 5 development blocks of Hazaribagh. In the north-eastern part of this belt, there is only one block with more than 60 per cent of land under forests. In general, the topography is rugged and the soil is infertile in most parts of this belt. As such percentage of net area sown is usually less than 20 per cent in thickly forested areas whereas it is 21-40 per cent in rest of the belt. In fact, a very high percentage of area in this region would have been barren if there would not have been this forest cover.

Percentage of net area sown is usually medium to high in the majority of the development blocks outside the northern forest belt in the region. Only 26 blocks (22 blocks with more than 40 per cent of land under forests and 4 blocks with a high percentage of land under non-agricultural activities, i.e. mining and manufacturing) have a very low percentage of land under cultivation and most of them lie in the northern part.

Area sown more than once as a percent to net area sown varies between 8 and 19 while the averages for the region and State are 13.1 and 33.3 per cent respectively. It is because of the agriculture's total dependence on monsoon rains which is highly uncertain and seasonal in character. Intensive cultivation of crops is, therefore, not possible without irrigation. Irrigation facilities, however, are too meagre. As such gross irrigated area constitutes less than 10 per cent of the gross cultivated area (Table 2.3). Palamau district shows a relatively higher percentage under irrigated area (20 per cent of the gross cultivated) which is due to some irrigation facilities available through 'bandhs', wells and tanks in the northern part of the district. Important sources of irrigation in the region are wells, tanks, rivers and artificial reservoirs. Of 209,000 hectares of gross irrigated area, 75,000 hectares (35.9 per cent) are irrigated by wells, 65,000 hectares (31.1 per cent) by 'bandhs' and rivers and remaining 69,000 hectares (33.0 per cent) by tanks and canals.

Cropping Pattern

The cropping pattern in the region shows little diversification as foodgrains occupy nearly 70 per cent of the gross cropped area (Table 2.4). Rice is the single predominant crop which generally occupies more than 50 per cent of the total cropped area in all districts except Palamau where paucity of rain restricts rice cultivation. Maize is the second important crop which shares nearly 6 per cent of the total cropped area in the region. Except Ranchi, all other districts have a higher percentage of cropped area given to maize than wheat because it can be grown even on uplands where irrigation is difficult. Area under maize constitutes 2-13 per cent of the total cropped area. Wheat with 2-5 per cent of total cropped area is at the third position in majority of the districts. If seasonwise distribution of crops is examined, Aghani (Kharif) crops seem to dominate the region with highest acreage (about 60 per cent) though the percentage may vary from district to district. As Palamau falls in the rainshadow belt of the 'pat' region, rainfall

TABLE 2.3

Chota Nagpur : Cultivated Area and Irrigated Area (1975–76)

DISTRICT/ REGION/ STATE	Total Area	NET AREA SOWN		AREA SOWN MORE THAN ONCE		TOTAL CROPPED AREA	GROSS IRRIGATED AREA	
	(thousand hectares)	(thousand hectares)	(% to the total area)	(thousand hectares)	(% to the net area sown)	(thousand hectares)	(thousand hectares)	(% to the total cropped area)
(1)	(2)	(3)	(4)	(5)	(6)	(7)	(8)	(9)
Hazaribagh	1110	219	19.7	37	16.9	256	20	7.8
Giridih	688	183	26.6	16	8.7	199	16	8.0
Dhanbad	299	95	31.8	9	9.5	104	8	7.7
Ranchi	1822	767	42.1	102	13.3	869	64	7.4
Palamau	1273	312	24.5	58	18.6	370	75	20.3
Singhbhum	1357	404	29.8	38	9.4	442	26	5.9
Chota Nagpur	6549	1980	30.2	260	13.1	2240	209	9.3
Bihar	17330	8465	48.8	2822	33.3	11287	3362	29.8

Source: Directorate of Statistics and Evaluation, Bihar.

is comparatively less as such aghani crops are restricted to lowlands and only 37.3 per cent of its total cropped area is under these crops. As maize (bhadai crop) may be grown even with little moisture,it is the major crop of the uplands. Bhadai crops, therefore, occupy 32.2 per cent of the total cropped area. Wheat is the most important rabi crop of the region. Compared to aghani crops it has less importance in the region except Palamau where it occupies 30 per cent of the cultivated area. Garma (or summer crops) crops are insignificant in the region as they occupy only 1 per cent of the total cropped area. Being summer crop, they need plenty of water and irrigation is, therefore, extremely important. Lack of irrigation in the region is the main cause for its little importance.

So far as production of various crops are concerned, the Chota Nagpur contributes about 18 per cent of the total production of rice in Bihar, though it shares 23 per cent of the total acreage under rice. This is a reflection of subsistance farming and yields are generally lower than those in the plains of Bihar. About 13 per cent of the total acreage under maize in Bihar is shared by this region and almost the same percentage of production too. Rest of the crops occupy greater share of land in the region but have less production (Table 2.5).

Crop Yields

As can be seen from the table 2.6, there is considerable variation in yields among districts. Crop yields show marked fluctuation partly due to variations in rainfall within the region. Although measures for the introduction of new technology are underway the progress is slow because of the lack of response of the farming community.

Average size of farms is small. Besides, undulating topography and general poverty of farmers restrict the use of tractors. As is evident from table 2.7, the region has such a small number of tractors that the total cultivated area served by a tractor varies between 3000 and 80000 hectares from one district to another. Traditional method of farming by iron and wooden ploughs is more common and convenient for the farmers who have small holdings and little money to invest in farming practices. As such number of such ploughs are very high and 1-3 hectares of cropped area is served by an iron and wooden plough. Statistics on fertiliser consumption by districts of the region reveal lower consumption in comparison to other districts of Bihar. Of the total consumption of NPK fertilisers within the region, Ranchi consumes more than 57 per cent. Hazaribagh, Palamau and Singhbhum consume about 33 per cent and rest is

TABLE 2.4

Chota Nagpur : Area under Principal Crops (1975-76)

Area given in thousand hectares. Figures within brackets are percentage of area under each crop to total cropped area of the district, region and state.

DISTRICT/ REGION/STATE	RICE	WHEAT	MAIZE	BARLEY	GRAM	PULSES	SUGAR-CANE	POTATO
(1)	(2)	(3)	(4)	(5)	(6)	(7)	(8)	(9)
Hazaribagh	144 (56.3)	9 (3.5)	26 (10.2)	2 (0.8)	3 (1.2)	5 (2.0)	2 (0.8)	8 (3.1)
Giridih	112 (56.3)	6 (3.0)	20 (10.1)	-	1 (0.5)	1 (0.5)	-	5 (2.5)
Dhanbad	77 (74.0)	5 (4.8)	7 (6.7)	-	1 (1.0)	-	-	1 (1.0)
Ranchi	503 (57.9)	26 (3.0)	15 (1.7)	1 (0.1)	10 (1.2)	13 (1.5)	-	13 (1.5)
Palamau	110 (29.7)	23 (6.2)	49 (13.2)	17 (4.6)	27 (7.3)	26 (7.0)	3 (0.8)	3 (0.8)
Singhbhum	359 (81.2)	9 (2.0)	12 (2.7)	-	6 (1.4)	6 (1.4)	-	1 (0.2)
Chota Nagpur	1305 (58.2)	78 (3.5)	129 (5.8)	20 (0.9)	48 (2.1)	51 (2.3)	5 (0.2)	31 (1.4)
Bihar	5266 (45.7)	1815 (16.1)	850 (7.5)	176 (1.6)	245 (2.2)	877 (7.8)	134 (1.2)	142 (1.3)

Source: Directorate of Statistics & Evaluation, Bihar.

TABLE 2.5

Chota Nagpur : Production of Principal Crops (1976-77)

(Production in thousand metric tons. Figures in brackets are percentage share of each district/region to total production of the state)

DISTRICT/ REGION/ STATE	RICE	WHEAT	BARLEY	MAIZE	GRAM	PULSES	SUGAR-CANE	POTATO
(1)	(2)	(3)	(4)	(5)	(6)	(7)	(8)	(9)
Hazaribagh	60 (1.26)	10 (0.40)	1 (1.12)	21 (2.12)	1 (0.71)	2 (0.36)	69 (1.65)	53 (4.33)
Giridih	62 (1.30)	8 (0.32)	-	19 (1.92)	1 (0.71)	-	14 (0.34)	38 (2.33)
Dhanbad	28 (0.59)	5 (0.20)	-	5 (0.50)	-	-	5 (0.12)	2 (0.15)
Ranchi	360 (7.53)	23 (0.93)	-	22 (2.22)	2 (1.42)	3 (0.53)	2 (0.05)	65 (4.85)
Palamau	78 (1.63)	15 (0.61)	5 (5.62)	54 (5.44)	6 (4.26)	9 (1.60)	90 (2.16)	12 (0.89)
Singhbhum	316 (6.61)	3 (0.12)	-	9 (0.91)	1 (0.71)	2 (0.36)	1 (0.02)	4 (0.30)
Chota Nagpur	904 (18.92)	64 (2.58)	6 (6.74)	130 (13.11)	11 (7.81)	16 (2.85)	181 (4.34)	179 (13.35)
Bihar	4778 (100)	2470 (100)	89 (100)	992 (100)	141 (100)	563 (100)	4176 (100)	1341 (100)

Source: Directorate of Statistics and Evaluation, Bihar.

shared by Giridih and Dhanbad. Rabi crops consume more fertiliser in the Chota Nagpur than Kharif crops (Table 2.8). Per hectare consumption of fertiliser in the Chota Nagpur is quite low and varies between 2.3 Kg in Dhanbad and 6.4 Kg in Ranchi, whereas the average consumption of fertiliser in Bihar is 17.2 Kg.

TABLE 2.6

Chota Nagpur : Average Yields (in Kg) Per Hectare of Principal Crops - Rice, Wheat and Maize (1976-77)

DISTRICT/ REGION/ STATE	RICE	WHEAT	MAIZE
Hazaribagh	832	1242	781
Giridih	1052	1693	711
Dhanbad	1227	1422	726
Ranchi	830	1837	1355
Palamau	840	1458	622
Singhbhum	914	1355	1016
Chota Nagpur	882	1538	782
Bihar	929	1270	747

TABLE 2.7

Chota Nagpur : Cropped Area (in hectares) served per Iron and Wooden Plough and Tractor

DISTRICT/ REGION/ STATE	AREA SERVED BY AN IRON AND WOODEN PLOUGH	AREA SERVED BY A TRACTOR
(1)	(2)	(3)
Hazaribagh	1.27	11,794
Dhanbad	1.06	3,518
Ranchi	2.59	14,203
Palamau	1.79	4,216
Singhbhum	1.59	80,800
Chota Nagpur	5.82	33,757
Bihar	1.94	1,500

Source: Statistical Hand Book, Bihar, 1978.

TABLE 2.8
Chota Nagpur : Seasonwise Per Hectare (Cultivated Area) Consumption of NPK Fertilisers (in Kg); (1979-80)

DISTRICT/ REGION/ STATE	KHARIF	RABI	TOTAL
Hazaribagh	3.1	20.8	4.3
Giridih	2.3	24.9	3.6
Dhanbad	1.0	15.4	2.3
Ranchi	4.7	42.6	6.4
Palamau	2.8	5.2	2.6
Singhbhum	1.3	19.4	2.6
Chota Nagpur	3.0	20.5	4.9
Bihar	8.1	36.7	17.2

Source: Fertiliser Association of India, New Delhi, 1980.

Of the three fertilisers used in the region, nitrogen is used in the largest amount, a grater portion of which is given to Rabi crops. The Chota Nagpur region as a whole consumes only 5.2 per cent of the total fertiliser consumed within the State.

Forest Resources (Fig 8)

Apart from the agricultural resource base, forests are very important in the region. As is evident from the land-use pattern, forest cover is very high in Palamau (43.8 per cent) and Hazaribagh (45.7 per cent) and moderately high in Ranchi (23.3 per cent), Giridih (34.0 per cent) and Singhbhum (24.2 per cent). With an average rainfall of 1200 millimeters, the Chota Nagpur region is characterised by the 'moist deciduous' forest. Four months of the year i.e. June to September receive heavy monsoon rains and remaining months are comparatively dry. The districts of Singhbhum, Ranchi, Palamau, Giridih and Hazaribagh in Chota Nagpur together share more than 70 per cent of the total forest area of the State.

The vallyes and basins with humid climate and deep soil are dominated by Sal (**Shorea Robusta**) trees of multi-species. Some of the companions of Sal are mangoes (**Mangifera indica**), jamun (**Eugenia jambolana**), teak (**Tecotona Grandis**), jackfruit (**Artocarpus itegrifolia**), gamhar (**Gmelina arborea**), mahua (**Basia Latifolia**), kusum (**Schleirshza Terjuga**), and semal.

Sabai, dhak and piar grow on the drier and steeper slopes where the soil cover is also thin. Palas is a tree of wasteland. Thus the areas unsuited to farming in Chota Nagpur are also economically important as they provide valuable forest products.

Important forest products of the region are timber, firewood, bamboo, sabai grass, kendu leaves, lac, medicinal herbs and the like. The commercial and economic value of the forest largely depends on the quality of timber produced. Sal, teak, paisal, and gamhar are the important trees found in the region which make valuable timber. Sal is the dominant species found over a wider area in the region. Teak, though not a native tree, thrives well in the moist climate of Singhbhum. Some of the other trees which produce timber and firewood are katha, jamun, mahua, etc. There are several saw mills in the region. Bamboo is grown in all parts of the forest belt but Palamau and Hazaribagh are especially important. It is one of the raw materials for paper industry. As there is no paper factory within the region, most of the bamboo grown here is sent to Dehri-on-Son paper factory or to West Bengal where a number of paper manufacturing units are located. Bamboo is also used in basket-making and it has developed as a cottage industry in the region. Daltonganj, Garhwa, Latehar, Chatra, Hazaribagh and Bundu are some of the centres. Sabai grass is used in making ropes and papers. The bulk of the product is exported to Calcutta. The important industry using this raw material in the region is the Mahalaxmi Fibre Works at Ormanjhi. Katha, an important ingredient of betel is obtained from Acacia Catechu trees, which occupy nearly 2 per cent of the forest are in Palamau, one of the largest producers of Katha in the country. Kendu leaves are used for bidi making and are produced on a commercial basis in the forests of Palamau and Singhbhum. These are exported to all parts of the country. Lac insects thrive well on palas, kusum and ber trees in the region. Lac collection is a seasonal occupation so farmers do it in their spare times. Stick - lac is collected from the scattered hosts in the forests and is brought to the village hat for sale. Here it is purchased by the local businessmen who sell it to wholesale merchants or factory owners. Districtwise production of sticklac during 1975-76 has been shown in fig. 8.

Mineral Resources (Fig 9)

Minerals are the most important resource of the region. Chota Nagpur popularly known as the 'mineral treasury of India' possesses all the key minerals of economic importance like coal, iron ore, manganese, chromite, bauxite, limestone, mica, copper, kyanite, china clay, fire clay and dolomite. Their distribution in

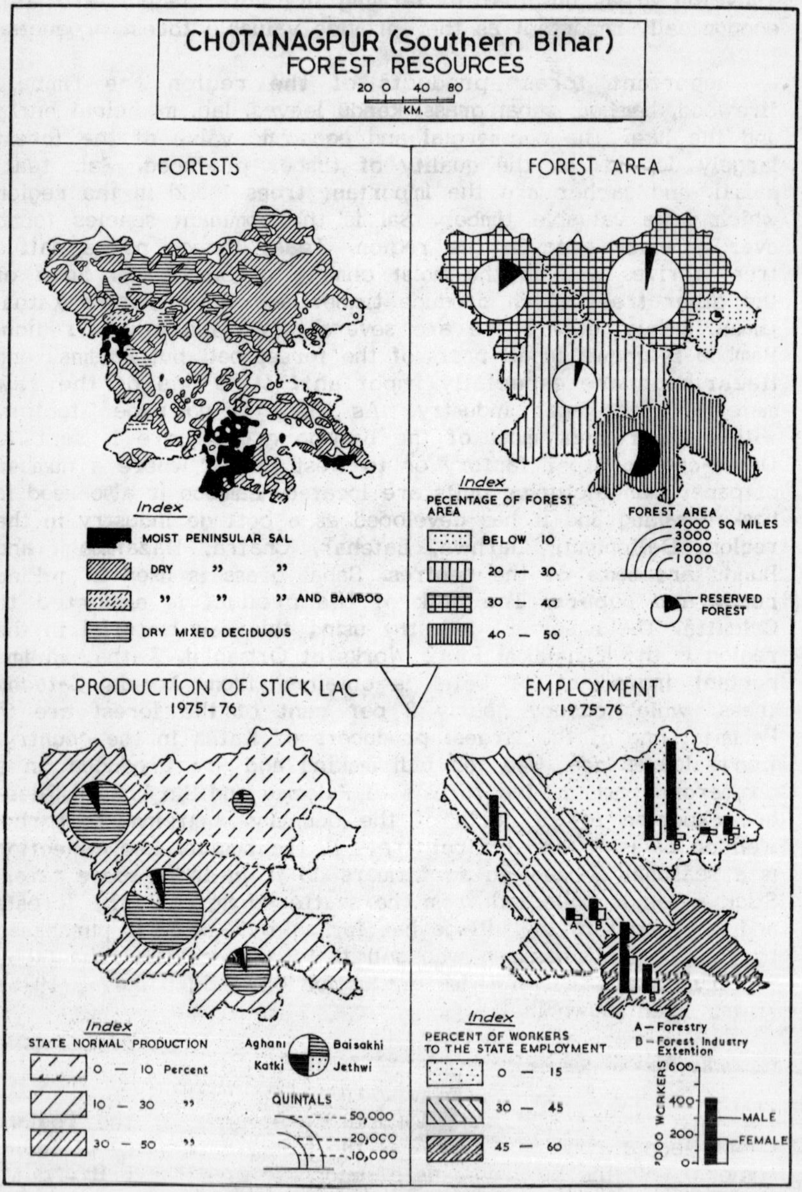
CHOTANAGPUR (Southern Bihar)
FOREST RESOURCES
20 0 40 80
KM.
FORESTS
Index
MOIST PENINSULAR SAL
DRY " "
" " " AND BAMBOO
DRY MIXED DECIDUOUS
FOREST AREA
Index
PECENTAGE OF FOREST AREA
BELOW 10
20 — 30
30 — 40
40 — 50
FOREST AREA
4000 SQ MILES
3000
2000
1000
RESERVED FOREST
PRODUCTION OF STICK LAC
1975-76
Index
STATE NORMAL PRODUCTION
0 — 10 Percent
10 — 30 "
30 — 50 "
Aghani
Baisakhi
Katki
Jethwi
QUINTALS
50,000
20,000
10,000
EMPLOYMENT
1975-76
Index
PERCENT OF WORKERS TO THE STATE EMPLOYMENT
0 — 15
30 — 45
45 — 60
A — Forestry
B — Forest Industry Extention
'000 WORKERS
600
400
200
0
MALE
FEMALE

Fig. 8

the region is associated with the occurrences of geological formation of rocks of different ages ranging from the oldest i.e. archaean to the latest i.e. recent pleistocene.

Table 2.9 shows the production of some of the important minerals in Bihar for 1968 and 1974 and the areas of their occurrences. Except for china clay, dolomite, limestone and mica which occur in other parts of the Stage as well, all other minerals mentioned in the table are found in the Chota Nagpur only.

TABLE 2.9

Production and Occurrence of Important Minerals in Bihar (1968, 1974)

MINERALS	PRODUCTION IN TONNES		AREA OF OCCURRENCE
	1968*	1974@	
(1)	(2)	(3)	(4)
Apatite	6290	9060	In the copper belt near Ghatsila
Asbestos	265	1929	West of Chaibasa in Singhbhum
Barytes	97	-	Singhbhum
Bauxite	460783	284384	West of Lohardaga and Palamau
Beryl	N.A	N.A	Palamau
China Clay	135387	135773	Santhal Pargana, Palamau, Singhbhum
Chromite	233	82	Singhbhum
Coal	23702000	35495000	Damodar Valley and Palamau
Copper	475744	818183	Hazaribagh, Singhbhum
Dolomite	478	452	Palamau, Singhbhum, Shahabad
Graphite	N.A	1236	Palamau
Iron Ore	4891979	5708875	Palamau, Singhbhum
Kaolin	N.A	N.A	Singhbhum
Kyanite	64108	30579	Lapsa burn in Singhbhum
Manganese Ore	23652	8406	Singhbhum
Limestone	2195161	3387446	Shahabad, Palamau, Damodar Valley
Mica	8888	6031	Hazaribagh, Giridih, Monghyr, Bhagalpur, Gaya

Sources to Production figures:

* India Bureau of Mines, Nagpur.

@ Bihar Statistical Handbook, 1978.

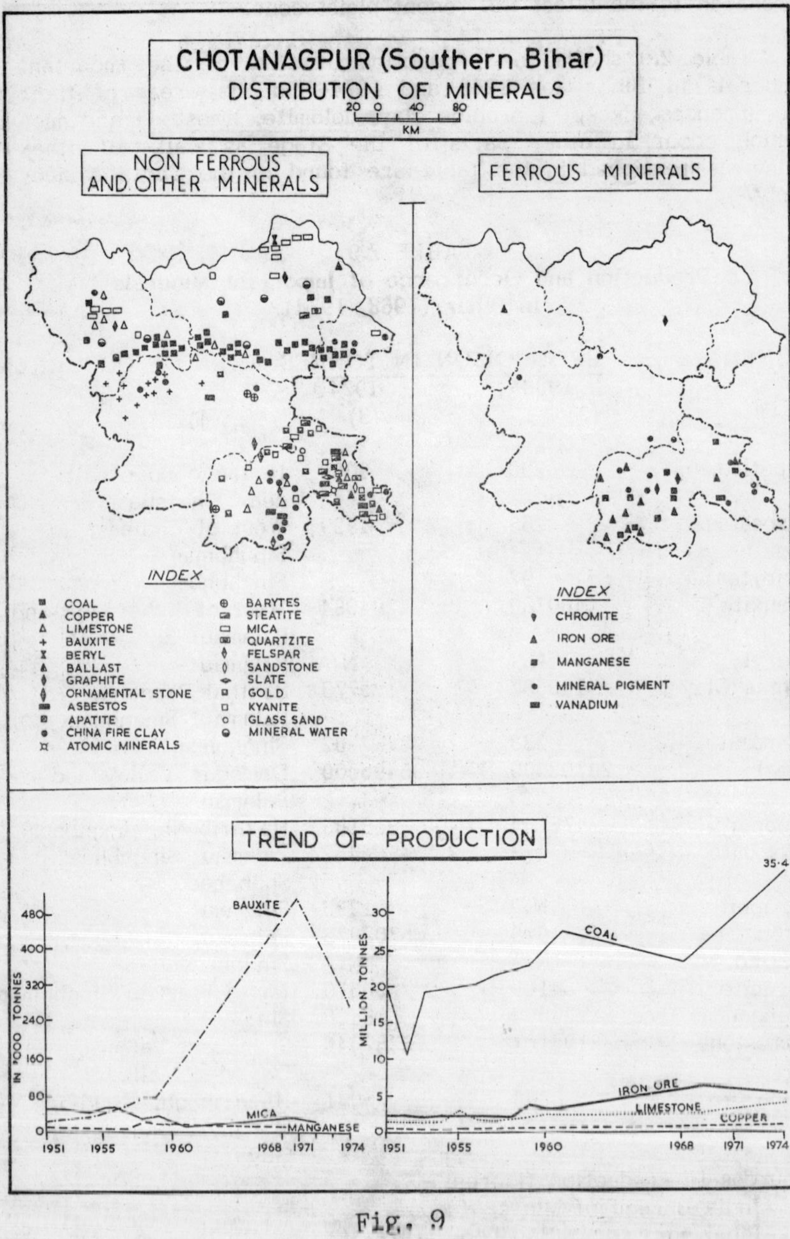
CHOTANAGPUR (Southern Bihar)
DISTRIBUTION OF MINERALS
20 0 40 80
KM
NON FERROUS AND OTHER MINERALS
FERROUS MINERALS
INDEX
COAL
COPPER
LIMESTONE
BAUXITE
BERYL
BALLAST
GRAPHITE
ORNAMENTAL STONE
ASBESTOS
APATITE
CHINA FIRE CLAY
ATOMIC MINERALS
BARYTES
STEATITE
MICA
QUARTZITE
FELSPAR
SANDSTONE
SLATE
GOLD
KYANITE
GLASS SAND
MINERAL WATER
INDEX
CHROMITE
IRON ORE
MANGANESE
MINERAL PIGMENT
VANADIUM
TREND OF PRODUCTION
IN '000 TONNES
480
400
320
240
160
80
0
BAUXITE
MICA
MANGANESE
1951
1955
1960
1968
1971
1974
MILLION TONNES
30
25
20
15
10
5
0
35·4
COAL
IRON ORE
LIMESTONE
COPPER
1951
1955
1960
1968
1971
1974

Fig. 9

Chota Nagpur produces about 40 per cent of coal, 100 per cent of India's copper, 91 per cent of apatite, 75 per cent of kyanite, 40 per cent of iron ore and more than 50 per cent of mica, bauxite and china clay. The region contains about 80 per cent of India's known deposits of coal and nearly 100 per cent of its coking coal. Recently large deposits of high grade uranium have been found in Jadugora in Singhbhum.

Coal reserves are concentrated in Dhanbad, Hazaribagh, Giridih and Palamau districts. The main coal fields of the region are:

1. Damodar valley coalfieds - (a) The Jharia Coalfield is roughly sickle - shaped extending over an area of 450 sq. km. in Dhanbad district. As regards potentialities and development, it is the most important coal field in the country (Ministry of Mines and Fuels, 1963a). (b) Raniganj coalfield is the birthplace of coalmining industry in the country and contributes 33 per cent of India's present coal production. Greater part of this belt lies in West Bengal while a small portion to the west of Barakar river falls within Dhanbad district (Ministry of Mines and Fuels, 1963b). (c) East Bokaro, and (d) West Bokaro coalfields are situated in Hazaribagh district and cover an area of 208 (Ministry of Mines and Fuels, 1963c) and 259 (Ministry of Mines and Fuels, 1972a) sq. km. respectively. (e) Ramgarh coalfield is known for its metallurgical coal reserves. It's areal extent is about 98 sq. km. and is located close to West Bokaro and South Karanpura coalfield (Ministry of Mines and Fuels, 1972b). (f) North Karanpura, and (g) South Karanpura coalfields occupy an area of 1230 and 53 sq km. respectively (Chakraborty, 1972). Geographically, North Karanpura coalfield falls within Hazaribagh district but it extends into Ranchi and Palamau districts also. Vast areas of this coalfield are still undeveloped and the regional exploration conducted by the Geological Survey of India has revealed its potentialities in vast reserves of metallurgical and thermal grade coal. Total reserves of these coalfields (excluding Raniganj and South Karanpura coalfields have been estimated to be 43,147 million tons.

2. Giridih, Itkhori and Chope coalfields of Hazaribagh and Giridih districts are comparatively smaller in areal extent but they contain good coal.

3. Auranga, Hutar and Daltonganj coalfields in Palamau district together cover an area of about 612 sq. km.

Iron ore is associated mainly with the Pre-Cambrian rocks. Its deposits occur in a series of prominent hills known as the

Iron Ore Series and the Kolhan series stretching from the south west part of Singhbhum into Keonjhar and Subarnrekha districts of Orissa. Iron content in these ores is very high. Chief iron-ore mining centres are at Noamundi, Gua, Jamda, etc.

Mica belt extends over a wide area with northern part of Hazaribagh as its centre. 80 per cent of the mica production comes from this part of the mica belt. Mica splitting has developed in the region mainly as household industry and its important centres are located within the mica belt.

Copper generally occurs in nature as native copper or in combination with other minerals. Here in the region it is found in the form of chalcopyrites. The copper belt is about 129 kms. long and it passes through Kharsawan, Seraikela and Dhalbhum where it curves to south-east through Rekha mines and Musabani ending in the south-eastern part of Bahragora. The major portion of copper produced in the country is utilised by the Indian Copper Corporation Limited for the manufacture of yellow metal sheets and rolled brass for utensil industry. The total reserves of ores are estimated to be 3.85 million tons.

Bauxite is used commercially as the source of aluminium. Bauxite deposits in the region are found in numerous highly dissected hillocks forming conspicuous scarps in western Ranchi and southern Palamau. The total reserve of bauxite in the impartant 'pats' is estimated to be 1,300,000 tonnes. As this part of the region is highly dissected and inaccessible, it is expected that when properly surveyed smaller plateaus might also come into prominence.

Water Resources (Fig 10)

The rivers of the region are mostly non-perennial. Because of the impervious nature of rocks and steep gradients, underground water storage is minimum and the Geological Survey of India has described the districts of the region as unsuitable for even moderate groundwater development (Roy and Sinha, 1968). On the other hand pressure on water utilisation is increasing day by day because of the industrial and urban growth of the region.

The major river basins of the region are of the Damodar, the Subarnrekha, the Koel, and the Sankh (Fig 10). Water potential of the region as estimated by the Irrigation Commission report of the Bihar Government (1975) is summarised in table 2.10.

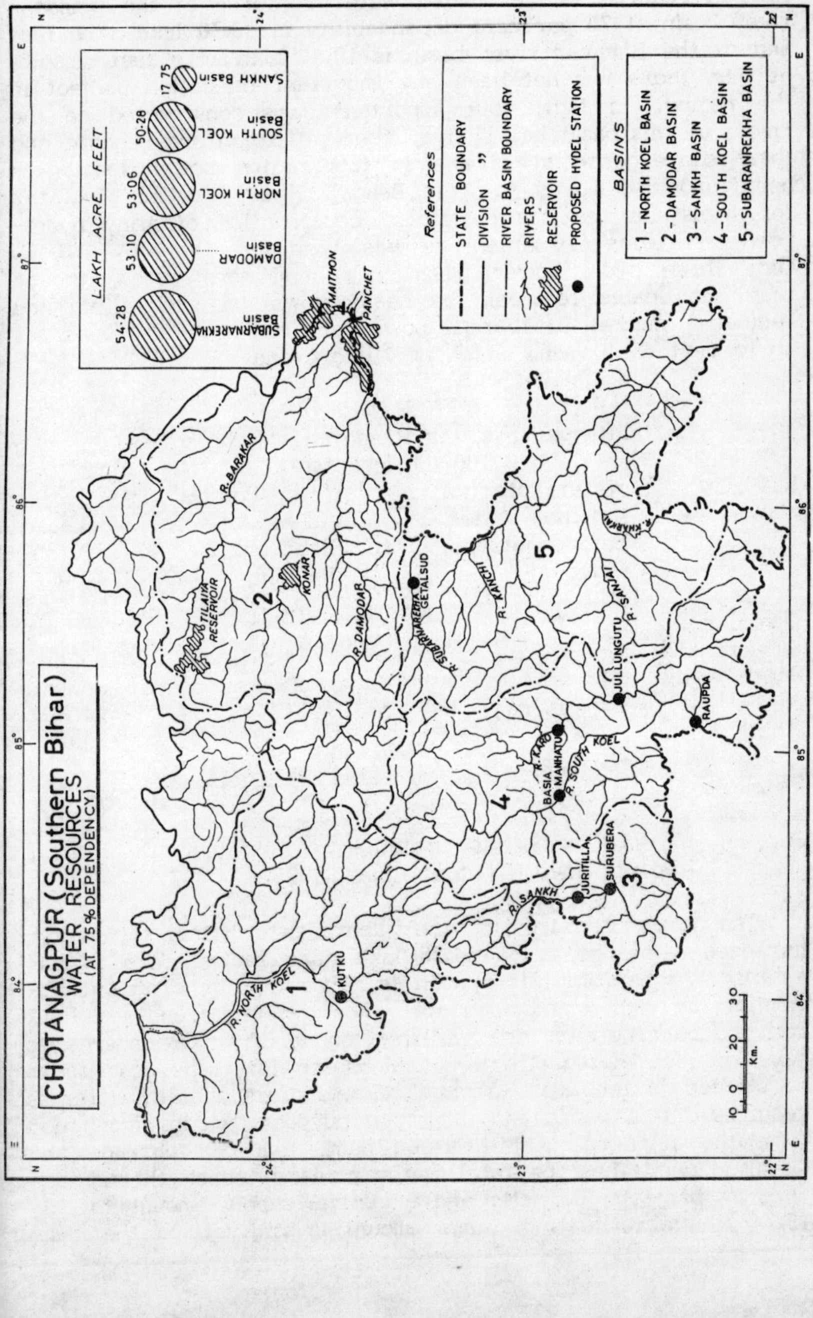

CHOTANAGPUR (Southern Bihar)
WATER RESOURCES
(AT 75% DEPENDENCY)
LAKH ACRE FEET
54·28 SUBARNAREKHA Basin
53·10 DAMODAR Basin
53·06 NORTH KOEL Basin
50·28 SOUTH KOEL Basin
17·75 SANKH Basin
References
STATE BOUNDARY
DIVISION "
RIVER BASIN BOUNDARY
RIVERS
RESERVOIR
PROPOSED HYDEL STATION
BASINS
1-NORTH KOEL BASIN
2-DAMODAR BASIN
3-SANKH BASIN
4-SOUTH KOEL BASIN
5-SUBARANREKHA BASIN
R. NORTH KOEL
KUTKU
TILAIYA RESERVOIR
KONAR
R. BARAKAR
MAITHON
PANCHET
R. DAMODAR
R. SUBARNAREKHA
GETALSUD
R. KANCHI
R. KARO
BASIA
MANHATU
R. SOUTH KOEL
R. SANKH
JURITILLA
SURUBERA
JULLUNGUTU
R. SANJAI
R. KHARKAI
RAUPDA
10 0 20 30
Km.

Fig. 10

The Damodar river basin is drained by the Damodar, the Barakar and a number of their tributaries. On the basis of the rainfall records, the estimated water resource of the Damodar river basin at 75 per cent dependability is 33.70 lakh acre feet and of the Barakar river basin is 19.40 lakh acre feet. Inspite of this, there has not been any important irrigation project in the region. In fact, four important dams constructed on the rivers of this basin i.e. Tilaiya, Konar, Maithon and Panchet and their submergence areas are in this region but irrigation is being provided mostly to West Bengal. Heavy demand of water for industrial use has restricted construction of many hydel-power stations (10 units) as was proposed early by D.V.C. Only three hydel power units have been constructed, though they are unable to meet the heavy power demand within the region. A number of thermal power stations have also been set up to meet the demand which is still growing.

TABLE 2.10

Chota Nagpur : Water Resources of the Rivers

(In 100000 acre feet)

RIVER	Water Potential in other states before entering Bihar	Water Potential in Bihar portion only	Total Water Potential
Damodar	-	53.10	53.10
Subarnrekha	11.72	54.28	66.00
South Koel	-	50.28	50.28
Sankh	6.36	17.75	24.11
North Koel	-	53.06	53.06
Total	18.08	228.47	246.55

Source: Water Resources of Bihar, Irrigation Commission Report, Government of Bihar, 1975.

The water resource of the Subarnrekha within the region has been estimated to be 54.28 lakh acre feet at 75% dependability. As artificial irrigation is necessary for crop cultivation in the region and adequate water resources and excellent dam and barrage sites are available, about 13 irrigation schemes have been completed. There are plans for few more schemes to be started in the area. About 2.76 lakh acre feet of water is required for domestic and industrial purposes which is supplied from the Hatia dam, Sitarampur dam, Jodugora barrage and Getalsud dam. Thus the total water already tapped through irrigation projects, domestic and industrial supply amount to only 15.74 lakh acre feet. A large amount is still left in the basin unused for which suitable irrigation and water supply schemes may be planned. There is only one hydroelectric power project at Getalsud in the region.

Water resources of the South Koel basin have not been assessed properly for want of appropriate discharge figures. Therefore, the available assessment is a very rough estimate which is approximately 50.28 lakh acre feet. Inspite of great need for irrigation and availability of water, no major scheme has yet been started. There are five minor schemes which irrigate about 22,000 acres only. Similarly, there is no hydel-power station in the basin, though its potentiality was assessed as early as 1954 and a report was prepared. (Government of India, 1954)

The Sankh river basin has approximately 17.75 lakh acre feet of water resource at 75% dependability rate. At present 9 minor schemes have been initiated in the basin but there is a proposal for 26 storage dams and 16 diversion barrages to be constructed in the basin. After their completion they would be able to irrigate 370.50 sq. km. of area in the basin. Though the hydroelectric power potential of this river basin has been assessed to be 155 M.W. of firm power, there is no hydro-electricity generation scheme at present. Six power stations have been proposed to utilises the available resource.

The North Koel Basin is a part of the Son river basin, but its major portion lies within the region. It is proposed to initiate few irrigation schemes to irrigate about 311.88 sq. km. of area in Palamau and Ranchi districts. The water resource potential of this river is estimated to be 53.06 lakh acre feet. There is no hydroelectric power scheme in this basin which could have been helpful in the region's development.

Power Resources

Coal, oil and water are the important sources of power generation. There are three thermal power stations one each at Patratu, Bokaro and Chandrapura and five hydroelectric power stations within the region but all of them are located in the eastern part of the region (Fig 11). As is apparent from the figure, maximum power demand is for the industrial purposes. Dhanbad and Singhbhum districts have a very high consumption of power within the region.

Human Resources

Population forms an integral part of the region's resource.

For balanced developent of regions, it is necessary to have harmony between the number of people (and within it, workers) and manpower demand of the sectors of production and services. It, therefore, becomes essential to study the nature and trend of population growth and its demographic, economic and cultural traits which help to ascertain the development of the human potential of the region, its degree of utilisation and also to provide a framework for preparing developmental strategies.

In this backgroud, region's population growth, density, distribution and other characteristics like sex ratio, literacy rate, economic participation ratio, ethnic composition have been analysed.

Changes in Population (1901-1981)

A comparative analysis of the population change between 1901 and 1981 of the Chota Nagpur region and Bihar will help to establish the region's position in the state because such comparisons have often been found to be useful in visualising regional characteristics (Britton, 1967). Similarly inter-district and intra-district variations during past eight decades may prove to be useful in assessing the region's growth potentialities. To measure the rate of change, decadal variations in population size expressed in percentage have been used (Table 2.11).

It is evident from the table 2.11 that the region has experienced a positive population change though with varying magnitude all through eight decades since 1901 and its rate of increase has always been higher than the State's average growth-rate. Inter-district variations are however sharp. During 1911-21 the growth rate has been low and even negative in certain areas. This conforms however, to the whole country and the region was no exception. Palamau, Dhanbad and Singhbhum experienced a slow growth while Hazaribagh and Ranchi had negative growth-rate. Since 1921, all the districts have gained population but the decadal variations show a fluctuating trend. Since 1951, however, the district level, the regional level (Chota Nagpur) and the State level figures show higher growth rate (15 per cent and above).

Population Distribution and Density

The Chota Nagpur region had 19.6 per cent of the State's total population in 1971 as against 15.6 per cent in 1901. Among the districts, Hazaribagh ranks first with more than 3 million people in 1971 and Dhanbad is the last with 1.4 million popula-

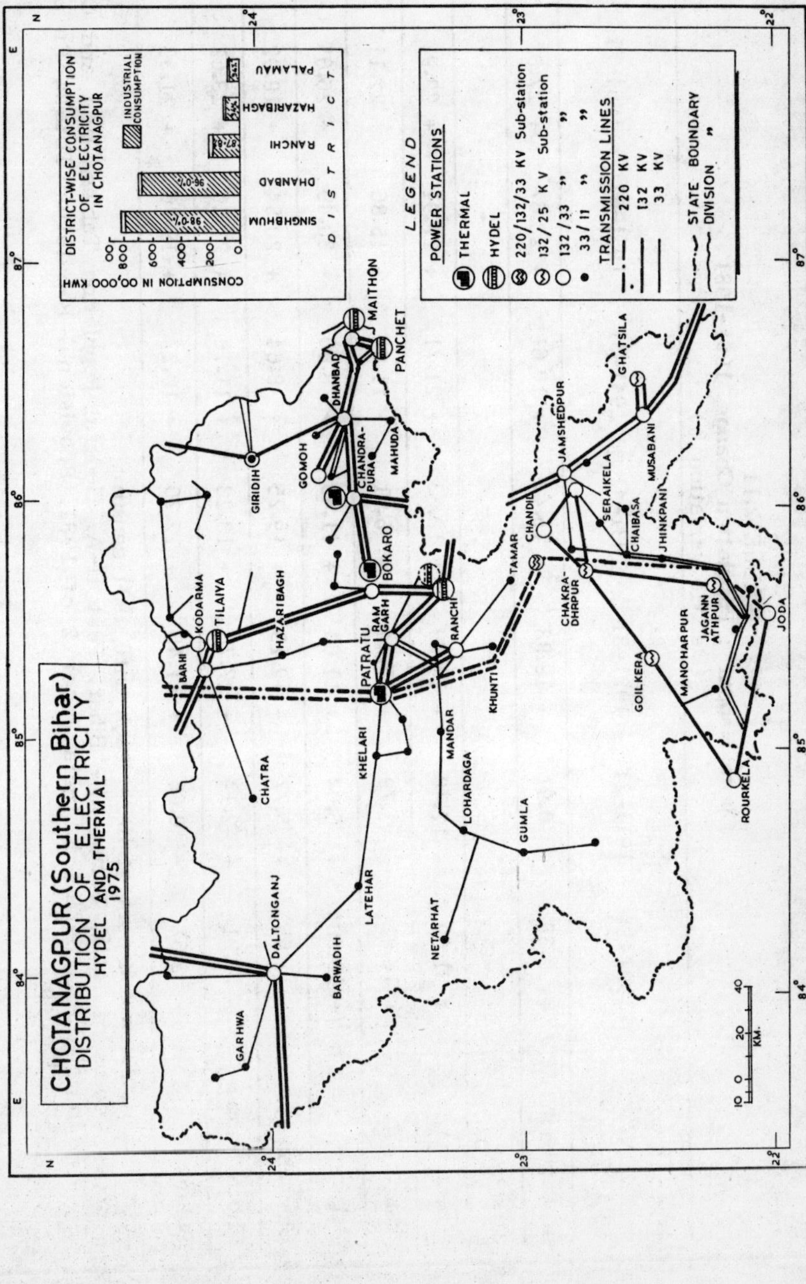
CHOTANAGPUR (Southern Bihar)
DISTRIBUTION OF ELECTRICITY
HYDEL AND THERMAL
1975
DISTRICT-WISE CONSUMPTION OF ELECTRICITY IN CHOTANAGPUR
INDUSTRIAL CONSUMPTION
CONSUMPTION IN 00,000 KWH
SINGHBHUM
DHANBAD
RANCHI
HAZARIBAGH
PALAMAU
DISTRICT
LEGEND
POWER STATIONS
THERMAL
HYDEL
220/132/33 KV Sub-station
132/25 KV Sub-station
132/33 " "
33/11 " "
TRANSMISSION LINES
220 KV
132 KV
33 KV
STATE BOUNDARY
DIVISION "
GARHWA
DALTONGANJ
BARWADIH
LATEHAR
NETARHAT
CHATRA
KHELARI
LOHARDAGA
GUMLA
MANDAR
KHUNTI
RANCHI
TAMAR
PATRATU
RAM GARH
HAZARIBAGH
BARHI
KODARMA
TILAIYA
BOKARO
GIRIDIH
GOMOH
CHANDRAPURA
MAHUDA
DHANBAD
MAITHON
PANCHET
CHANDIL
JAMSHEDPUR
GHATSILA
MUSABANI
SERAIKELA
CHAIBASA
JHINKPANI
CHAKRADHRPUR
GOILKERA
MANOHARPUR
JAGANNATHPUR
JODA
ROURKELA
KM.

Fig. 11

TABLE 2.11

Chota Nagpur : Population Change, 1901-1981

(Decade variation %)

DISTRICT/ REGION/ STATE	1901-11	1911-21	1921-31	1931-41	1941-51	1951-61	1961-71	1971-81
Hazaribagh	+ 9.39	- 0.91	+ 18.83	+ 15.42	+ 10.61	+ 23.67	+ 27.32	+ 33.41
Giridih*	-	-	-	-	-	-	-	+ 25.91
Dhanbad	+ 31.99	+ 12.40	+ 15.89	+ 13.33	+ 21.71	+ 27.91	+ 23.97	+ 43.50
Ranchi	+ 16.81	- 3.79	+ 17.44	+ 6.91	+ 11.09	+ 15.86	+ 22.11	+ 17.15
Palamau	+ 10.90	+ 6.64	+ 11.64	+ 11.48	+ 8.00	+ 20.49	+ 26.65	+ 27.37
Singhbhum	+ 11.65	+ 5.77	+ 12.19	+ 19.25	+ 8.64	+ 20.54	+ 18.92	+ 17.29
Chota Nagpur	+ 14.21	+ 2.14	+ 17.78	+ 13.23	+ 11.18	+ 21.10	+ 23.61	+ 25.59
Bihar	+ 3.67	- 0.66	+ 11.45	+ 12.20	+ 10.27	+ 19.76	+ 21.33	+ 23.90

* Giridih was a part of Hazaribagh until 1971 census.

Source: Census of India, Series 4 - Bihar, Part II-A, General Population Tables, 1971 and Census of India, 1981, Series 1, India Paper 2 of 1981, Provisional Population Totals, Rural-Urban Distribution.

tion (Table 2.12). But 1981 Census reveals change in this order. Division of Hazaribagh into 2 districts - Hazaribagh and Giridih brought down Hazaribagh from the Ist to the 3rd rank. Dhanbad with a fast increase in population is pushed up to the 4th position in this ranking. Thus in the new ranking Ranchi secures the first position and Giridih is placed last.

But if the percentage share of each district is observed during last eight decades, Dhanbad appears as the only district where population concentration has been fairly significant. During 1901, it had only 9 per cent of the total population as against 15 per cent in 1981. Ranchi shows a gradual decline in its share during all eight decades. Palamau, Hazaribagh and Singhbhum show slight fluctuations and their relative share has not changed significantly.

In order to bring out the unevenness in the distribution of population the index of population concentration is computed. By obtaining the difference between the percentage of population and percentage of area (Mitra and Singh, 1971) areas of high and low population concentration may be found. The formula for its computation is as follows:

$$I.C = \frac{1}{2} X \frac{K}{i = 1} Xi - Yi$$

Where:

I.C = Index of Concentration
i = Concentration in a Small unit
K = Total number of small units
Xi = Percent of population in the ith areal unit
Yi = Percent of area of that particular place contained in the ith areal unit

Index of population concentration prepared for the districts of Bihar (Sharma, 1977) reveals that except Dhanbad all other districts of the Chota Nagpur have negative values reflecting very low concertratio of population compared to their area. Even Dhanbad's value which is on the positive side (7.65) is low compared to districts of Bihar plains.

An attempt is made to work out the index of population concentration for each of the development blocks of the region. Based on the breaks in the value range seven groups were identified (Table 2.13). A very high percentage (54.6) of the blocks show negative population concentration which means that compared to their area, they have less population. Most of the

TABLE 2.12

Chota Nagpur : Relative Share of Population (1901–1981)

(Population figures are in millions; Figures in bracket are percentages to total population of the region)

DISTRICT/ REGION	1901	1911	1921	1931	1941	1951	1961	1971	1981
Hazaribag	1.16 (27.4)	1.28 (26.2)	1.27 (25.4)	1.50 (25.7)	1.73 (26.1)	1.92 (26.0)	2.37 (26.6)	3.02 (27.4)	2.19 (15.8)
Giridih*	-	-	-	-	-	-	-	-	1.73 (12.5)
Dhanbad	0.39 (9.2)	0.51 (10.6)	0.58 (11.6)	0.67 (11.4)	0.76 (11.4)	0.92 (12.5)	1.18 (13.2)	1.47 (13.3)	2.10 (15.2)
Ranchi	1.18 (27.6)	1.38 (28.2)	1.32 (26.6)	1.55 (26.5)	1.60 (25.1)	1.85 (25.0)	2.14 (23.9)	2.61 (23.6)	3.06 (22.1)
Palamau	0.62 (14.5)	0.69 (14.1)	0.73 (14.8)	0.82 (14.0)	0.91 (13.8)	0.99 (13.4)	1.19 (13.3)	1.50 (13.6)	1.92 (13.8)
Singhbhum	0.91 (21.3)	1.01 (20.9)	1.07 (21.6)	1.31 (22.4)	1.57 (23.6)	1.70 (23.1)	2.05 (23.0)	2.44 (22.1)	2.86 (20.6)
Chota Nagpur	4.26 (100)	4.87 (100)	4.97 (100)	5.85 (100)	6.63 (100)	7.38 (100)	8.93 (100)	11.04 (100)	13.86 (100)

* Giridih was a part of Hazaribagh until 1971 Census.

Source: Census of India, Series 4 - Bihar, Part II A, General Population Tables, 1971, and Census of India 1981, Series 1, India, Paper 2 of 1981, Provisional Population Totals, Rural - Urban Distribution.

Blocks of the northern, western and southern parts of the region fall in this category. Remaining blocks with positive index values may be grouped into two broad categories each consisting of 3 sub-groups. It is clear from the table that only ten blocks have index values of more than 50.0 depicting high concentration of population. In fact, these are the blocks marked with fast industrial and urban growth and are located in three distinct patches in the eastern part of the region. The other group with index value of 0.1 to 50.0 is distributed mostly along the transport routes and around the areas with higher values. Thus it can be summarised that majority of blocks have low concentration of population because of vast rugged and forested terrain. Only few blocks have high concentration of population which are located mostly in the plain areas with favourable terrain or have mining and manufacturing activities to attract population. Distribution of population is, therefore, extremely uneven.

TABLE 2.13

Chota Nagpur : Index of Population Concentration:1971

GROUPS	VALUE RANGE	NUMBER OF BLOCKS
I	Negative Values - 0.10 to - 70.00	83
II	Positive Values: 0.01 to 10.00	31
III	10.01 to 30.00	21
IV	30.01 to 50.00	7
V	50.01 to 75.00	3
VI	75.01 to 100.00	3
VII	100.01 to 300.00	4

In terms of population density, Palamau, Ranchi, Hazaribagh and Singhbhum had a density of 119, 142, 167, and 181 persons per sq km (1971) respectively which were less than the State's average of 324 persons per sq km. Dhanbad with 490 persons per sq km. had the highest density within the region. Density of population for blocks is shown in Fig. 12. Topography, resource availability and their utilisation and the nature of economic activity seem to influence the population distribution. Blocks with high to very high density of population (more than 300 person per sq. km) are few and are located mostly in the mining and manufacturing areas of Dhanbad, Ranchi, Hazaribagh, Giridih and Singhbhum. In Palamau, only Daltonganj block has a high density. Large number of blocks in the northern, western and southern parts of the region have a very low density of population, which is even lower than the region's average (168 persons per sq. km).

Rural and Urban Population

Proportion of urban population to total population is one of the indicators of region's economic character as the process of urbanisation has long been recognised as a concomitant of social and economic development.

Decadal variations in the rural and urban components of population for the districts, region and the State is shown in Table 2.14.

The proportion of urban population is in general higher than the state average in all districts except Palamau. Dhanbad has more than 50 per cent (1981) of population in urban areas which is the highest figure among all districts of Bihar. Comparison of 1971 and 1981 figures reveal increase in urban population in all districts. Palamau with only 5.6 per cent (1981) of urban population is the least urbanised district.

So far as distribution of urban population at the block level is concerned, of 152 blocks only 42 blocks (27.6%) have urban population. Thus a large number of blocks in the region are completely rural. Even among the urbanised blocks, two features of the pattern of urbanisation are noteworthy. In areas of relatively low population concentration the share of urban centres as places of immigration and of important activities is generally high. Secondly, there are 'small towns' which owe their urban status due to mining activity and these cannot be called as towns in the functional economic sense.

Sex Ratio

Sex ratio expressed as number of females per 1000 males, varies markedly among the districts of the region as well as between rural and urban areas (Table 2.15).

As is evident from the table 2.15, Hazaribagh and Ranchi are the only districts in the region where females outnumber males in the rural areas, a reflection of outmigration of males from rural areas elsewhere either to mining areas or industrial towns. Female population is particularly low in more industrialised and urbanised districts of Dhanbad and Singhbhum.

TABLE 2.14

Chota Nagpur : Rural and Urban Components (Percentage): Decadal Variations (1901-1981)

(R and U refer to Rural and Urban Components respectively)

DISTRICT/ REGION/ STATE	1901		1911		1921		1931		1941		1951		1961		1971		1981	
	R	U	R	U	R	U	R	U	R	U	R	U	R	U	R	U	R	U
1	2	3	4	5	6	7	8	9	10	11	12	13	14	15	16	17	18	19
Hazari-bagh	96.9	3.1	97.1	2.9	96.5	3.5	96.6	3.4	95.2	4.8	93.1	6.9	91.5	8.5	87.1	12.9	84.9	15.1
Giridih	-	-	-	-	-	-	-	-	-	-	-	-	-	-	-	-	85.8	14.2
Dhanbad	-	-	-	-	97.9	2.1	97.6	2.4	94.8	5.2	91.4	8.6	75.5	24.5	56.5	43.5	49.3	50.7
Ranchi	96.8	3.2	96.6	3.4	96.1	3.9	95.8	4.2	95.4	4.6	93.2	6.8	90.5	9.5	86.3	13.7	79.1	20.9
Palamau	98.5	1.5	98.3	1.7	97.3	2.7	97.1	2.9	97.5	2.5	96.2	3.8	95.3	4.7	95.3	4.7	94.4	5.6
Singh-bhum	99.0	1.0	98.6	1.4	93.1	6.9	91.3	8.7	86.0	14.0	83.0	17.0	78.5	21.5	73.8	26.2	67.9	32.1
Chota Nagpur	97.9	2.1	97.7	2.3	95.9	4.1	95.4	4.6	93.4	6.6	91.0	9.0	86.7	13.3	81.0	19.0	76.1	23.9
Bihar	96.0	4.0	96.2	3.8	95.9	4.1	95.5	4.5	94.6	5.4	93.2	6.8	91.6	8.4	90.0	10.0	87.5	12.5

Source: Census of India, Series 4 - Bihar, Part II A, General Population Tables, 1971; and Census of India, Series 1 - India, Paper II of 1981, Provisional Population Tables

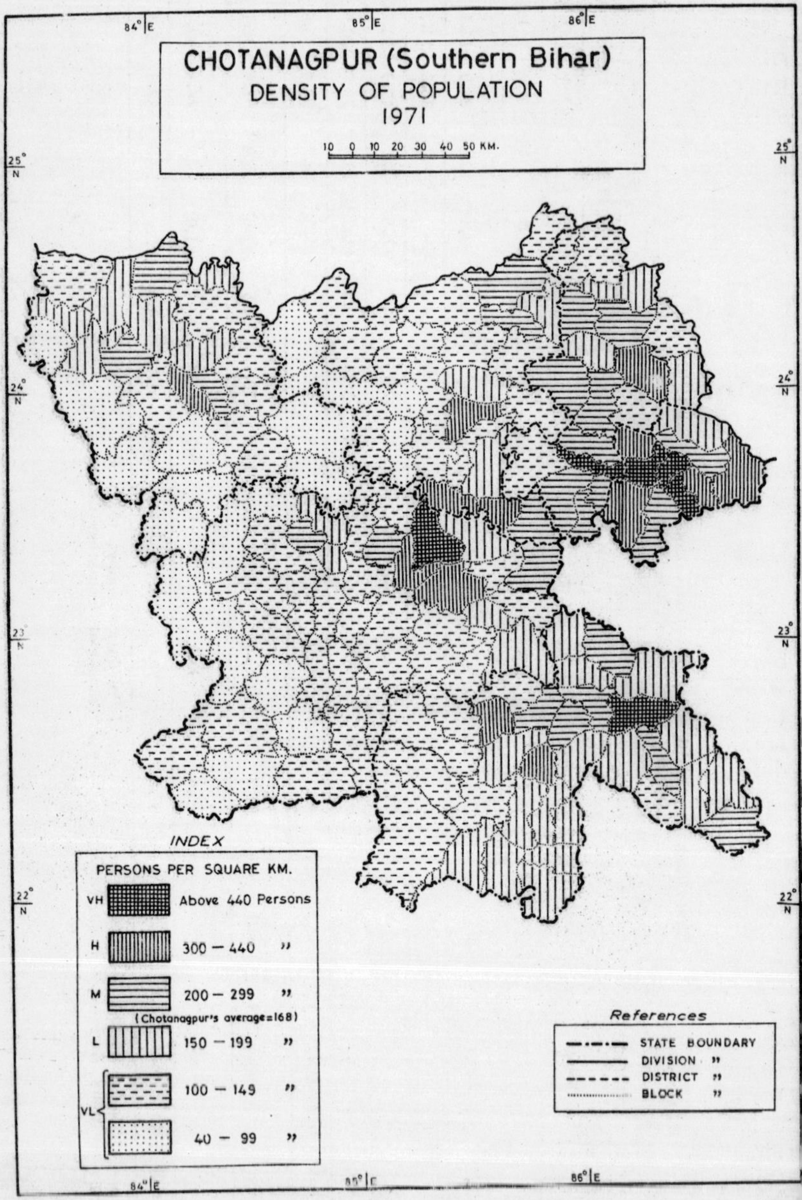
84° E
85° E
86° E
CHOTANAGPUR (Southern Bihar)
DENSITY OF POPULATION
1971
10 0 10 20 30 40 50 KM.
25° N
24° N
23° N
22° N
INDEX
PERSONS PER SQUARE KM.
VH Above 440 Persons
H 300 — 440 "
M 200 — 299 "
(Chotanagpur's average=168)
L 150 — 199 "
VL 100 — 149 "
40 — 99 "
References
STATE BOUNDARY
DIVISION "
DISTRICT "
BLOCK "

Fig. 12

TABLE 2.15

Chota Nagpur : Sex Ratio (1971)

DISTRICT/ REGION/ STATE	RURAL	URBAN	TOTAL
Hazaribagh	1009	799	979
Dhanbad	893	675	792
Ranchi	1001	815	973
Palamau	970	842	963
Singhbhum	998	802	942
Chota Nagpur	987	764	942
Bihar	971	807	954

Source: Census of India, Series 4, Bihar, Part II A, General Population Tables, 1971.

Literacy Rate

Literacy rate is an important component of the cultural attributes of population as it provides a basis for jiudging the potentiality of the human resource. Economic development of a region affects the literacy rate on one hand and gets affected on the other. According to the census definition, literacy has been used as the ability of a person who can read and write with understanding in any language. Though the literacy defined this way may not be used for judging the quality of the work-force, it can be used at least for measuring the level of development.

TABLE 2.16

Chota Nagpur : Literacy (1971)

(Figures in percent)

DISTRICT/ REGION/ STATE	LITERACY		
	RURAL	URBAN	TOTAL
Hazaribagh	12.84	40.63	16.42
Dhanbad	20.11	41.72	29.51
Ranchi	18.03	56.14	23.24
Palamau	13.62	45.61	15.12
Singhbhum	15.77	54.22	25.86
Chota Nagpur	15.54	47.93	21.68
Bihar	17.17	44.92	19.94

Source: Census of India, Series 4, Bihar, Part II A General Population, Tables 1971.

It is apparent from table 2.16 that urban literacy rate is usually higher than rural and total literacy rates. The Chota Nagpur region in general, has higher urban and total literacy rate than the State's average. At the district level, Ranchi and Singhbhum have more than 54 per cent of their urban population literate. In rest of the districts it varies between 40 and 46 per cent. Rural literacy, on the contrary, is quite low and varies between 12 and 20 per cent. Due to wide gap between rural and urban literacy rates, the percentage for the total population comes between these two extremes and varies between 15 and 29 percent.

Intra-regional variations observed at the block-level are quite distinct (Fig 13). It reveals the following pattern:

(a) Mostly rural blocks of the region have low to very low literacy rate (less than 20 percent). As such large part of the region (116 blocks) belong to this category and some of them have even less than 10 percent of literacy. But Ranchi district is an exception to some extent; firstly because none of its blocks has very low literacy (less than 10 percent); and secondly, because some of the rural blocks (e.g Kolebira, Bano, etc.) have a higher literacy than the region's average. This has been mainly because of the efforts of the Christian Missionaries in this area.

(b) Blocks with urban population usually have a high literacy. As such distribution of blocks with high literacy has been highly uneven and most of them are located in the eastern part of the region in the mining - manufacturing belts. In fact, only three blocks (Golmuri, Ranchi and Dhanbad) have high to very high literacy (41-60 percent) in the region and they appear as the 'islands' around which some of the blocks have moderate literacy (21-40 per cent). Besides these three main clusters, few other blocks with moderate literacy are distributed isolately in the region.

Economic Participation Ratio (Fig 14)

This generally is a reflection of the region's economy. Higher percentage of workers would mean a well developed economy with more avenues for employment. An analysis of the comparison between the change in the economic participation ratio and the rate of population change during the same period could have brought out some interesting results by way of showing shifts in the economic activities of the people if there had been any. Because of change in the definition of workers, such a comparison becomes difficult. Hence, 1971 data on worker's

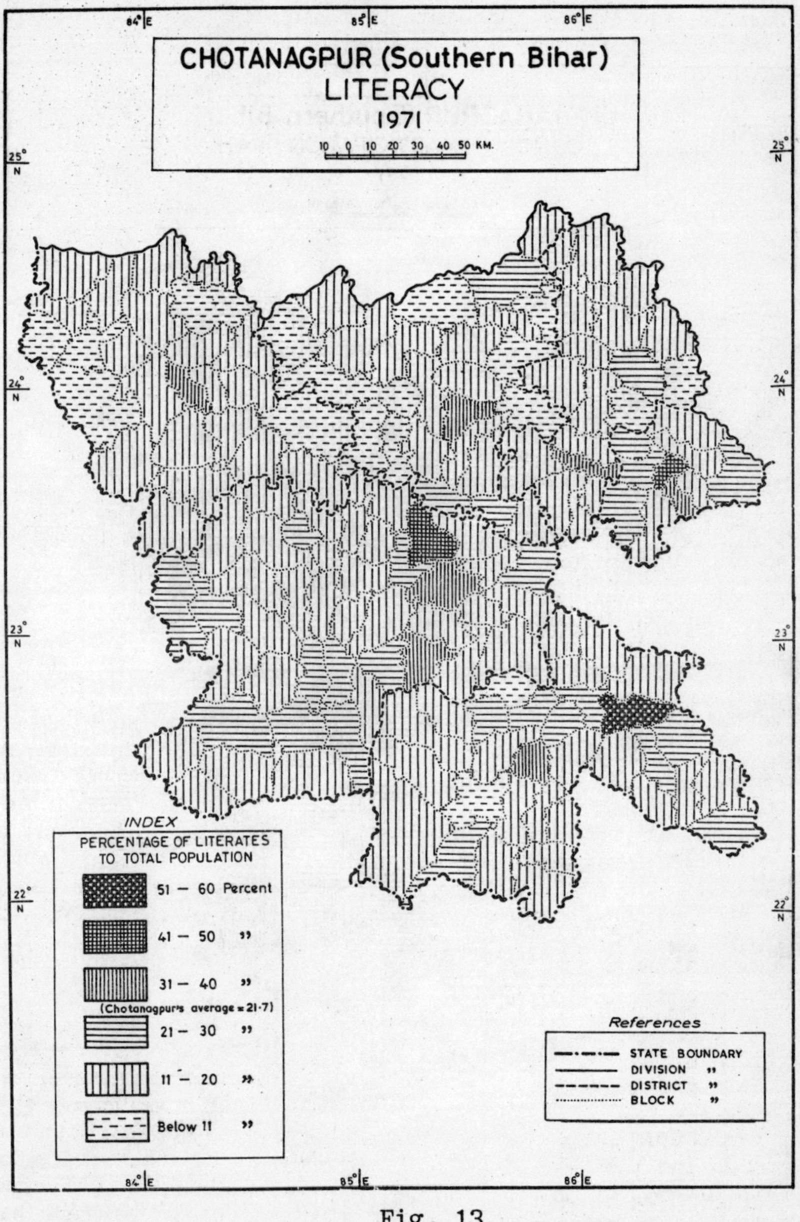
CHOTANAGPUR (Southern Bihar)
LITERACY
1971
10 0 10 20 30 40 50 KM.
84° E
85° E
86° E
25° N
24° N
23° N
22° N
INDEX
PERCENTAGE OF LITERATES TO TOTAL POPULATION
51 — 60 Percent
41 — 50 "
31 — 40 "
(Chotanagpur's average = 21·7)
21 — 30 "
11 — 20 "
Below 11 "
References
STATE BOUNDARY
DIVISION "
DISTRICT "
BLOCK "

Fig. 13

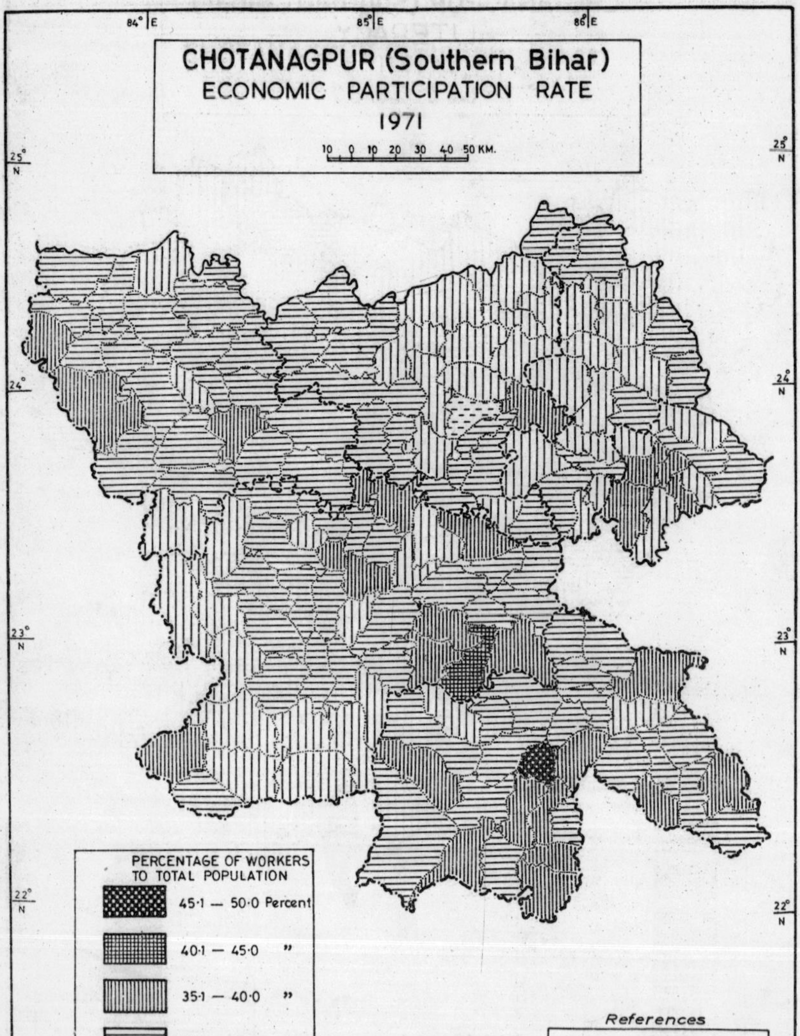
CHOTANAGPUR (Southern Bihar)
ECONOMIC PARTICIPATION RATE
1971
10 0 10 20 30 40 50 KM.
84° E
85° E
86° E
25° N
24° N
23° N
22° N
PERCENTAGE OF WORKERS TO TOTAL POPULATION
45·1 — 50·0 Percent
40·1 — 45·0 "
35·1 — 40·0 "
30·1 — 35·0 "
25·1 — 30·0 "
21·1 — 25·0 "
References
STATE BOUNDARY
DIVISION "
DISTRICT "
BLOCK "

Fig. 14

population at the block level have been used to describe the pattern of economy in the region (Fig 14).

Percentage of workers to total population in the Chota Nagpur region is slightly higher (31.85) than Bihar (31.03). Among the Blocks, more than 57 per cent of the blocks have higher percentage of workers than the average for Chota Nagpur. These blocks are distributed in the region in small patches and include mostly urban and industraial areas of the region.

As regards occupational structure of the workers, large part of the region (77 per cent of the blocks) have more than 80 per cent of their workers engaged in agricultural activities. Only 6 per cent (9 blocks) of the blocks have more than 40 per cent workers in industrial activities (mining and manufacturing) and these are located in Dhanbad and Singhbhum districts. Of all districts, Palamau is mostly agricultural as almost the entire area has more than 80 per cent of its workers in agricultural activities. In remaining districts, majority of the blocks are agricultural, but there are few groups of blocks particularly outside the forest belt with predominance of non-agricultural workers.

Scheduled Caste and Scheduled Tribe Population

Chota Nagpur contains about 14.9 per cent of the scheduled caste population of the State and nearly 25 per cent of the region's total is contained by Palamau alone. Concentration of scheduled tribe population is much more than the scheduled caste population as the region shares 70 per cent of the State's total scheduled tribe population. Singhbhum and Ranchi districts have fairly high concentration of scheduled tribe population as these districts form part of the tribal belt of Central India which includes neighbouring districts of Madhya Pradesh and Orissa also.

Distribution of scheduled caste and scheduled tribe population at the block level shows some distinguished patterns. More than 50 per cent of the scheduled caste and scheduled tribe population of the region is concentrated within a group of 59 blocks distributed almost contiguously in districts of Hazaribagh, Palamau and Ranchi in the western central part of the region. In general, blocks of the northern part of the region (districts of Palamau, Hazaribagh, Giridih and Dhanbad) have comparatively higher percentage of scheduled caste population than scheduled tribe population whereas in the southern part of the region, it is just the reverse. Percentage of scheduled caste and

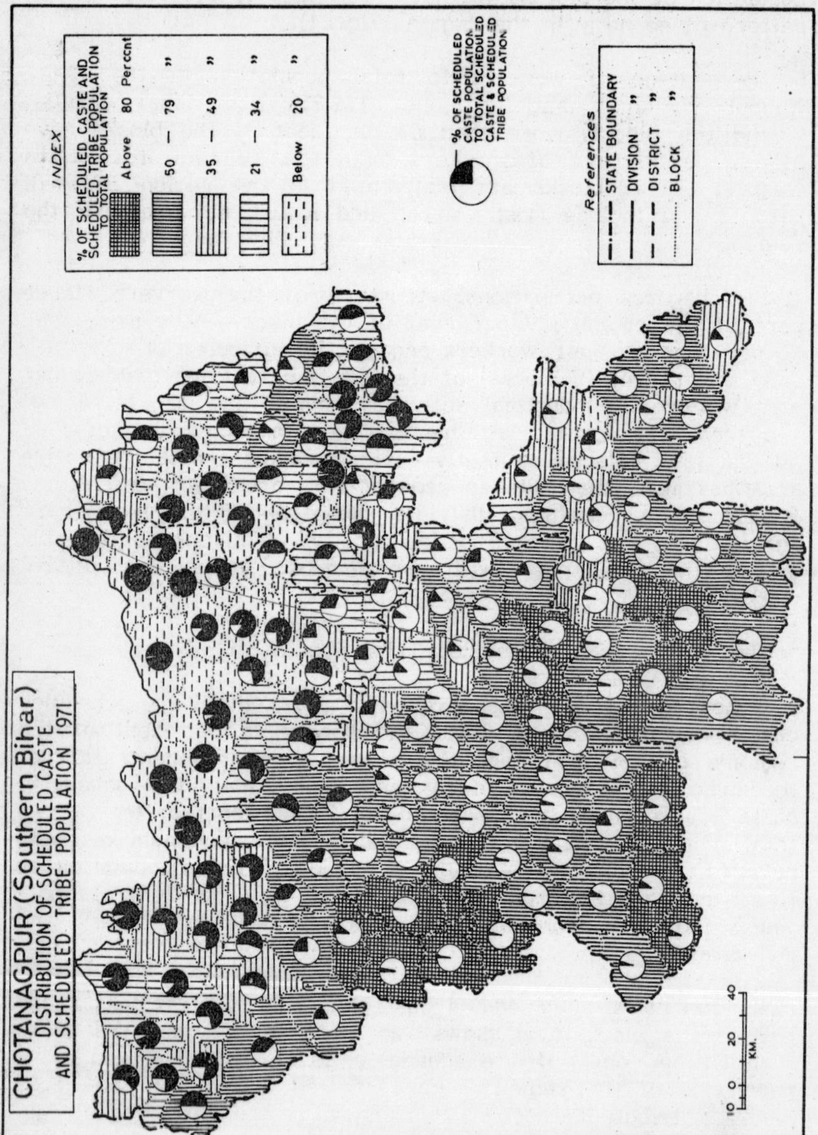
CHOTANAGPUR (Southern Bihar)
DISTRIBUTION OF SCHEDULED CASTE
AND SCHEDULED TRIBE POPULATION 1971
INDEX
% OF SCHEDULED CASTE AND SCHEDULED TRIBE POPULATION TO TOTAL POPULATION
Above 80 Percent
50 — 79 ”
35 — 49 ”
21 — 34 ”
Below 20 ”
% OF SCHEDULED CASTE POPULATION TO TOTAL SCHEDULED CASTE & SCHEDULED TRIBE POPULATION
References
STATE BOUNDARY
DIVISION ”
DISTRICT ”
BLOCK ”
10 0 20 40
KM.

Fig. 15

scheduled tribe population is generally low in the eastern part of the region particularly in the mining-manufacturing areas where large number of people have migrated from outside the region.

Thus it can be summarised that the resource potential of the region in general is very high both in terms of natural as well as human resources. But at present these resources are not being properly utilised in all parts of the region, which presents a highly imbalanced picture on the whole. Development of qualitative aspects of human resources would certainly help in overcoming the physical constraints to economic development. For example, scientific management of farming would increase agricultural production even in limited area of agriculture. Similarly, consciousness among the local people towards developing various natural resources of the region can only bring fruitful results.

THREE

Process and Patterns of Industrialisation:
Spatial and Temporal

INDUSTRIALISATION AND ECONOMIC DEVELOPMENT

Industrialisation is considered as vital for rapid economic development of a country. But it has different implications for the development of a system of regions within a country. Spatial and temporal patterns of industrialisation are influenced in the initial stages of development by the distributional pattern of economic activities and resources. The degree of importance of the resources or industries - national, regional and local - influence the initial pattern and this is dependent on the strategy employed in planning at these area levels. There are instances in India wherein the basic and heavy industries located in certain regions are a part of the national policy and unless a comple- mentary strategy for the development of resources and industries of regional importance is formulated by the State for purposes of establishing the forward and backward linkages for different set of activities, distortions in the sectoral and spatial patterns of development are bound to occur. The Chota Nagpur region is one such example.

If we compare the per capita income and the sectoral composition of income of the districts of the Chota Nagpur at two points of time that is 1955-56 and 1664-65 (Table 3.1) it would be clear that there is a positive association between the manufacturing sector of economy and per capita income. Likewise the low level of population would provide a paradox in which per capita income would appear to be relatively high. During 1955-56 Dhanbad derived 56 per cent of its income from manufacturing and its per capita income was Rs.391/-. It secured first position in both respects among all other districts of the region and was the most prosperous district. It retained its position in 1964-65 also by way of deriving 69 per cent of its income from manufacturing and having per capita income of Rs.882/-. Its total income was also highest among all districts (Rs.115.36 crores). Palamau on the other hand, was the least industrialised district both in 1955-56 and 1964-65 as the percentage share of manufacturing sector to the total income was 14 per cent only in 1955-56 (higher than Ranchi only) and 13 per cent in 1964-65. Per capita income was Rs.125/- in 1955-56 and Rs.140/- in 1964-65. These were the lowest figures in respective years.

Comparison of these figures also reveals that there has been a gradual increase in the percentage share of manufacturing sector to the total income of the districts from 1955-56 to 1964-65, though the rate has varied from one district to another. Per capita income has increased more or less in a similar fashion.

Agricultural income per head is generally lower than non-agricultural income all over the world, but the difference narrows down with the higher level of development. It is so because successful industrial development attracts labour from agriculture no doubt, but the reducing number of workers in the agricultural activity is able to produce more through the application of science and technology and agricultural efficiency is raised (Mountjoy, 1966). A more prosperous agricultural sector provides market for the products of a new or expanding industries.

Industrialisation may, therefore, be viewed as a process of transformation of the economic structure of a region during which dominance shifts from primary to secondary sector of economy. As such shifting distribution of labour among major kinds of activity, i.e. primary, secondary and tertiary (Clark, 1951) may be used to identify and classify the stages of economic development. Rostow (1960) views that an economy moves from a traditional stage through a take-off period to sustained growth, maturity and a stage of mass consumption. In order to assess the shift from one sector of economy to another, percentage of labour in all three sectors of economy classified as agriculture, industry (mining and manufacturing) and service for 152 blocks of the Chota Nagpur for two census years of 1961 and 1971 have been worked out and compared (Table 3.2). This exercise helped to identify and group the development blocks according to (a) increase in percentage of labour in single or a combination of two sectors (Fig 16) and (b) highest percentage of labour in any of the three sectors in 1971 (Fig 17). Of 152 blocks, 127 blocks showed an increase in the percentage share of agriculture and service during 1961-71. The proportions of workers in industry increased in 25 Blocks only, and a majority of them (19 blocks) had experienced it in combination with agriculture or service. Thus only six blocks had experienced increase in the proportion of workers in industrial

TABLE 3.1

Chota Nagpur : Per Capita and Sectoral Composition of Income (1955-56; 1964-65)

DISTRICT	PER CAPITA INCOME (In Rupees)		PERCENTAGE OF INCOME DERIVED FROM AGRICULTURE		MANUFACTURING		SERVICE	
	1955-56	1964-65	1955-56	1964-65	1955-56	1964-65	1955-56	1964-65
1	2	3	4	5	6	7	8	9
Dhanbad	391	882	25.80	5.55	56.00	69.45	18.20	25.00
Singhbhum	277	411	33.28	23.21	53.85	51.62	12.87	25.17
Ranchi	143	232	72.24	60.60	8.77	14.45	18.99	24.95
Hazaribagh	140	298	58.22	29.21	18.22	45.79	23.56	25.00
Palamau	125	140	62.33	61.94	13.87	13.07	23.80	24.99

Source: (a) Resource Development Regions and Divisions of India, Planning Commission, Government of India, New Delhi, 1964, pp 52-53.

(b) Regional Development Plan for South East Resource Region, Town and Country Planning Organisation, Government of India, New Delhi, 1976.

sector exclusively. Palamau emerged as the only district where not even a single block had experienced increase in the proportion of industrial workers.

With regard to the highest percentage of labour in any of the three sectors (Fig 17) the analysis revealed that majority of the blocks (122 blocks) had more than 75 per cent of workers engaged in agricultural activity with small proportions in secondary and tertiary activities. Of the remaining 30 blocks of the region, only 7 Blocks had more than 40 per cent of workers in industry. However, Jharia is the only Block which has more than 73 percent of workers in industry.

TABLE 3.2
Chota Nagpur : Employment Change (Percentage) During 1961-71

DISTRICT	BLOCK	AGRICULTURE		INDUSTRY		SERVICE	
		1961	1971	1961	1971	1961	1971
1	2	3	4	5	6	7	8
RANCHI	Kanke	40.4	35.4	16.6	14.9	43.0	49.7
	Namkum	66.0	39.0	15.7	34.1	18.3	26.9
	Ratu	71.8	73.2	12.9	17.3	15.3	9.5
	Bero	92.7	93.5	3.2	1.9	4.1	4.6
	Karra	85.3	87.2	9.7	5.1	5.0	7.7
	Lapung	88.6	91.2	7.6	4.3	3.8	4.5
	Lohardaga	83.8	79.7	6.7	5.7	9.5	14.6
	Bhandra	83.8	79.7	6.7	5.7	9.5	14.6
	Kuru	89.8	91.8	5.1	2.9	5.1	5.3
	Kisco	90.0	86.1	7.2	10.2	2.8	3.7
	Mandar	90.2	89.5	5.3	4.2	4.5	6.3
	Chanho	90.2	89.5	6.9	4.2	4.5	6.3
	Burmu	80.9	71.0	11.9	20.5	7.1	8.5
	Ormanjhi	86.1	89.7	9.2	5.8	4.7	4.5
	Angara	90.8	89.4	5.5	3.8	3.7	6.8
	Silli	77.1	82.6	10.2	6.7	12.7	10.7
	Sonahatu	89.4	92.7	6.4	2.7	4.2	4.6
	Bundu	77.1	85.3	10.1	4.7	12.8	10.0
	Tamar	89.6	92.0	5.6	3.4	4.8	4.6
	Erki	89.4	95.5	9.2	2.4	1.4	2.1
	Murhu	89.9	91.0	6.9	3.3	3.2	5.7
	Torpa	91.2	91.1	6.0	3.8	2.8	5.1
	Rania	91.2	91.1	6.0	3.8	2.8	5.1
	Basia	91.3	91.1	5.5	3.4	3.2	5.5
	Kamdara	92.7	93.0	4.8	2.6	2.5	4.4

	Kolebira	91.7	90.9	5.5	4.6	2.8	4.5
	Jaldega	91.7	90.9	5.5	4.6	2.8	4.5
	Simdega	87.5	84.7	5.3	4.1	7.2	11.2
	Thethaita-ngar	93.3	92.6	3.7	3.1	3.0	4.3
	Bolba	93.0	89.9	5.3	5.1	1.7	5.0
	Kurdeg	90.4	93.6	6.0	3.2	3.6	3.2
	Gumla	87.4	83.9	6.4	4.5	6.2	11.6
	Raidih	91.1	89.4	5.9	4.4	3.0	6.2
	Palkot	88.4	94.0	8.8	2.5	2.8	3.5
	Dumri	93.2	91.4	4.7	3.4	2.1	5.2
	Chainpur	92.1	89.6	4.7	3.4	3.2	7.0
	Ghaghra	94.8	94.7	3.3	1.8	1.9	3.5
	Sisai	95.1	93.2	3.5	2.4	1.4	4.4
	Verno	95.1	93.2	3.5	2.4	1.4	4.4
	Senha	93.4	93.0	4.5	3.3	2.1	3.7
	Bishunpur	88.3	91.2	6.5	3.1	5.2	5.7
	Bano	93.7	91.6	3.6	2.6	2.7	5.8
	Khunti	84.1	85.0	9.6	6.0	6.3	9.0
HAZARI-BAGH	Hazari-bagh	55.6	45.0	11.0	8.9	33.4	46.1
	Churchu	71.9	66.0	22.5	29.2	5.6	4.8
	Barkagaon	87.4	91.0	9.0	5.6	3.6	3.4
	Keredari	80.3	84.9	13.8	11.4	5.9	3.7
	Tandwa	89.0	93.5	6.7	2.8	4.3	3.7
	Katkamsandi	83.5	87.7	7.3	3.3	9.2	9.0
	Ichak	88.8	89.5	5.6	5.3	5.6	5.2
	Barhi	87.1	90.5	5.2	2.8	7.7	6.7
	Jainagar	87.7	86.7	7.5	4.8	4.8	8.5
	Kodarma	47.3	50.9	36.7	25.5	16.0	23.6
	Markacho	89.2	92.7	8.0	3.9	2.8	3.4
	Barkatha	92.7	94.1	3.8	2.1	3.5	3.8
	Bagodar	86.1	88.0	5.2	3.1	8.7	8.9
	Bishungarh	90.0	93.6	6.3	2.6	3.7	3.8
	Gumia	71.9	65.2	20.9	21.4	7.2	13.4
	Peterbar	89.7	70.6	6.1	9.3	4.2	20.1
	Jaridih	84.0	87.1	8.7	5.5	7.3	7.4
	Kasmar	90.6	90.3	5.5	3.7	3.9	6.0
	Gola	82.7	92.1	9.8	3.4	7.5	4.5
	Ramgarh	65.2	62.5	14.8	17.7	20.0	19.8
	Mandu	57.2	49.5	35.7	45.6	7.1	4.9
	Patratu	51.3	33.7	37.5	46.3	11.2	20.0
	Chatra	79.9	87.1	8.0	4.7	12.1	8.2
	Simaria	90.9	95.6	5.5	1.7	3.6	2.7
	Pratappur	78.3	93.2	11.7	2.7	10.0	4.1
	Hunterganj	79.6	92.1	10.5	3.0	9.9	4.9
	Chauparan	90.7	91.8	4.3	3.3	5.0	4.9

	Itkhori	91.8	94.4	4.1	1.7	4.1	3.9
	Giridih	42.4	46.4	40.8	30.6	18.4	23.0
	Pirtanr	91.3	92.7	3.4	2.9	5.3	4.4
	Dumri	87.9	87.2	4.6	3.9	7.5	8.9
	Nawadih	85.2	81.2	9.3	9.4	5.5	9.4
	Bermo	16.3	12.5	60.5	55.9	23.2	31.6
	Birni	93.0	94.5	4.1	1.7	2.9	3.8
	Dhanwar	92.6	91.6	4.1	2.7	3.3	5.7
	Gawan	74.8	84.0	17.6	9.9	7.6	6.1
	Satgawan	90.1	92.2	4.9	2.1	5.0	5.7
	Tisri	71.9	75.8	24.3	18.1	3.8	6.1
	Deori	90.9	95.6	7.5	1.4	1.6	3.0
	Jamua	89.7	91.8	6.0	2.4	4.3	5.8
	Bengabad	84.6	92.0	10.8	3.9	4.6	4.1
	Gande	86.2	93.8	9.7	2.5	4.1	3.7
PALAMAU	Daltonganj	55.0	55.7	11.5	8.5	33.5	35.8
	Chainpur	82.2	91.5	7.9	2.9	9.9	5.6
	Bishrampur	85.4	92.4	6.0	2.5	8.6	5.1
	Hussainabad	74.4	84.5	14.4	7.9	11.2	7.6
	Hariharganj	76.1	87.7	14.3	4.9	9.6	7.4
	Chhatarpur	87.8	95.4	8.5	1.7	3.7	2.9
	Patan	90.8	93.4	5.4	3.4	3.8	3.2
	Manatu	89.5	95.1	5.3	2.0	5.2	2.9
	Panki	88.0	94.5	6.6	2.2	5.4	3.3
	Lesliganj	92.2	93.8	4.0	2.6	3.8	3.6
	Latehar	82.4	88.2	6.8	2.8	10.8	9.0
	Garu	83.5	89.6	12.3	2.4	4.2	8.0
	Mahuadanr	86.8	89.3	5.5	2.2	7.7	8.5
	Barwadih	74.4	80.2	8.1	5.0	17.5	14.8
	Manika	90.0	94.0	4.4	1.2	5.6	4.8
	Balumath	87.9	94.4	6.9	1.8	5.2	3.8
	Chandwa	79.7	84.2	8.4	5.7	11.9	10.1
	Garhwa	72.2	84.1	11.7	4.9	16.1	11.0
	Ranka	90.7	94.6	6.0	2.2	3.3	3.2
	Bhandaria	88.7	93.0	5.2	2.1	6.1	4.9
	Dhurki	90.2	96.9	6.3	1.4	3.5	1.7
	Untari	82.2	91.7	5.9	3.2	11.9	5.1
	Bhawnathpur	88.9	93.2	6.9	4.1	4.2	2.7
	Manjhiaon	89.5	93.3	5.7	2.8	4.8	3.9
	Meral	87.9	96.2	6.4	1.0	5.7	2.8
DHANBAD	Dhanbad	10.2	7.7	59.0	53.2	30.8	39.1
	Jharia	4.7	3.0	70.7	70.7	24.6	26.3
	Gobindpur	82.5	83.2	8.3	6.9	9.2	9.9
	Tundi	91.2	92.6	5.4	3.0	3.4	4.4
	Nirsa	44.6	37.6	36.4	44.1	18.9	19.3
	Baliapur	78.7	64.4	19.8	24.2	11.5	11.4
	Baghmara	28.5	23.5	56.7	60.7	14.8	15.8
	Chandan-						

	kiyari	71.8	72.5	17.0	14.5	11.2	13.0
	Chas	84.9	49.3	9.9	17.8	5.2	32.9
	Topchanchi	69.3	63.3	9.3	8.4	21.1	28.3
SINGHBHUM	Chaibasa	73.1	60.7	10.6	9.6	16.3	29.7
	Tantnagar	88.9	94.2	7.9	2.8	3.2	3.0
	Manjhari	88.9	94.2	7.9	2.8	3.2	3.0
	Kumardungi	87.0	91.6	9.5	5.2	3.5	3.2
	Majhgaon	87.0	91.6	9.5	5.2	3.5	3.2
	Jagannath-pur	69.1	67.4	16.3	17.0	14.6	15.6
	Noamundi	69.1	67.4	16.3	17.0	14.6	15.6
	Jhinkpani	85.4	83.4	10.1	9.3	4.5	5.3
	Tonto	85.4	83.4	10.1	9.3	4.5	5.3
	Manoharpur	74.1	76.6	11.7	12.9	14.2	10.5
	Goilkera	86.6	93.0	7.0	3.3	6.4	3.7
	Sonua	80.5	85.9	12.1	8.3	7.4	5.8
	Bangaon	80.5	85.9	12.1	8.3	7.4	5.8
	Chakradhar-pur	64.7	77.5	18.2	8.9	17.1	13.6
	Khuntpani	64.7	77.5	18.2	8.9	17.1	13.6
	Seraikela	75.8	77.4	7.0	7.8	17.2	14.8
	Gobindpur	93.7	94.9	2.4	2.3	3.9	2.8
	Kharsawan	72.9	84.3	11.0	4.7	16.1	11.0
	Kuchai	85.8	91.2	9.4	5.8	4.8	3.0
	Chandil	78.5	87.0	10.6	6.2	10.9	6.8
	Ichagarh	86.3	94.0	9.0	2.3	4.7	3.7
	Nimdih	83.4	93.8	6.3	1.7	10.3	4.5
	Adityapur	63.0	56.9	18.2	26.8	18.8	16.3
	Golmuri	10.0	9.0	50.1	55.3	39.9	35.7
	Potka	87.2	86.6	7.4	7.5	5.4	5.9
	Patamda	87.6	93.7	6.8	3.0	5.6	3.3
	Ghatsila	71.5	72.2	12.8	16.5	15.7	11.3
	Dhalbhumgarh	80.6	84.8	11.0	7.6	3.4	7.6
	Chakulia	82.1	87.5	5.7	4.6	12.2	7.9
	Bahragora	83.3	89.7	8.0	4.3	8.7	6.0
	Dumaria	76.0	66.5	16.7	25.9	7.3	7.6
	Musabani	76.0	66.5	16.7	25.9	7.3	7.6

Source: Census of India, 1961, and 1971, Series IV Bihar, General Population Tables.

Wide variations are thus observed in the economic landscape of the region. Shift from primary sector to secondary and tertiary sectors of economy is very nominal indicating a slow economic transformation of the region. All parts of the region have vast potentialities for industrial development of one kind or the other. But industrial development has taken place only around existing mining and manufacturing centres. Inspite of the Government's consistent efforts, there has not been much

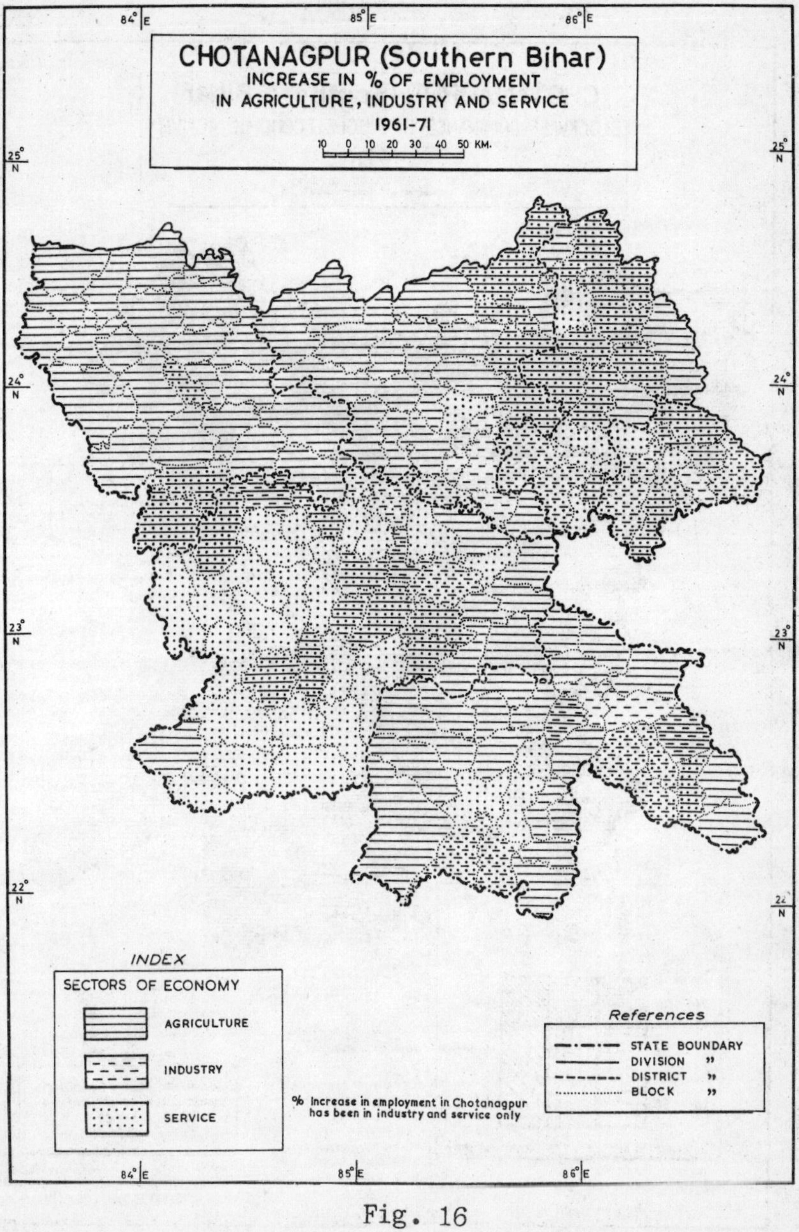
CHOTANAGPUR (Southern Bihar)
INCREASE IN % OF EMPLOYMENT
IN AGRICULTURE, INDUSTRY AND SERVICE
1961-71
10 0 10 20 30 40 50 KM.
84° E
85° E
86° E
25° N
24° N
23° N
22° N
INDEX
SECTORS OF ECONOMY
AGRICULTURE
INDUSTRY
SERVICE
% Increase in employment in Chotanagpur has been in industry and service only
References
STATE BOUNDARY
DIVISION "
DISTRICT "
BLOCK "

Fig. 16

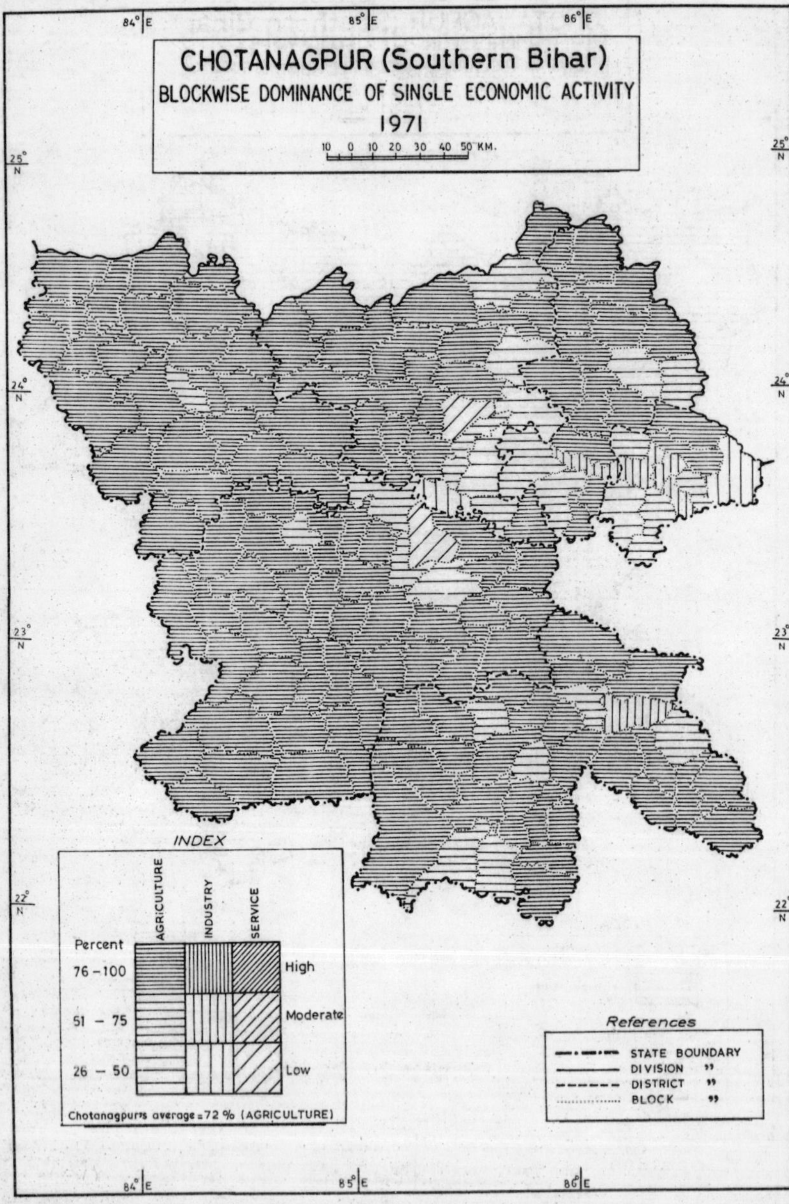

CHOTANAGPUR (Southern Bihar)
BLOCKWISE DOMINANCE OF SINGLE ECONOMIC ACTIVITY
1971
10 0 10 20 30 40 50 KM.
84° E
85° E
86° E
25° N
24° N
23° N
22° N
INDEX
AGRICULTURE
INDUSTRY
SERVICE
Percent
76 - 100
51 - 75
26 - 50
High
Moderate
Low
Chotanagpur's average = 72 % (AGRICULTURE)
References
STATE BOUNDARY
DIVISION "
DISTRICT "
BLOCK "

Fig. 17

development outside these areas. Such centres, therefore, appear as bold but isolated features in the agricul- tural backgrounds. In order to gain insight into the develop- mental problems at the sub-regional level, an attempt is made to study the process and patterns of industrialisation in the Chota Nagpur region. Main objectives are:

(i) to analyse the manufacturing growth and change since independence and its present industrial structure;

(ii) to understand the dynamic elements which have been responsible for differences in industrial development at sub-regional levels; and

(iii) to identify areas of high, moderate and low levels of development and select these centres/nodes which have acted as nuclei for industrial development.

MANUFACTURING : GROWTH AND CHANGE

Growth in manufacturing and change have been measured through (i) increase in the number and types of industrial units since independence; and (ii) change in the proportion of industrial workers during 1961-71 according to broad industry groups. Employment figures using absolute numbers for 1961 and 1971 are difficult to be compared because of change in the definition of workers. As such proportion of workers in different industry groups to total workers has been used wherever changes in employment have been referred.

Growth in Manufacturing Activity

Industrialisation is a recent phenomenon in the region. Though iron and copper smelting was known to the region since ancient times, mining of these minerals along with others started on a commercial basis very late. The first coal mine was opened at Giridih in 1851. The entire period of industrial development may be subdivided into two parts - pre-independence and post-independence periods. Industrial growth prior to independence was slow and concentration of industrial units was mostly in the Damodar Valley. The post-independence period however has witnessed a sudden upsurge of industries within the region with some diversification and emergence of new locations.

Pre-Independence Stage

Though the coal mining industry started in the region in 1851 and a number of coal mines and related industries got ground since then, there was no other major industrial establishment within the region until 1911 when India's first iron and steel plant set up by J.N. Tata at Jamshedpur started its production. During and after the First World War, the British Government's favourable policy for industrial development encouraged a number of industrial establishments to be set up within the region, mostly in the Damodar Valley coal belt. Coke oven plants and by-product plants naturally dominated in number over other industrial units because of coal mining industry. But gradually different types of industrial units were also established. These were Shalimar Tar products at Lodna, Dhanbad (1934); cement plant at Khelari, Ranchi (1936); Engineering Works at Kumardhubi, Dhanbad (1936); lead smelting and refining unit at Tundoo, Dhanbad (1942); refractory units in and around Dhanbad during 1939-45; fertiliser factory at Sindri, Dhanbad (1945) and Indo-Ashai Glass Works at Bhadainagar, Hazaribagh (1946). All of these were based on the local raw material.

Post-Independence Stage

Since independence the region has witnessed a remarkable industrial growth. During early years of independence i.e. 1947-50, Damodar Valley Corporation was set up (1948) as a multipurpose project to implement two phased programme. It's first phase of development has been completed during which four dams with connected hydro-electric stations were constructed at Tilaiya, Konar, Maithon and Panchet. In addition, a thermal power station at Bokaro was also set up. Indian Aluminium Company erected an alumina plant at Muri near Ranchi in 1948 using the bauxite reserves of the 'Pat' region. Fertiliser unit at Sindri was expanded with the addition of a coke-oven and a thermal plant.

Industrial growth has been spectacular since 1950. Twelve coal washeries have come up since then. They are located at West Bokaro (1951), Jamadoba (1952), Lodna (1955), Kargali (1958), Dugda I (1962), Bhojudih (1962), Pathardih (1965), Chasnala (1968), Dugda II (1968), Kathara (1969), Swang (1970) and Gidi (1970). The Central Coking Coal-Field Limited, is planning to establish a big coal washery near Ramgarh to utilise raw coal mined in the Ramgarh coalfield.

An iron and steel plant was set up at Bakaro in 1965 which was to be completed in two phases. The work of the first phase has been completed and production has started. A mini steel plant called M/s Alloy Steel Ltd. was also established at Patratu in 1972.

Refractory industries have grown mainly in two areas in the Damodar Valley coal field. One belt is spread between Ramgarh and Patratu comprising units like Hindustan Steel Refractories at Merar (1960), India Firebricks and Insulation Private Limited. at Ranchi Road (1960) and Karanpura Development Company Limited at Sirka (1970). Another belt lies along the Grand Trunk Road between Dhanbad and Chirkunda. Kharkari Firebricks at Kharkari (1957), Allied Refractories at Gobindpur (1974), Valley Refractories (1970) and Maithon Ceramics (1972) both located at Kumardhubi are some of the units lying in the Dhanbad-Chirkunda belt.

Four new cement factories were established in the region one each at Chaibasa, Banjhari, Japla and Sindri. Sindri plant uses the byproduct 'carbonate sludge' of the fertiliser factory as its raw material. Six sulphuric acid plants - two at Jamshedpur, one each at Sindri, Jadugora, Gumia and Golmuri; one micanite factory at Jhumri Tilaiya, superphosphate factory at Sindri (1960), copper smelter at Ghatsila, Mahalakshmi Fibre Works using the Sabai grass at Ormanjhi (1962), Indian Tube Ltd. at Jamshedpur (1954), Heavy Engineering Corporation at Hatia (1967) are the important large and medium size factories of the region.

Changes in Employment in Major Industrial Groups—1961-71

Before 1961, the main criterion for economic classification was income which was changed to work in 1961. The 1961 census thus inflated the number of workers as it included all people who worked for income or helped in household duties without money. In 1971, therefore, the definition was changed again to include only those people under this category who worked full time in some economic activity. Because of this change in the definition of workers, 1971 census witnessed a drop in the total number of workers everywhere and did not present a realistic picture.

For the present study, therefore, change refers to difference in the proportion of workers in a particular sector at two points of time, i.e. 1961 and 1971. As such actual change in the number of workers can not be worked out, only a trend can be noticed. Table 3.3 depcits the districtwise percentage of workers in major industrial groups during two census years of 1961 and 1971 for the Chota Nagpur region. It is apparent from the table that industrial groups 32 (Rubber, Petroleum and Coal products), and 36 (mineral based industries) share more than 50 per cent of manufacturing employment in 1971 in the Chota Nagpur region as a whole with the exception of Singhbhum

TABLE 3.3

Chota Nagpur : Employment in Major Industrial Groups as Percentage of Total Employment in Manufacturing (1961 and 1971)

INDUSTRY		HAZARIBAGH		DHANBAD		RANCHI		PALAMAU		SINGHBHUM		CHOTA NAGPUR	
CODE	NAME	1961	1971	1961	1971	1961	1971	1961	1971	1961	1971	1961	1971
1	2	3	4	5	6	7	8	9	10	11	12	13	14
20-21	Food & Beverage	7.6	8.0	5.1	8.0	9.5	5.8	15.5	22.5	2.8	4.5	5.2	6.9
22	Tobacco Products	1.6	2.0	1.1	1.8	1.7	1.8	6.9	7.5	8.8	14.9	5.3	6.0
23-27	Textiles	5.6	7.6	4.4	8.1	9.9	10.2	10.9	25.7	2.4	6.9	4.4	8.9
28	Wood & Wood Products	4.4	0.4	3.2	1.3	7.7	1.5	6.7	0.9	1.8	0.6	3.3	0.9
29	Paper & Paper Products	0.1	0.6	0.1	0.5	0.1	0.2	0.8	5.7	-	0.2	0.1	0.5
30	Printing & Publishing	0.4	1.6	0.9	2.8	2.6	0.4	1.0	0.4	0.4	0.6	0.7	1.2
31	Leather & Leather Products	1.2	5.4	1.1	7.1	1.9	0.9	2.2	1.0	0.6	15.3	0.9	7.5

Table 3.3 (contd.)

1	2	3	4	5	6	7	8	9	10	11	12	13	14
32	Rubber, Petroleum & Coal products	0.1	56.1	1.0	28.3	0.1	6.6	0.1	5.6	1.7	12.3	1.1	23.3
33	Chemicals & Chemical Products	2.7	0.6	23.6	0.1	0.6	2.5	2.1	-	0.3	7.2	5.3	2.9
34-35	Non-metallic mineral Products	66.8	8.8	35.5	25.5	40.3	58.7	38.1	14.7	6.6	16.9	26.9	27.0
36	Basic metals	3.2	0.1	12.9	1.5	11.8	1.6	3.3	-	52.8	5.1	30.8	2.2
37	Machinery & Electrical Equipments	0.7	0.2	2.2	0.1	3.2	0.6	0.4	0.2	4.8	6.1	3.3	2.1
38	Transport Equipment	1.9	2.4	3.8	2.6	6.2	3.4	4.3	9.9	15.5	3.4	9.6	3.2
39	Miscellaneous Manufacturing Industries	4.2	6.2	4.7	12.3	4.4	5.8	7.7	5.9	1.5	6.0	3.1	7.4
2&3	TOTAL (Manufacturing)	100.0	100.0	100.0	100.0	100.0	100.0	100.0	100.0	100.0	100.0	100.0	100.0

Source: Census of India, 1961, Series 4, Bihar, Part II - B (i) General Economic Tables;
Census of India, 1971, Series 4, Bihar, Part II - B (i) General Economic Tables.

where employment is shared rather uniformly by all groups. Table 3.4 shows the difference in the percentage employment during two census years for the Chota Nagpur region. Gain or loss in the percentage of share of each industrial group has been marked by positive and negative signs. Industrial group 28 (wood and wooden products) has lost employment in all districts. Five industrial groups 22, 23-27, 29, 32 and 39 have gained employment in all districts and the region too while rest of the groups have gained in some and lost in others.

TABLE 3.4

Chota Nagpur : Gain or Loss in the Percentage Share of Employment by Major Industrial Groups during 1961-1971

INDUSTRY GROUP	I HAZARI-BAGH	II DHAN-BAD	III RANCHI	IV PALA-MAU	V SINGH-BHUM	VI CHOTA NAGPUR
20-21	0.4	2.5	-3.7	0.7	1.7	1.7
22	0.4	0.7	0.1	0.6	6.1	0.7
23-27	2.0	3.7	0.3	14.8	4.5	4.5
28	-4.0	-1.9	-6.2	-5.8	-1.2	-2.4
29	0.5	0.4	0.1	4.9	0.2	0.4
30	1.2	1.9	-2.2	-0.6	0.2	0.5
31	4.2	6.0	-1.0	-1.2	14.7	6.6
32	56.0	27.0	6.5	5.5	10.6	22.2
33	-2.1	-23.5	1.9	-2.1	6.9	-2.4
34-35	-58.0	-10.0	18.4	-23.4	10.3	0.1
36	-3.1	-11.4	-10.2	-3.3	-47.7	-28.6
37	-0.5	-2.1	-2.6	-0.2	1.3	-1.2
38	0.5	-1.2	-2.8	5.6	-12.1	-6.4
39	2.0	7.6	1.4	-1.8	4.5	4.3

SPATIAL DISTRIBUTION OF MANUFACTURING INDUSTRY AND ITS STRUCTURE

Process of industrialisation starts within a region either spontaneously with the start of an industry under favourable conditions or it is implanted with considerable planning and effort. In either situation two basic questions emerge. Where an industry is located and why? What type of industry is this? These together influence future growth on the one hand and are guided by a variety of living conditions and levels of development on the other. As such the analysis of the pattern of distribution of manufacturing industries over space, serves to identify those locational factors which were instrumental in their establishments. Such a study also helps in evaluating the potential for growth.

It is thus obvious that during 1961-71 there is a tendency towards diversification as industrial groups other than metallic and nonmetallic based industries have gained employment.

Locational Factors

While setting up an industry, choice before the project analyst often lies between two or three locations. An optimal location is selected after examining the cost of assembling the necessary raw materials, the cost of processing and the cost of marketing the product at all locations in mind. It is very difficult to provide 'pure rules' of optimal location for the individual firm because wide range of industries and wide variety of firms, each with its own input combinations and market characteristics have varying considerations while selecting a particular location.

Two main approaches to the study of these factors of industrial location are apparent - one theoretical, formulated mainly by geographers. The theoretical approach attempts to search for an abstract general theory of industrial location which can explain the existing structure of industrial location and changes in that structure. The empirical approach tries to list the factors which might be important in the location of particular industries together with examples of situations where they have in fact been important. Thus attempt is not to formulate a general theory but is limited to provide a descriptive picture.

All these theories put forward in search of an abstract model for the optimum location of a firm may be grouped under three approaches to industrial location theory. They are:

(i) the least cost approach propagated by Weber (1909) and Hoover (1948) attempts to explain location in terms of the minimisation of factor costs;

(ii) market area analysis elaborated by Losch (1940), Harris (1954) and Richardson (1969) emphasises more on the demand factor, i.e. market; and

(iii) the profit maximisation approach followed by Isard (1956), and Greenhut (1956) is the logical outcome of the other two.

Question does arise whether firms actually do 'maximise' profits. March and Simon (1958) have suggested that firms sought locations giving a satisfactory level of profits and growth. Finally, human behaviour is also an important factor as there might be some personal consideration in selecting an industrial location and Pred (1967) has emphasised the importance of these factors.

It is thus apparent that there are many problems in formulating a general theory of industrial location as locational factors are different for a wide range of firms. Location decisions, therefore, in practice, are based on one or a combination of several factors. They may be grouped in a few categories as it is difficult to rank then in any order of importance because it varies from firm to firm (Glasson, 1974).

1. Labour - quality and quantity
2. Transport and communication
3. Site and premises
4. Government aid
5. Environmental factors - in the widest sense.

Many of the locational determinants listed here depend on 'agglomeration economies' derived not from a specific geographical position but from the stimulus given by the concentration of firms. The social and institutional factors of communication and information as well as customary modes of contact, therefore, attract firms to the city in developing countries. Personal relations play a more frequent and more persuasive role in human contacts of all types, including business contacts. The choice of location for an industry between the city and the hinterland in the early stages goes in favour of the city because of external economies in terms of common services and inventories, sources of finance and complementary producers. With time, stability and specialisation enters the production processes and managerial functions respectively. Demand becomes more predictable which enables the firm to internalise some of its functions previously being done outside. At this stage the industry might think of moving to a location outside city with advantages in transport, cost, labour or any such factor.

Distribution pattern and structure of industries

Distribution of manufacturing industry over space in the Chota Nagpur region has been discussed with reference to the sieze and kind of industry in the following pages. It will help to explain (a) the guidling factors in the location of industries within the region; (b) differences in manufacturing characteristics between various parts of the region; (c) differing degrees of spatial disperson or concentration of each major industry groups; and (d) industrial complexes and inter industry relations.

Distribution of industrial units by size

The region has the major share of the large scale industrial units of Bihar including both public and private sectors that is 20 out of 24 units. If these are taken separately, of the 11 public sector undertakings and 13 private sector enterprises, 10 units each in public and private sectors respectively, are located within the region mostly in and around Ranchi and Jamshedpur. Besides these large-scale industrial units, there are about 368 medium size plants and 906 small scale units within the region. Table 3.5 and Figs 18-19 highlight the structure and spatial pattern of industries in the region. These reveal the following features:

The ratio between large - medium and small scale industrial units for the Chota Nagpur region is 1 : 2.3. Corresponding ratios for districts are 1 : 9.9 for Palamau, 1 : 3.3 for Hazaribagh, 1 : 3.2 for Ranchi, 1 : 2.0 for Singhbhum, 1 : 1.8 for Giridih and 1 : 1.2 for Dhanbad. Palamau and Dhanbad again present the contrast as number of small scale units per large-medium size plant is roughly ten times ore whereas in Dhanbad it is almost the same revealing the dominance of large-medium size plants. Rest of the districts have two to three times more small scale units than the large-medium size plants.

(a) Dhanbad has the highest number of large-medium size plants (109 units) while Palamau has only 11 units.

(b) Hazaribagh ranks first with 200 small scale units whereas Palamau records only 109 units which is again the lowest figure among all districts.

(c) If all units are taken together Hazaribagh and Singhbhum with 260 and 259 units share first and second position respectively. Palamau is the only district with less than 200 units (120 units only).

(d) Areal variations in the location of these industrial units are sharper at the Block level. Most of these units are concentrated within a few Blocks in each district. For example, Kanke and Nankum Blocks in Ranchi have 196 industrial units (92 per cent of the total units in the district); Hazaribagh, Kodarma and Ramgarh Blocks in Hazaribagh have 197 units (76 per cent of the total); Giridih, Bermo and Gumia Blocks in Giridih have 179 units (88 per cent of the total); Dhanbad and Jharia Blocks have 177 units (74 per cent of the total); Daltonganj and Garhwa Blocks in Palamau have 73 industrial units (61 per cent of

TABLE 3.5

Chota Nagpur : Distribution of Industrial Units by size and type, 1978

(Note: L = Large; S = Small)

DISTRICT/ BLOCK	AGRO-BASED		FOREST BASED		LIVE-STOCK BASED		TEX-TILES		METAL BASED		ENGG. INDUS-TRIES		CHEMI-CALS		NON METAL-LIC		MISCE-LANE-OUS		TOTAL	
	L	S	L	S	L	S	L	S	L	S	L	S	L	S	L	S	L	S	L	S
1	2	3	4	5	6	7	8	9	10	11	12	13	14	15	16	17	18	19	20	21
RANCHI	4	2	7	37	-	22	4	-	11	22	11	47	4	24	10	6	-	1	51	161
Kanke	-	2	4	34	-	22	2	-	8	21	5	33	3	20	6	6	-	1	28	139
Namkum	4	-	1	-	-	-	-	-	2	1	6	11	1	1	2	-	-	-	16	13
Ormanjhi	-	-	-	-	-	-	1	-	-	-	-	-	-	-	-	-	-	-	1	-
Ratu	-	-	-	-	-	-	1	-	-	-	-	-	-		-	-	-	-	1	-
Burmu	-	-	-	-	-	-	-	-	-	-	-	-	-	-	1	-	-	-	1	-
Khunti	-	-	-	-	-	-	-	-	-	-	-	-	-	-	1	-	-	-	1	-
Simdega	-	-	-	2	-	-	-	-	-	-	-	1	-	2	-	-	-	-	-	5
Silli	-	-	-	-	-	-	-	-	1	-	-	1	-	-	-	-	-	-	1	1
Gumla	-	-	-	1	-	-	-	-	-	-	-	-	-	1	-	-	-	-	-	2
Kisko	-	-	1	-	-	-	-	-	-	-	-	-	-	-	-	-	-	-	1	-
Palkot	-	-	1	-	-	-	-	-	-	-	-	-	-	-	-	-	-	-	1	-
Lohardaga	-	-	-	-	-	-	-	-	-	-	-	1	-	-	-	-		-	-	1

Table 3.5 (contd.)

1	2	3	4	5	6	7	8	9	10	11	12	13	14	15	16	17	18	19	20	21
HAZARIBAGH	1	4	1	45	-	6	-	-	4	105	3	15	2	6	49	5	-	14	60	200
Hazaribagh	1	2	1	26	-	2	-	-	2	28	1	5	-	-	5	-	-	3	10	66
Kodarma	-	1	-	9	-	-	-	-	1	18	1	7	-	-	30	3	1	7	32	45
Patratu	-	-	-	3	-	-	-	-	1	14	1	2	-	-	2	-	-	2	4	21
Ramgarh	-	1	-	4	-	-	-	-	-	18	-	-	1	6	11	2	-	1	12	32
Barhi	-	-	-	1	-	2	-	-	-	3	-	-	-	-	1	-	-	-	1	6
Katkamsandi	-	-	-	-	-	-	-	-	-	2	-	-	-	-	-	-	-	-	-	2
Jainagar	-	-	-	-	-	-	-	-	-	5	-	-	-	-	-	-	-	-	-	5
Chauparan	-	-	-	-	-	-	-	-	-	6	-	-	-	-	-	-	-	-	-	6
Bishungarh	-	-	-	-	-	2	-	-	-	3	-	-	-	-	-	-	-	-	-	5
Mandu	-	-	-	2	-	-	-	-	-	5	-	1	1	-	-	-	-	1	1	9
Chatra	-	-	-	-	-	-	-	-	-	3	-	-	-	-	-	-	-	-	-	3
GIRIDIH	-	3	1	19	-	8	-	1	2	83	4	9	6	7	59	-	-	1	72	131
Tisri	-	-	-	-	-	-	-	-	-	7	-	-	-	-	2	-	-	-	2	7
Birni	-	-	-	-	-	-	-	-	-	6	-	-	-	-	-	-	-	-	-	6
Bermo	-	1	-	3	-	-	-	-	1	4	-	-	2	2	-	-	-	-	3	10
Dhanwar	-	-	-	-	-	-	-	-	-	3	-	-	-	-	-	-	-	-	-	3
Gumia	-	-	1	4	-	-	-	-	-	18	-	1	3	1	1	-	-	-	5	24
Giridih	-	2	-	12	-	6	-	1	1	41	4	6	1	6	56	-	-	1	62	75
Dumri	-	-	-	-	-	2	-	-	-	4	-	-	-	-	-	-	-	-	-	6

Table 3.5 (contd.)

1	2	3	4	5	6	7	8	9	10	11	12	13	14	15	16	17	18	19	20	21
DHANBAD	1	1	2	15	-	13	-	-	28	17	17	46	35	33	26	5	-	1	109	131
Dhanbad	1	1	-	9	-	5	-	-	5	10	8	31	10	12	12	2	-	1	36	71
Jharia	-	-	2	6	-	7	-	-	3	6	2	10	13	19	2	-	-	-	22	48
Nirsa	-	-	-	-	-	-	-	-	4	-	2	2	4	2	2	3	-	-	12	7
Baghmara	-	-	-	-	-	1	-	-	1	1	-	3	-	-	-	-	-	-	1	5
Chas	-	-	-	-	-	-	-	-	14	-	2	-	1	-	5	-	-	-	22	-
Gobindpur	-	-	-	-	-	-	-	-	1	-	3	-	5	-	3	-	-	-	12	-
Baliapur	-	-	-	-	-	-	-	-	-	-	-	-	2	-	-	-	-	-	2	-
Topchanchi	-	-	-	-	-	-	-	-	-	-	-	-	-	-	2	-	-	-	2	-
PALAMAU	-	-	7	65	-	-	-	-	-	24	-	7	-	5	4	8	-	-	11	109
Daltonganj	-	-	3	22	-	-	-	-	-	11	-	7	-	3	1	7	-	-	4	50
Garhwa	-	-	2	15	-	-	-	-	-	-	-	-	-	2	-	-	-	-	2	17
Hussainabad	-	-	-	4	-	-	-	-	-	5	-	-	-	-	2	1	-	-	2	10
Latehar	-	-	-	14	-	-	-	-	-	-	-	-	-	-	-	-	-	-	-	14
Hariharganj	-	-	-	4	-	-	-	-	-	8	-	-	-	-	-	-	-	-	-	12
Ranka	-	-	-	2	-	-	-	-	-	-	-	-	-	-	1	-	-	-	1	2
Lesliegan j	-	-	-	2	-	-	-	-	-	-	-	-	-	-	-	-	-	-	-	2
Chainpur	-	-	-	2	-	-	-	-	-	-	-	-	-	-	-	-	-	-	-	2
Bishrampur	-	-	2	-	-	-	-	-	-	-	-	-	-	-	-	-	-	-	2	-

Table 3.5 (contd.)

1	2	3	4	5	6	7	8	9	10	11	12	13	14	15	16	17	18	19	20	21
SINGHBHUM	1	12	8	51	-	-	1	-	25	15	20	44	4	32	25	14	1	6	85	174
Golmuri	-	-	2	12	-	-	1	-	12	10	14	25	1	12	18	2	1	2	49	63
Chaibasa	-	7	-	14	-	-	-	-	-	4	-	3	-	10	-	12	-	1	-	51
Chakra-dharpur	-	5	-	12	-	-	-	-	-	1	-	-	-	6	1	-	-	1	1	25
Chandil	-	-	4	4	-	-	-	-	-	-	-	-	-	-	1	-	-	-	5	4
Noamundi	-	-	-	4	-	-	-	-	-	-	-	1	-	2	-	-	-	-	-	7
Chakulia	1	-	-	-	-	-	-	-	1	-	-	3	-	1	-	-	-	-	2	4
Ghatshila	-	-	-	4	-	-	-	-	1	-	-	1	-	-	-	-	-	-	1	5
Seraikela	-	-	-	-	-	-	-	-	1	-	-	1	-	-	1	-	-	-	2	1
Musabani	-	-	-	1	-	-	-	-	2	-	-	-	-	-	-	-	-	-	2	1
Adityapur	-	-	1	-	-	-	-	-	8	-	6	10	3	1	2	-	-	2	20	13
Goilkera	-	-	1	-	-	-	-	-	-	-	-	-	-	-	-	-	-	-	1	-
Jhinkpani	-	-	-	-	-	-	-	-	-	-	-	-	-	-	1	-	-	-	1	-
Gobindpur	-	-	-	-	-	-	-	-	-	-	-	-	-	-	1	-	-	-	1	-
CHOTA NAGPUR	7	22	26	232	-	49	5	1	70	266	55	168	51	107	173	38	1	23	388	906

Source: Complied from the List of Small, Medium and large size Industrial units, Department of Industries and Technical Education, Bihar, 1978.

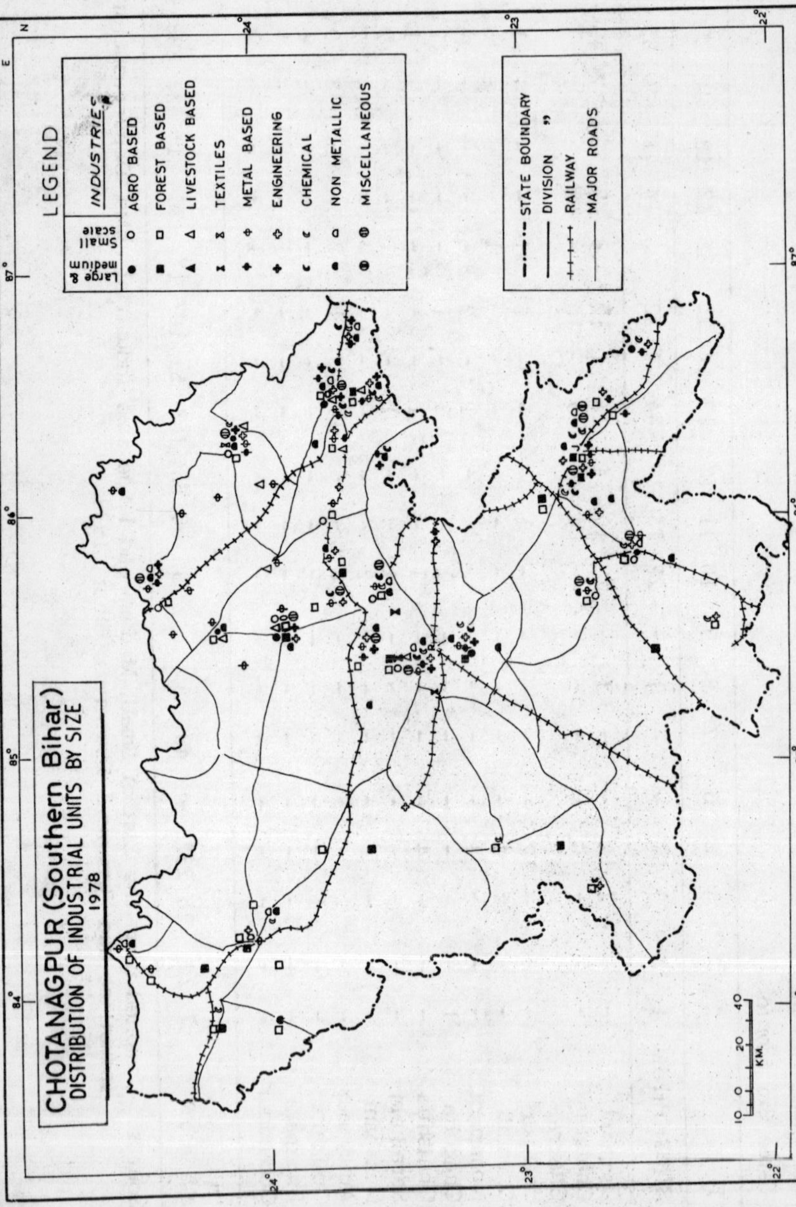
CHOTANAGPUR (Southern Bihar)
DISTRIBUTION OF INDUSTRIAL UNITS BY SIZE
1978
LEGEND
Large & medium
Small scale
INDUSTRIES
AGRO BASED
FOREST BASED
LIVESTOCK BASED
TEXTILES
METAL BASED
ENGINEERING
CHEMICAL
NON METALLIC
MISCELLANEOUS
STATE BOUNDARY
DIVISION "
RAILWAY
MAJOR ROADS
10 0 20 40
KM.
N
E
84°
85°
86°
87°
24°
23°
22°

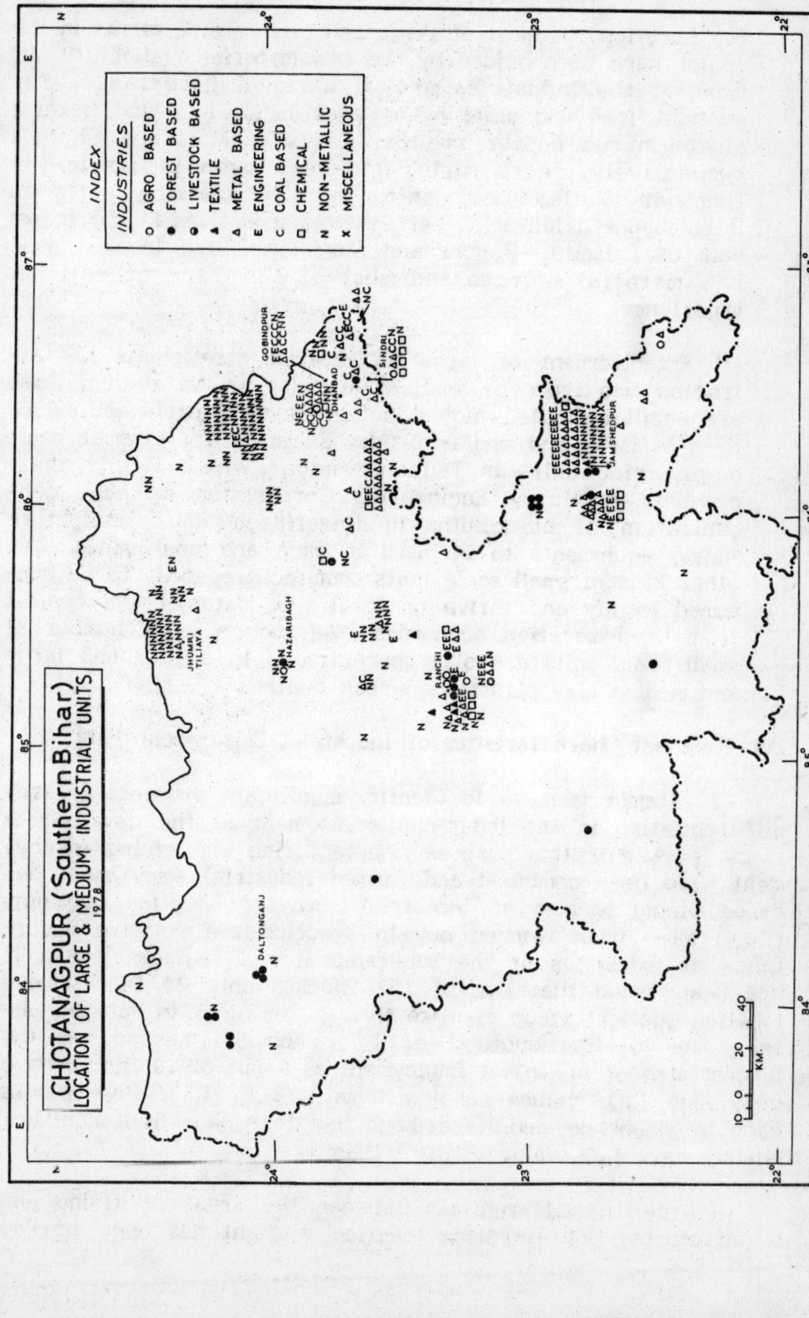
CHOTANAGPUR (Southern Bihar)
LOCATION OF LARGE & MEDIUM INDUSTRIAL UNITS
1978
INDEX
INDUSTRIES
AGRO BASED
FOREST BASED
LIVESTOCK BASED
TEXTILE
METAL BASED
ENGINEERING
COAL BASED
CHEMICAL
NON-METALLIC
MISCELLANEOUS
DALTONGANJ
JHUMRI TILIAYA
HAZARIBAGH
GOBINDPUR
DHANBAD
SINDRI
RANCHI
JAMSHEDPUR
KM.

Fig. 19

the total) and Golmuri, Adityapur and Chaibasa Blocks in Singhbhum have 196 units which is 76 per cent of the total.

(e) Locations of most of large and medium size plants in the region have been guided by the raw material availability and most of the industries are of national importance. For example, iron and steel industry at Jamshedpur and Bokaro; aluminium and copper smelting plants at Muri and Ghatsila respectively, refractories and coke oven plants in the Damodar Valley coal belt, mica processing units in Hazaribagh-Giridih mica belt, shellac industries in the forest belt of Palamau, Ranchi and Singhbhum, are located near raw material sources and most of them are of national importance.

(f) Establishment of large and medium size plants has attracted two types of small scale units in the region. Some are ancillary units which manufacture small parts and supply them to large and medium plants. Examples are of small scale engineering units in Jagannathnagar which supply their products to Heavy Engineering Corporation or huge concentration of blacksmiths in Hazaribagh who manufacture mining equipments to be used in mica and coal mines. The other kind of small scale units manufacture goods to be consumed locally and thrive on local raw material and benefit from 'agglomeration economies'. As such a large number of small scale units are also concentrated in and around large and medium size plants and urban centres.

Sub-Regional Characteristics of Industrial Employment 1971

An attempt is made to identify significant elements of area differentiation in the industrial employment at the development block level. For this purpose manufacturing and mining employment have been combined and termed industrial employment because mining is also an industrial activity. Location quotients (L.Q.) have been worked out to describe the relative importance of industries at the sub-regional and regional levels. It has been found that out of 152 Blocks, only 24 Blocks have location quotient value of more than 1. No Block in Palamau district has location quotient of 1 or above. Dhanbad has the largest size of industrial employment as 6 out of 10 Blocks have very high L.Q. values ranging from 1.19 to 4.73. Five Blocks each in Singhbhum and Hazaribagh and four each in Ranchi and Giridih have L.Q. value of more than 1.

In order to differentiate between the areas of mining and manufacturing concentration location quotient has been worked out separately for both activities. Based on these values, three kinds of concentration of mining or manufacturing activity may be observed at the Block level (Fig 20 and 21). Location quotient values below 0.5 mark low concentration, 0.6 - 1.5 mark medium concentration and values above 1.5 show high concentration of particular industries. It is evident from the map that vast areas within the Chota Nagpur region have low values for mining or manufacturing activity. Medium to high concentration of mining activity is restricted to an elongated belt running in an east-west direction covering parts of Dhanbad, Giridih, Hazaribagh and Ranchi districts and also to few isolated patches in Singhbhum and other districts.

Locational Patterns of Major Industry Groups

All industries of the region have been grouped into nine categories - agro-based, forest-based, livestock-based, textiles, metal based, engineering, chemicals including rubber and coal products, non-metallic mineral based and miscellaneous industries.

Agro-based, livestock-based and textile industries do not seem to be important within the region. Agro-based industries include rice, flour and oil mills and bakeries. Few such units are located within the region mostly in urban centres to meet the local need. Livestock-based industries (e.g. manufacturing of leather goods) are small scale catering mostly to the needs of local people. There are four medium size textile factories in Ranchi and one in Singhbhum which manufacture yarn or are engaged in printing and dyeing.

Forest-based industries include saw mills, paper and shellac industries. Saw mills and shellac industries are very important within the region and are scattered over a wide area. There is only one unit manufacturing paper products.

Metal based industries include iron and steel manufacturing and associated industries; zinc, copper, aluminium and tin smelting; manufacture of sundry hardwares, wires, buckets, pipes, brass and bell metal and so on. Of these, iron and steel industry is the most important and is widely scattered in the region compared to other metal based industries. Besides two large scale iron and steel plants, there are several medium size industrial units manufacturing iron and steel products. Aluminium, copper and zinc smelting plants usually export the metal outside the region.

A wide range of engineering industry has developed within the region due to mining and manufacturing activities. Iron and

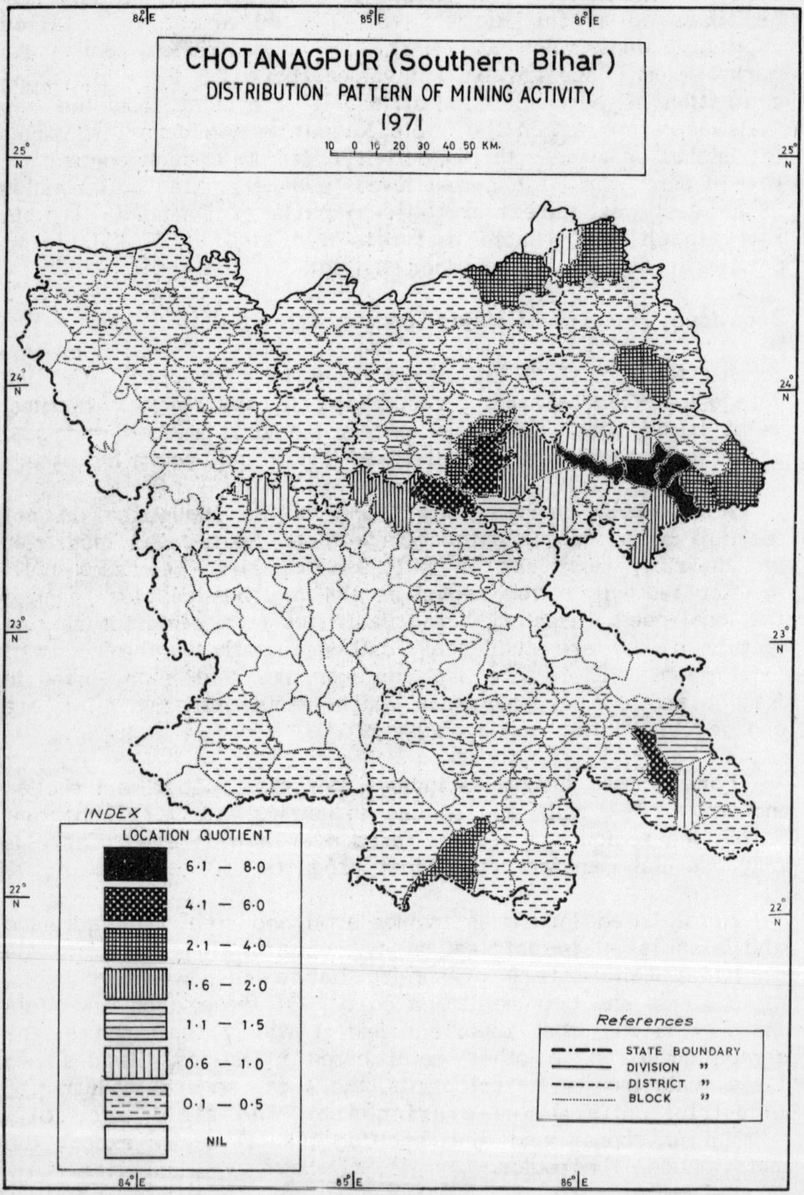
CHOTANAGPUR (Southern Bihar)
DISTRIBUTION PATTERN OF MINING ACTIVITY
1971
10 0 10 20 30 40 50 KM.
84° E
85° E
86° E
25° N
24° N
23° N
22° N
INDEX
LOCATION QUOTIENT
6·1 — 8·0
4·1 — 6·0
2·1 — 4·0
1·6 — 2·0
1·1 — 1·5
0·6 — 1·0
0·1 — 0·5
NIL
References
STATE BOUNDARY
DIVISION "
DISTRICT "
BLOCK "

Fig. 20

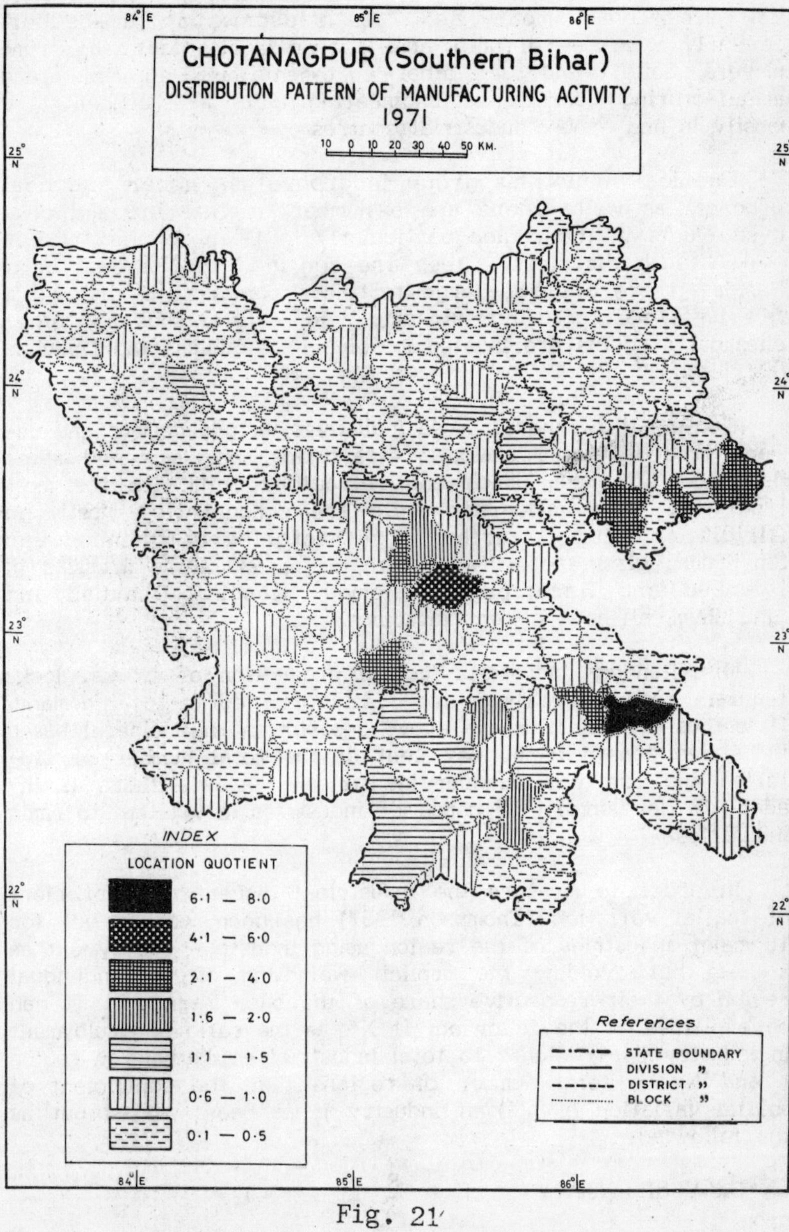
CHOTANAGPUR (Southern Bihar)
DISTRIBUTION PATTERN OF MANUFACTURING ACTIVITY
1971
10 0 10 20 30 40 50 KM.
84° E
85° E
86° E
25° N
24° N
23° N
22° N
INDEX
LOCATION QUOTIENT
6·1 — 8·0
4·1 — 6·0
2·1 — 4·0
1·6 — 2·0
1·1 — 1·5
0·6 — 1·0
0·1 — 0·5
References
STATE BOUNDARY
DIVISION "
DISTRICT "
BLOCK "

Fig. 21

steel plants at Jamshedpur encouraged the establishment of Heavy Engineering corporation at Jagannathnagar, Tata Electrical Locomotive Company and Tata Yadogawa at Jamshedpur. Similarly a number of units are engaged in manufacturing prime movers, boilers and such other equipments used in mining and manufacturing operations. Engineering units are concentrated mostly in and around industrial centres.

Chemical industries group incorporates rubber and coal products as well. There are a number of coal tar and coke oven plants in the region particularly in Dhanbad, Hazaribagh, and Giridih districts. These are confined to the coal belt. Besides, there are two large fertiliser plants at Sindri and a few units manufacturing sulphuric acid, caustic soda and other chemical products are located in Ranchi, Singhbhum and Dhanbad districts.

Non-metallic mineral based industries include cement and cement products, glass, mica, refractories, ceramics and stone dressing. Of these, mica and refractory units are the most important. Mica processing units are concentrated mostly in Giridih and and Hazaribagh; refractories in Dhanbad and Singhbhum; glass factories in Hazaribagh; and stone dressing in Dhanbad and Hazaribagh. Palamau, Ranchi, Dhanbad and Singhbhum, all have cement factories.

Miscellaneous industries include production of clocks, locks fountain pens, etc. These are mostly oriented to local demand. It is thus evident from the above description that mineral based industries constitute 60 per cent of the total number of factories and are thus leading industries. Besides, there is inadequate development of consumer industries in relation to basic industries.

In order to measure the industrieal dispersion, coefficient of spatial variation (Thompson 1957) has been worked out for 18 major industries of the region using industrial employment as a base but avoiding the implicit weighting of the individual region by their respective share of the base magnitude. It can be explained as the following. If X^r_j is the ratio of employment in industry j in region r to total industrial employment in region r and N the total number of regions then the coefficient of spatial variation (C.S.V) of industry j has been worked out as the following:

$$\text{C.S.V of industry} \quad j = \frac{S}{\bar{X}_j}$$

where;

$$S = \frac{(X_j^r - X_j)^2}{N} \quad ; \text{ and}$$

$$X_j = \frac{r \; x_j^r}{N}$$

Thus C.S.V. is simply the standard deviation of the proportion of employment in industry j in the districts divided by the mean proportion of industry j for the region. Higher C.S.V. means higher concentration and vice versa.

TABLE 3.6

Chota Nagpur : Degree of Industrial Dispersion

Industry Code	Industry	Coefficient of Spatial Variation (CSV)	Rank
20-21	Food & Beverage	0.670	13
22	Tobacco Products	0.911	8
23	Textile Cotton	1.179	3
24	Textile Jute	1.066	6
26	Textile Silk	0.615	16
27	Textile Miscellaneous	0.619	15
28	Wood & Wood Products	0.389	17
29	Paper and Paper Products	1.457	2
30	Printing & Publishing	0.802	11
31	Leather & Leather Products	0.888	9
32	Rubber, Petroleum and Coal Products	0.871	10
33	Chemical & Chemical Products	1.165	4
34	Non metallic mineral products-Cement, Mica	0.925	7
35	Non metallic mineral products-Earthenware, Earthen Pottery	1.153	5
36	Basic Metals	0.798	12
37	Machinery & Electrical Equipment	1.653	1
38	Transport Equipment	0.647	14
39	Miscellaneous manufacturing Industries	0.347	18

Table 3.6 refers to the coefficient of spatial variation for 18 industrial groups of the region and their ranks according to values. Because of low numbers of manufacturing units in industries like paper and paper products, textiles, chemicals and machine building, high concentration is observed in their distribution. On the other hand, industries like metallic and non-metallic mineral based industries, food and beverage and wood products are distributed in large number in different districts and thus they show dispersal.

This explains what types of industries are distributed evenly or unevenly within the region. Thus the locational pattern of various industries by type and size suggests that large-medium size plants in the region have developed around raw materials of national importance. They show very little diversification. Small scale industries are widely distributed but they have not developed their links with large industries.

AGGLOMERATION ECONOMY AND NODALITY

Concentration of industries whether it be large-medium or small in few centres reflects two kinds of pulls - raw material availability and agglomeration economies. When a set of activities occur at a given location and belong to a group (subsystem) of activities which are subject to important production, marketing or other interrelations, they from industrial complexes. Nature of these complexes may vary. For example, an industrial complex (a multi-plant unit) may consist of two or more stages in a series of successive stages of production from raw materials to the final product; it may consist of a cluster of plants putting out two or more products from a single raw material (that is engaged in the output of a process-related product line); or it may consist of more or less integrated establishments engaged in activities (the preceding, the following are the allied activities) related to a major activity (for example: publishing).

On these lines we can identify few industrial complexes, though of varying nature, within the region. For example, Jamshedpur and Bokaro industrial complex of iron and steel industry; Dhanbad-Jharia-Sindri industrial complex of refractories, coke ovens, fertiliser and chemicals; Ramgarh-Patratu power complex; and Jagannathnagar industrial complex for engineering industry. Such industrial complexes if planned properly could be very useful in accelerating economic growth as it reduces current expenditures, capital investments and permits more effective use of the infrastructure and auxiliary and servicing establishments. The territorial division of labour in

USSR refers to this kind of planning where economic regions are selected on the basis of their potentiality and needs, and inter-related industries are developed for the optimal development of the economy. It is, therefore, necessary to study the nature of inter-industry relationships because some of the industries are directly linked with each other whereas some benefit from similarities in technology and, therefore, are 'clustered together'.

Florence (1953) recognised four types of integration between metal industries of Central England (i) vertical integration (i.e. links between refining of nonferrous metals and production of nonferrous hardware products); (ii) convergent integration (i.e. manufacture of bolts, car bodies, tyres, etc, feeding convergently into the motor assembly industry); (iii) diagonal integration (e.g. foundaries and tool manufacturers serving a number of local industries); and (iv) indirect integration (e.g. food industries which tend to balance the male employment in the metal industries with their majority in female workers). The rationale of this extreme localisation does not lie in the present distribution of resources. Mc Carty, Hook and Knos (1956) in their study of the machinery industries of the United States tested three alternative hypotheses by regression analysis and found that an aggregation hypotheses gave the most significant results. They concluded that 'birds of a feather flock together' might summarise location behaviour of industries Alagh (1972) in an examination of the regional aspects of Indian industrialisation has pointed out that industries in India have grown in relatively self-contained technologically inter-linked regional clusters associated with 'agglomeration economies'. Cluster of industries which have developed together in Bihar as identified by Lakadawala, Alagh and Sarma (1974) include large public-sector industries like heavy machinery, railway equipment, fertilisers and iron and steel industry.

At the sub-regional level two types of clustering are obvious. Industries belonging to the same group are located mostly in rural settlements whereas in urban centres different kinds of industries have agglomerated - some of them catering to the local needs whereas others serve the regional and national markets. Table 3.7 shows location of large and medium size industries. Only 85 settlements - rural as well as urban, share 388 large and medium size industrial establishments within the region. Of these, 43 are urban settlements sharing 76.5 per cent of total industrial units. Remaining 23.5 per cent of industrial units are shared by 42 rural settlements of varying population size.

TABLE 3.7

Chota Nagpur : Distribution of Large and Medium Size Units by Location, 1978

SETTLEMENT	POPULATION	TOTAL UNITS	AGRO-BASED I		FOREST BASED II		LIVE STOCK BASED III		TEXTILES IV		METAL BASED V		ENGINEERING BASED VI		RUBBER PETROLEUM, COAL VII		CHEMICALS VIII		NON-METALLIC IX		MISCELLANEOUS X	
			A*	B**	A	B	A	B	A	B	A	B	A	B	A	B	A	B	A	B	A	B
1	2	3	4	5	6	7	8	9	10	11	12	13	14	15	16	17	18	19	20	21	22	23
URBAN																						
Jamshedpur	356783	49			2	118			1	89	16	36000	10	21747			1	216	18	1542	1	100
Ranchi	175934	23	2	102	3	268			2	216	5	268	4	642			3	201	4	530		
Bokaro city	94007	23									15	21063	2	350	1	675	1	85	4	259		
Dharbad	79838	23	1	50							7	534	3	540	5	270	1	50	6	646		
Jagannath nagar	55663	7	1	290							2	4571	3	4555					1	100		
Hazaribagh	54818	7	1	200	1	56													5	460		
Kerkend	51314	1													1	368						
Sindri	46385	11			1	67					2	100			2	107	4	3942	2	409		
Jharia	45236	4			1	100					1	50			2	588						
Giridih	40308	49											2	189					47	8163		
Chakradhar-pur	34967	1																	1	50		
Daltonganj	32367	3			3	247																
Jhumri-Tilaiya	29097	22									1	57							21	3082		
Adityapur	28226	20			1	67					10	1179	4	305			3	180	2	104		
Bhowrah	25597	1													1	124						
Doranda	23954	1			1	50																
Ramgarh Cantt	23052	7									1	100							6	725		

Table 3.7 (contd.)

1	2	3	4	5	6	7	8	9	10	11	12	13	14	15	16	17	18	19	20	21	22	23
Gumia	20884	3			1	62									1	189	1	200				
Bhuli	20876	1									1	568										
Ghatshila	18351	1									1	2811										
Bermo	17325	2									1	50			1	826						
Jamadoba	16646	2									1	128			1	390						
Sijua	16346	3									1	50			2	140						
Kumardhubi	15986	3									1	1775	1	334	1	87						
Gomoh	15986	1																	1	50		
Garhwa	15228	2			2	300																
Patratu	14502	3									1	884							2	300		
Chas	13152	1																	1	172		
Chirkunda	12945	4									2	100			1	50			1	105		
Japla	10563	1																	1	1254		
Maithon	10163	1											1	238								
Pathardih	9906	5									2	622			3	717						
Bokaro	9374	1													1	500						
Tenudam	9037	2													1	591			1	50		
Dugda	8753	1													1	857						
Chandrapura	8544	1									1	100										
Khelari	8104	1																	1	374		
Kodarma	7559	5																	5	600		
Domchanch	7559	2											1	59					1	563		
Jhinkpani	7506	1																	1	1108		
RURAL																						
Giddi	7026	1													1	239						
URBAN																						
Barkakana	6935	1											1	576								
Muri	6712	1									1	483										
Chakulia	6646	2	1	50							1	151										

Table 3.7 (contd.)

1	2	3	4	5	6	7	8	9	10	11	12	13	14	15	16	17	18	19	20	21	22	23
Jadugoda	6558	2									2	415										
Narkum	5753	3	1	56	1	51													1	327		
RURAL																						
Barni	4974	1																	1	50		
URBAN																						
Sini	4903	1									1	749										
RURAL																						
Rajaulatu	4609	2									2	118										
Nirsachatti	4408	4									1	393			2	100			1	61		
Kandra	3513	1																	1	605		
Baliapur	3502	2													2	100						
Tatisilwai	3350	3											2	1126			1	126				
Govindpur	3251	12									2	100	2	107	5	261			3	231		
Kuju	2981	1											1	79								
Chandil	2912	5			4	250													1	50		
Ramka	2880	1																	1	50		
Topchanchi	2615	1																	1	50		
Rerma	2604	1																	1	100		
Kharagdiha	2247	1																	1	100		
Tisri	2166	2																	2	484		
Ormanjhi	1965	1							1	573												
Buti	1853	1																	1	51		
Renla	1793	3			2	150													1	100		
Marar	1478	4																	4	670		
Tundoo	1456	1									1	361										
Amjhore	1259	1																	1	50		
Hirodih	1215	1									1	350										

Table 3.7 (contd.)

1	2	3	4	5	6	7	8	9	10	11	12	13	14	15	16	17	18	19	20	21	22	23
Jhinjhari	1099	1																	1	50		
Tapkara	1020	1			1	50																
Kalamati	947	1																	1	57		
Hehal	902	1							1	56												
Mugma	847	4																	4	485		
Kamre	825	1									1	118										
Goilkera	825	1			1	52																
Haldipokhar	674	1																	1	50		
Lokai	635	3																	3	330		
Chota Ambcna	635	1																	1	50		
Sihodih	445	1																	1	150		
Barahganda	357	5																	5	718		
Pachamba	327	2																	2	334		
Murmu	322	1			1	100																
Ghoranjo	300	1																	1	100		
Bhadaninagar	198	1																	1	679		
Jarar	114	1											1	50								
Baniadih	11	2											1	500	1	294						
Grand Total: 86 Settlements		388	7	749	26	1988	-	-	5	934	85	73968	39	31397	36	7413	15	5000	174	26828	1	100
Percentage of Industrial Units		100	1.8		6.7				1.3		21.9		10.2		9.2		3.9		44.8		0.2	
Total Employment	148377																					
Percentage of Employment		100		0.5		1.3				0.6		49.8		21.2		5.0		3.4		18.1		0.1

Note: * A = Number of Industrial Units;
** B = Number of Persons employed.

Source: Compiled from the list of industrial units, Directorate of Industries, Bihar, 1978.

It is also apparent from the table that only 11 medium size towns in the population range of 20,000-49,999 persons accomodate the largest number of industrial units (122 units). Four class II cities contain 61 industrial units, the average number of units being about 15 which is higher than the previous group. This figure is the highest (36 units average) for Class I cities having population above 100,000 persons.

Jamshedpur (Class I city) and Giridih (Class III) each with 49 industrial units share the first rank among individual settlements having the highest numbers of industrial units. But if the nature of industrial units is taken into consideration, Jamshedpur is the only city with a much diversified industrial base as industrial units of Giridih are basically dependent on mica mining and its processing.

Other industrial centres like Kodama, Dom chanch and Jhumri Tilaiya which are located in the mica belt, are also primarily dependent on mica mining and processing. It is rather astonishing to find that no sophisticated industry using processed mica as its raw material has been set up in the mica belt or even outside the belt in the Chota Nagpur region. Probably the greatest restrain has been imposed by the market factor. As such, mica processing centres whether it be rural or urban, export mica to other parts of the country outside the region.

Industrial centres located in an elangated belt between Dhanbad and Khelari which covers major portion of the Damodar and Khelari Valley coal belt show comparatively more diversified industrial base than mica processing centres. Coal based industries dominate within the belt but they have developed in association with other metallic and non metallic minerals. As such refractories, coal washeries, engineering units manufacturing coal-mining equipments, fertiliser, cement, glass, stone crushing and dressing together with few agro and forest based industries catering to local and regional needs have developed side by side within the belt. Certain centres located on trunk routes of roads and railways within the belt have naturally attracted higher number of diverse industries. Ranchi, Dhanbad, Bokaro, Sindri, Ramgarh, Hazaribagh, Patratu, Jagannathnagar and Namkum are some of the important centres within this belt.

Jamshedpur-Adityapur industrial complex in the southern part of the region is the most important industrial centre as it has about 69 industrial units belonging to metal, engineering, chemical, nonmetallic mineral, forest and miscellaneous groups. Iron ore, copper, and manganese (as raw material) sources at close proximity has helped to build the most promising iron and steel complex at Jamshedpur.

Chandil, Daltonganj and Garhwa are some of the isolated industrial centres outside the important belts of industrial development which have developed basically as collecting centres for forest products like shellac, timber and kendu leaves.

Most of the large and medium size plants located within the region cater to national and regional markets and a great majority of them are close to raw material sources. But preference of few urban centres over others for the sitting of various industrial units reveal that such centres offer some additional advantages in terms of agglomeration economy and nodality (Perloff et. al. 1960). The existing distribution of population and economic activities among and within the settlements in itself becomes a factor in their differential growth rates. This might explain the clustering of diverse industries in the urban settlements with 20,000 + population and nodal character in terms of accessibility. Centres with "punctiform grouping of business enterprises" (Johnson, 1970) grow at a higher rate than centres with a cluster of similar industries because such a grouping by communicative power of its proffered goods and services can stimulate and improve the quantity and quality of production.

To sum up, this study of spatial and temporal aspects of the process of industrialisation has brought to focus the fact that there are two types of industrial structures and spatial organisations both of which have the inherent weaknesses. The basic and heavy industries have tended to develop industrial complexes in select localities and are foot-loose so far as their integration with the rest of the regional economy is concerned. Small industries, though locally and regionally important are weak in their extent of diversification and forward linkages with non-primary activities found mostly in towns. What is implied in the degree of dispersal and diversification as between large and small scale is only relative in an area of diversified natural resource base and extreme poverty.

FOUR

Process and Patterns of Urbanisation:

Spatial and Temporal

THE PROCESS OF URBANISATION

Urbanisation refers to the proportion of the total population concentrated in urban centres or else to a rise in this proportion which means transformation of the agrarian society into a non-agrarian one. Thus in the process, economic activities and people tend to be attracted towards those central places or nodes where "... the individual has the greatest freedom to interact", (Lukermann, 1966 p. 170). Because all nodes do not have the same opportunity to grow those with higher population, greater accessibility and functional availability grow comparatively faster. Such a development leads to chages in the settlement structure and levels of specialisation. Areas get functionally organised around nodes of diffrent orders revealing differences in the levels of development. In totality, the functional organisation of settlements presents a heirarchy where the intensity of functional interaction among settlements decreases with the distance from the higher order centres.

Urbanisation may, therefore, be viewed as the process leading to functional organisation of settlements around nodes. Usually, urbanisation and growth of cities occur together. But they should not be confused because cities can grow without any urbanisation if the rural population grows at an equal or faster rate.

Although urban centres are known to exist in historical time, the breakthrough in the pace of urbanisation came only with the industrial revolution in Europe. Urbanisation has been faster in countries which have lately become industrialised. It is, therefore, widely accepted that industrialisation is bound up with increasing urbanisation. But it will be a wrong notion to accept that urbanisation is set in motion only by industrialisation. In fact, development of towns and cities is inevitable with economic progress caused by industrialisation, development of mining or agriculture or by commercialisation. Urban centres, on the other hand, accelerate economic growth as they help in transformation of the agrarian society into an industrial one in different ways. For example, they provide facilities for the location and expansion of non-agricultural enterprises in a greater variety of skills and occupational specialities. Besides, "... cities are the crucial places in underdeveloped countries in which the adaptation to new ways, new technologies, new consumption and production patterns and new social institutions is achieved", (Hoselitz, 1953, p.197). This change in the culture of the urban centres affects the traditional ways of life in the surrounding rural areas and make them susceptive to rapid changes brought about by the economic advancement. Thus urbanisation may be viewed as a cause as well as consequence of economic development. It is the extended definition of nodality and not metropolitanisation of development of city system as is typical of developed countries or in parts of India.

Clearly a close relationship exists between the process of urbanisation and economic development. The proportion of urban population (an index of urbanisation) and per capita income (an index or economic development) for five districts of the Chota Nagpur region have been shown in Table 4.1 When these two variables are tested statistically, the correlation coefficient value obtained is + .98 which is significant beyond .01 level and thus indicates a very high degree of positive correlation between the two. However, there is paradox in this process of urbanisation and economic development as it is not rooted to integrated development of the region as a whole.

TABLE 4.1

Chota Nagpur : Percentage of Urban Population (1971) and Per Capita Income (1966)

DISTRICTS	URBAN POPULATION (Percentage)	PER CAPITA INCOME (In 100 Rupees)
Hazaribagh	12.9	2.98
Dhanbad	43.5	8.82
Ranchi	13.7	2.32
Palamau	4.7	1.40
Singhbhum	26.2	4.11

The study of urbanisation at the sub-regional level may, therefore, be of immense value in assessing the pattern of economic development in past as well as in future. An attempt is made to study the scale and pace of urbanisation within the region, distribution of urban centres and their characteristics. This will help us (i) to examine the pattern of urbanisation at the sub-regional level and to identify areas with varying levels of urban development; (ii) to evaluate the impact of urban development on the industrial development and vice versa; and (iii) to assess the potentiality of urban centres as the guiding force in shaping the economic development within the region on the basis of their growth rates, occupational and other characteristics and basic amenities provided by them.

THE SCALE AND PACE OF URBANISATION

Although the process of urbanisation refers to quantitative and qualitative change of the demographic, social and economic aspects of rural life, the measurement of urbanisation is based mainly on the demographic aspect (Bose, 1970). As such, population data from the census publications have been taken as the basis of this study.

In measuring urbanisation the ratio of urban population to the total population is used. Urban hierarchy expressed in terms of the number of towns of different size-classes assuming size to be related to function is also another complementary measure of urbanisation. Besides, the rate of urban growth (an indicator of the pace of urbanisation) also helps in the analysis of the pattern of urbanisation at all levels.

According to 1971 census, Chota Nagur had 19 per cent of its population urban which was nearly double the average for Bihar (10 per cent). Corresponding figures for Chota Nagpur and Bihar in 1981 are 24 per cent and 13 per cent respectively (Table 4.2).

Though the region is in its initial stage of development urbanisation is more pronounced on account of the location of large industries on the one hand and recognition of a number of small mining settlements as urban on the other. Intra-regional variations are, however, sharp (Table 4.3). Palamau with 5.6 per cent of urban population (1981) and Dhanbad with 50.7 per cent of urban population emerge as the least and the most urbanised districts respectively. Other districts have higher percentage of urban population than Bihar, but only Dhanbad and Singhbhum have higher percentage than that of Chota Nagpur region.

An analysis of Table 4.2 also reveals that there has been an increase in the proportion of urban population during 1901-81 in all districts, the Chota Nagpur region and Bihar but the magnitude of increase has varied spatially. In 1901, Hazaribagh

TABLE 4.2
Chota Nagpur : Urbanisation (Percent of Urban Population to Total Population 1901–81)

DISTRICT/ REGION/ STATE	PRE INDEPENDENCE YEARS					POST INDEPENDENCE YEARS			
	1901	1911	1921	1931	1941	1951	1961	1971	1981
Hazaribagh	3.1	2.9	3.5	3.4	4.8	6.9	8.5	12.9	15.1
Giridih*	-	-	-	-	-	-	-	-	14.2
Dhanbad	-	-	2.1	2.4	5.2	8.6	24.5	43.5	50.7
Ranchi	3.2	3.4	3.9	4.2	4.6	6.8	9.5	13.7	20.9
Palamau	1.5	1.7	2.7	2.9	2.5	3.8	4.7	4.7	5.6
Singhbhum	1.0	1.4	6.9	8.7	14.0	17.0	21.5	26.2	32.1
Chota Nagpur	2.1	2.3	4.1	4.6	6.6	9.0	13.3	19.0	23.9
Bihar	4.0	3.8	4.1	4.5	5.4	6.8	8.4	10.0	12.5

* Giridih was part of Hazaribagh District until 1971 census.

TABLE 4.3
Chota Nagpur : Size of Urban Population (by Development Blocks 1971)

DISTRICT/ REGION	Total Number of Blocks	No. of Blocks in Different Percentage range of urban population				
		0.0 (Nil)	0.1 to 15.0 (Low)	15.1 to 25.1 (Moderate)	25.1 to 50.0 (High)	50.1 and above (Very High)
1	2	3	4	5	6	7
Hazaribagh	42	32	2	1	5	2
Dhanbad	10	4	1	1	2	2
Ranchi	43	34	2	4	1	2
Palamau	25	20	2	2	1	-
Singhbhum	32	20	5	-	6	1
Chota Nagpur	152	110	12	8	15	7

and Ranchi districts were more urbanised than other districts as well as the Chota Nagpur region as a whole. But after the location of the Iron and Steel Company at Jamshedpur in 1911, Singhbhum district had a rapid urban growth and in 1921 it surpassed all other districts in the degree of urbanisation and maintained its position till 1951. Dhanbad district was not at all urbanised in the beginning and the urban growth started only after 1911. During 1921-51, increase in the porportion of urban population was gradual but after that it has been rapid because of the growting mining and manufacturing activities. Pace of urbanisation has been moderate in all other districts except Palamau where it has been very slow all through due to fewer developmental activities. In general, post-independence years have witnessed comparatively higher increase in urban population than those of pre-independence years.

The spatial pattern of urbanisation at the block level highlights the polarised growth (Table 4.3). Majority of Blocks (110) are essentially rural (Table 4.3 and Fig 22) and include vast contiguous stretch of hilly and forested areas and interspersed plains. Urbanised Blocks are comparatively few (42) and are distributed unevenly. Some of them occur as isolated patches particularly in the northern and western parts where towns developed primarily as service centres but there has not been much change in the function of such towns over the years. As such these Blocks have low degree of urbanisation. On the contrary, in the eastern, central and southern parts of the region, urbanised blocks are distributed more closely particularly in the mining and manufacturing areas where several blocks are urbanised and form small clusters. In such areas highly urbanised Blocks act as nuclei around which urban growth has been spilling over particularly along the transport routes. This is further corroborated by the distributional pattern of towns.

Urban growth pattern has also been highly imbalanced in the region during last eighty years (Table 4.4). Though the region in general has a positive gain of urban population, remarkable decadal variations are observed both spatially (e.g + 36.03 per cent increase in Giridih to + 79.36 per cent increase in Ranchi during 1971-81) and temporally (e.g + 407.34 per cent increase during 1911-21 to + 32.28 per cent increase during 1941-51 in Singhbhum).

SIZE OF URBAN CENTRES

As a measure of urbanisation one of the drawbacks of the simple percentage of urban population is that it does not discri-

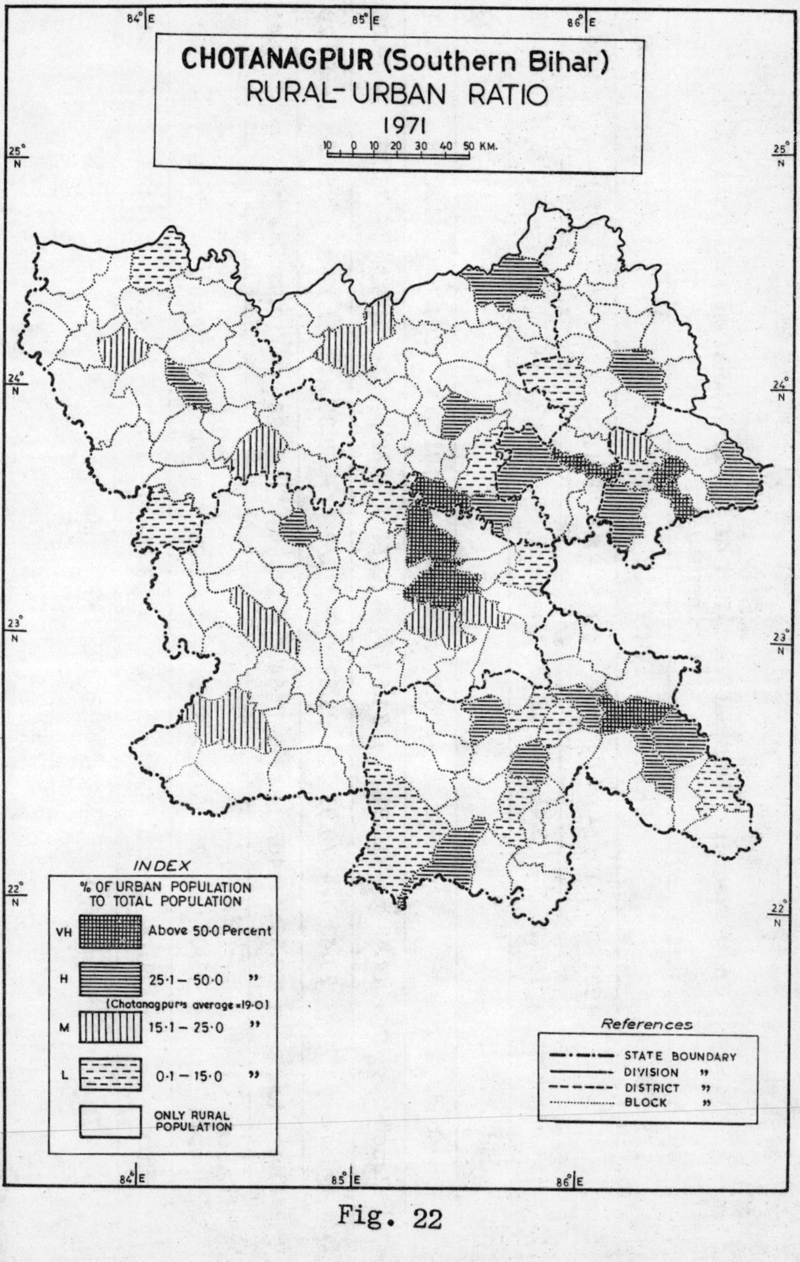
84° E
85° E
86° E
CHOTANAGPUR (Southern Bihar)
RURAL-URBAN RATIO
1971
10 0 10 20 30 40 50 KM.
25° N
24° N
23° N
22° N
INDEX
% OF URBAN POPULATION TO TOTAL POPULATION
VH Above 50·0 Percent
H 25·1 – 50·0 "
(Chotanagpur's average = 19·0)
M 15·1 – 25·0 "
L 0·1 – 15·0 "
ONLY RURAL POPULATION
References
STATE BOUNDARY
DIVISION "
DISTRICT "
BLOCK "

Fig. 22

TABLE 4.4
Chota Nagpur : Decadal Variation of Urban Population 1901-1981
(Percentage)

DISTRICT/ REGION	PRE INDEPENDENCE					POST INDEPENDENCE		
	1901-11	1911-21	1921-31	1931-41	1941-51	1951-61	1961-71	1971-81
Hazaribagh	+ 16.92	+ 5.41	+ 15.17	+ 63.58	+ 60.02	+ 51.12	+ 93.25	+ 59.45
Giridih*	-	-	-	-	-	-	-	+ 36.03
Dhanbad	-	-	+ 36.61	+141.18	+101.07	+264.79	+120.08	+ 67.21
Ranchi	+ 14.48	+ 10.91	+ 24.64	+ 19.14	+ 62.51	+ 61.92	+ 76.28	+ 79.36
Palamau	+ 20.43	+ 70.91	+ 23.57	- 5.70	+ 63.35	+ 51.77	+ 25.63	+ 53.20
Singhbhum	+ 69.66	+407.34	+ 33.64	+ 90.86	+ 32.28	+ 52.52	+ 45.19	+ 43.41
Chota Nagpur	+ 21.04	+ 76.05	+ 33.87	+ 63.05	+ 50.59	+ 79.39	+ 75.91	+ 58.07
Bihar	- 1.74	+ 8.17	+ 22.00	+ 33.66	+ 38.14	+ 42.03	+ 43.95	+ 54.40

* Giridih was part of Hazaribagh till 1971 census.

minate between different sizes of urban centres. A city with more than one lakh population is definitely more intensely urban than a small town or even five towns with 20,000 population. Also a large number of small towns would strengthen the pattern of organisation of the nodal settlement system unlike concentration of economic activities in one large city. These variations in intensity of urbanisation according to city size could be given appropriate values as weights might be helpful in calculating a refined index of the degree of urbanisation (Durand and Pelaez, 1965). But it is difficult to find a satisfactory basis for weighing these variations as they require a synthesis of data on the variations of a number of economic, social and demographic indices according to the size of urban centres.[1] Without attempting this, it is worthwhile to compare degrees of urbanisation in terms of the proportion of population in the six size-classes of towns.* (Table 4.5)

Distributional pattern of towns and their urban population by different size-classes (1981) suggests that the region like other parts of the world has a high percentage of urban population (58 per cent) concentrated within 14 cities (classes I and II) which constitutes just 16 per cent of the total urban settlements. Towns of less than 10,000 population (classes V and VI) are only few (23 per cent of the total towns) and they share only 4 per cent of urban population. In fact, intra-regional distribution pattern of towns by different size-classes reveal absence of highest and lowest orders of urban settlements in some of the districts. For example, there are only four cities of over one million population within the region, one each in Ranchi and Singhbhum and two in Dhanbad. Rest of the districts do not have class I cities. Similarly, Hazaribagh does not have a single town of less than 10,000 population. Palamau and Ranchi do not have classes V and VI towns respectively.

Largest group of towns in Chota Nagpur are those of classes III and IV which share almost equal percentages (28 and 27) respectively at the regional level. But the size of urban population contained by them varies significantly (27 percent in

---

1. Some of the indices have been exemplified in O.D.Duncan's study of the U.S. Census data for 1950 in his 'Community size and the Rural - Urban continum' in Hatt, Paul K. and Reiss, A.J. Jr.(Eds.) 'Cities and Society: The Revised Reader in Urban Sociology'; Glencoe, Illinois, The Free Press of Glencoe, 1957.

* Relevant data for the districts are given in Table 4.5

TABLE 4.5

Chota Nagpur : Distribution of Urban Settlements and their Population by Different Size - Classes (1981)

(Figures in brackets are percentages to total number of urban settlements and total urban population by districts/region.)

DISTRICT/ REGION	CLASS I Above 100000		CLASS II 50000-99999		CLASS III 20000-49999		CLASS IV 10000-19999		CLASS V 5000-9999		CLASS VI Less than 5000		TOTAL	
	No.of Towns	Popu-lation	No.of Towns	Popu-lation	No.of Towns	Popu-lation	No.of Towns	Popu-lation	No.of Towns	Popu-lation	No.of Towns	Popu-lation	No.of Towns	Popu-lation
Hazaribagh	-	-	2 (20)	150765 (45.5)	4 (40)	131773 (39.7)	4 (40)	49251 (14.8)	-	-	-	-	10 (100)	331789 (100.00)
Giridih	-	-	1 (9)	65446 (26.6)	2 (18)	80909 (32.9)	6 (55)	89537 (36.5)	1 (9)	7475 (3)	1 (9)	2441 (1)	11 (100)	245308 (100.00)
Dhanbad	2 (7)	340714 (31.9)	4 (13)	267945 (25.1)	12 (40)	356271 (33.4)	4 (13)	52210 (4.9)	7 (24)	47649 (4.5)	1 (3)	2077 (0.2)	30 (100)	1066366 (100.00)
Ranchi	1 (10)	487485 (76.1)	-	-	3 (30)	65911 (10.3)	5 (50)	77467 (12.1)	1 (10)	9318 (1.5)	-	-	10 (100)	640181 (100.00)
Palamau	-	-	1 (17)	51944 (48.1)	1 (17)	21515 (19.9)	2 (33)	26970 (24.9)	-	-	2 (33)	7663 (7.1)	6 (100)	108092 (100.00)
Singhbhum	1 (5)	457440 (49.9)	2 (9)	120586 (13.1)	6 (27)	221329 (24.1)	6 (27)	72338 (7.9)	6 (27)	42453 (4.6)	1 (5)	3327 (0.4)	22 (100)	917473 (100.00)
Chota Nagpur	4 (5)	1285639 (38.8)	10 (11)	656686 (19.8)	28 (31)	877708 (26.6)	27 (30)	367773 (11.1)	15 (17)	106895 (3.2)	5 (6)	15508 (0.5)	89 (100)	3310209 (100.00)

class III towns and 11 percent in class IV towns). Intra-regional variations are sharp in the percentage share of urban settlements and urban population between these two classes. But if towns are grouped under two categories only - more than 20,000 population (classes I, II and III) and less than 20,000 population (classes IV, V and VI) it would be clear that towns of higher order are less than 50 per cent of the total towns (89) but share almost 85 percent of urban population whereas lower order towns are more in number but share only 15 per cent of urban population. For further analysis, therefore, these two groups have been called 'effective towns' and 'quasi- urban towns', (Bose, 1978).

Temporal variations in the number and size of urban settlements prove to be important indicators of the pace of urbanisation. As such the chronological distribution of towns since 1901 and their population size in 1971 (Fig 23) presents the trend of urbanisation in the region. The sporadic growth of urban centres and urban population is a conspicuous feature particularly in the mining areas since independence. But the number and size of urban settlements have not changed much in the forested and hilly parts of Palamau, Hazaribagh and Ranchi.

During 1901-1981 there has been a significant change in the ratio of urban centres and urban population between two town-groups - 'effective and quasi-urban' (Table 4.6 and 4.7). Whereas percentages of towns and urban population in effective town- groups have increased all through this period, importance of quasi-urban towns has decreased with gradual fall in these percentages. It reveals a positive contribution of urban centres in the process of urbanisation within the region.

As regards the annual growth rate of urban settlements and urban population in the Chota Nagpur region, their patterns have been analysed for pre-independence (1901-51) and post-independence (1951-81) periods (Table 4.8). It is evident that the annual growth rate has increased during the post-independence period both in the cases of urban settlements (2.1 per cent per annum during 1901-51 to 3.5 per cent per annum during 1951-81) and urban population (3.0 per cent per annum during 1901-51 to 4.4 per cent per annum during 1951-81). Besides, the growth rate of urban population has always been higher than that of urban settlements. Among the districts, Dhanbad has recorded the highest growth rate in both urban settlements and urban population during pre as well as post-independence periods. Rest of the districts like the region as a whole have also experienced higher growth rate in urban population compared to urban settlements. They have also ex-

TABLE 4.6

Chota Nagpur : Percentage of Towns in Two Town Groups (1901-1981)

Town Groups	1901	1911	1921	1931	1941	1951	1961	1971	1981
Effective Towns	11.1	10.0	16.7	30.8	23.8	21.4	25.9	30.6	47.2
Quasi-urban Towns	88.9	90.0	83.3	69.2	76.2	78.6	74.1	69.4	52.8
Total	100.0	100.0	100.0	100.0	100.0	100.0	100.0	100.0	100.0

TABLE 4.7

Chota Nagpur : Percentage of Urban Population in Two Town Groups (1901-1981)

Town Groups	1901	1911	1921	1931	1941	1951	1961	1971	1981
Effective Towns	28.4	30.1	48.0	65.2	64.2	67.6	68.2	70.4	85.2
Quasi-urban Towns	71.6	69.9	52.0	34.8	35.8	32.4	31.8	29.6	14.8
Total	100.0	100.0	100.0	100.0	100.0	100.0	100.0	100.0	100.0

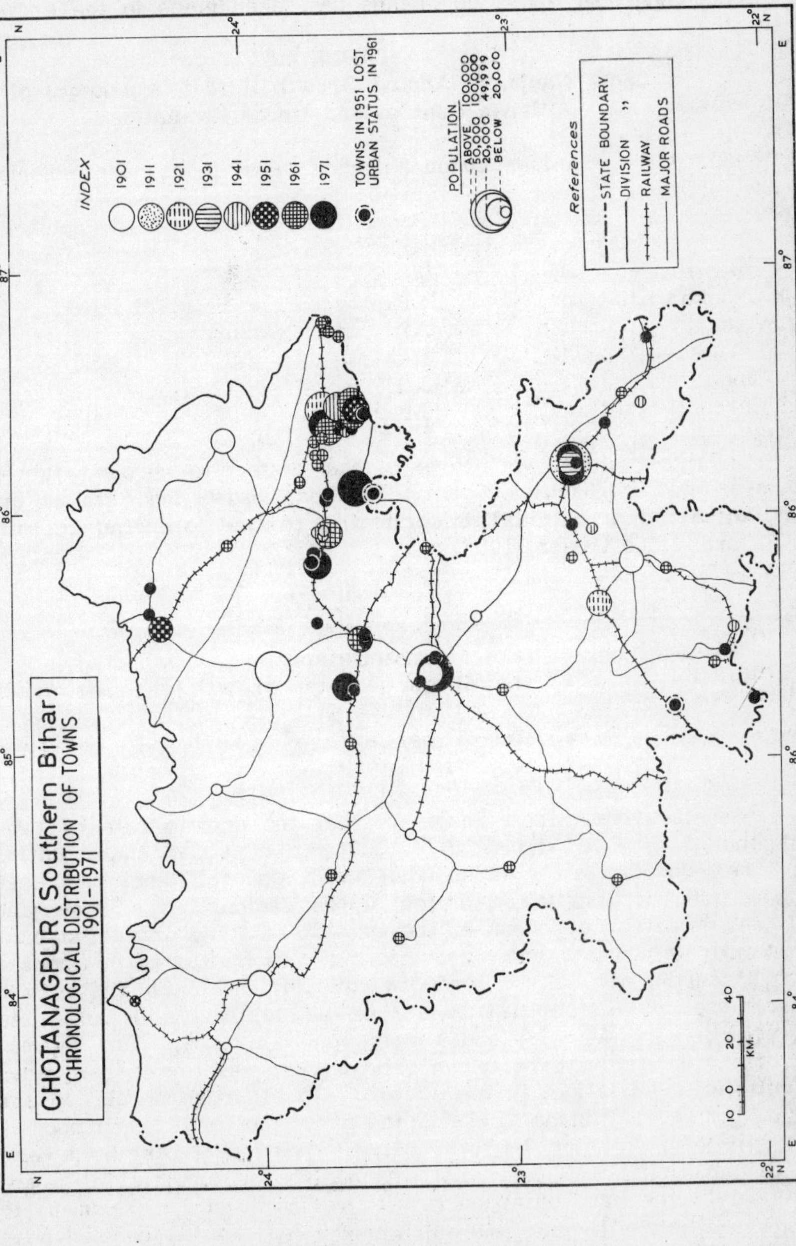
CHOTANAGPUR (Southern Bihar)
CHRONOLOGICAL DISTRIBUTION OF TOWNS
1901-1971
INDEX
1901
1911
1921
1931
1941
1951
1961
1971
TOWNS IN 1951 LOST URBAN STATUS IN 1961
POPULATION
ABOVE 100,000
50,000 100,000
20,000 49,999
BELOW 20,000
References
STATE BOUNDARY
DIVISION ,,
RAILWAY
MAJOR ROADS
10 0 20 40
KM.
84°
85°
86°
87°
24°
23°
22°
N
E

Fig. 23

perienced an increase in the growth rate of both urban settlements and urban population during post-independence period except Singhbhum where no change has taken place in the growth rate.

TABLE 4.8

Chota Nagpur : Annual Growth Rate (percentage) of Urban Centres and Urban Population

DISTRICT/ REGION	Pre Independence Period (1901-1951)		Post Independence Period (1951-1981)	
	Towns	Urban Population	Towns	Urban Population
Hazaribagh	1.8	2.3	4.7	4.9
Dhanbad	4.0	4.9	7.3	7.8
Ranchi	0.0	2.2	6.0	4.8
Palamau	0.8	2.4	2.5	3.1
Singhbhum	3.3	3.8	3.3	3.8
Chota Nagpur	2.1	3.0	3.5	4.4

Intra-regional variations in the pattern of urbanisation is presented in Table 4.9. An index to measure the rate of urbanisation is calculated according to the following formula (Durand and Pelaez, 1965).

$$r = 100 \frac{u - t}{100 + t}$$

Where: r = rate of urbanisation;
u = annual percentage growth rate of urban population;
t = annual percentage growth rate of total population.

It is evident from Table 4.9 that the growth rate of total population varied from 1.5 to 2.9 per cent per annum during three decades after independence. In general there has been positive increase in population of the region, but with varying growth rate. For example, the growth rate has increased constantly in Palamau and Hazaribagh. It has fluctuated in Dhanbad and Ranchi and has declined gradually in Singhbhum. The growth rate of urban population has been usually higher than the growth rate of total and rural population except for Palamau during 1961-71 where urban growth rate was lower than other districts. Variations in the growth rate of urban population are still sharper. During 1951-61, the growth rate of urban population varied from 4.1 per cent (Palamau, Hazaribagh and Singhbhum) to 11.4 per cent (Dhanbad). But during 1961-71 and 1971-81 the rate of urban growth varied from 2.3 (Palamau) to 7.5 (Dhanbad), 3.1 (Giridih) and 5.7 (Ranchi) percentages respectively. It thus appears from the analysis that the rate of urban growth is usually high in districts with new developmental activities particularly mining. But in later years, the pace of urban growth tends to slow down gradually probably because (a) developmental activities particularly industries have not been able to integrate themselves with the hinterland and (b) desired agglomeration of industries has not taken place which could have helped in maintaining the pace of urbanisation.

TABLE 4.9

Chota Nagpur : Rates of Total, Urban and Rural Population Growth and Rate of Urbanisation

DISTRICT/ REGION	Period	Annual Percent rate of growth			Rate of Urbanis-ation (r)
		Total (t)	Urban (u)	Rural	
1	2	3	4	5	6
Palamau	1951-61	1.9	4.1	1.8	2.2
	1961-71	2.4	2.3	2.4	-0.1
	1971-81	2.4	4.2	2.3	1.8
	1901-81	1.3	2.1	1.2	0.8
Hazaribagh	1951-61	2.1	4.1	2.0	2.0
	1961-71	2.4	6.4	2.0	3.9
	1971-81	2.9	4.6	-3.0	1.6
	1901-81	0.8	2.0	0.6	1.2
Giridih	1971-81	2.3	3.1	2.2	0.8
Ranchi	1951-61	1.5	4.7	1.2	3.2
	1961-71	2.0	5.5	1.5	3.4
	1971-81	1.6	5.7	0.7	4.0
	1901-81	1.1	2.2	0.9	1.1
Dhanbad	1951-61	2.4	11.4	0.5	8.8
	1961-71	2.1	7.5	-0.7	5.3
	1971-81	3.6	5.0	2.2	1.4
	1901-81	1.7	2.5	1.1	0.8
Singhbhum	1951-61	1.9	4.1	1.3	2.2
	1961-71	1.7	3.7	1.1	2.0
	1971-81	1.6	3.6	0.8	2.0
	1901-81	1.3	2.5	0.9	1.2
Chota Nagpur	1951-61	1.9	5.7	1.4	3.7
	1961-71	2.1	5.5	1.4	3.3
	1971-81	2.3	4.5	1.6	2.1
	1901-81	1.3	2.4	1.1	1.1

Still, urban growth in the Chota Nagpur region has been rapid compared to total and rural growth rates. However, the rate of urbanisation has always been lower than the urban growth rate and it is just 1.1 per cent per annum during 1901-81 which is undoubtedly very low. There is not much intra-regional variation in the rate of urbanisation (0.8 - 1.2 per cent per annum) during this period. This is because developmental activities started in the region only after independence and thus the average for the whole period is low. It is, therefore, worthwhile comparing the emerging pattern during 1951-81. Temporal and spatial variations are spectacular this period. The analysis suggests that:

(a) the rate of urbanisation has always been slower than the rate of urban growth;

(b) there has been a gradual decline in the rate of urbanisation from 1951 to 1981 except Ranchi where it has been just the reverse; and

(c) the rate of urbanisation has been generally less than 5 per cent per annum except Dhanbad where it has been more. It varied between 8.8 and 5.3 per cent per annum during 1951-61 and 1961-71 respectively.

It is clear from the preceding discussions that the Chota Nagpur region is more urbanised than other parts of the State. There has been a steady increase in the number of towns in general and effective towns in particular. The rate of growth has also been quite high (2.6 per cent annually) for urban population.

CITY-SIZE DISTRIBUTION

It is clear from he earlier discussions that the urban population in the Chota Nagpur region like other parts of the world is unevenly distributed. There is a great diversity in size, status, functions and character of towns and cities but together they form a system and are closely related to each other. Geographers have tried to search for an order in the distribution of urban centres and their space relations. These efforts have taken shape in the form of various theories of settlement put forward by W.Christaller (1933); Homer Hoyt (1939); A.Losch (1940); E.Ullman and C.D. Harris (1945), B.J.L. Berry and W.L. Garrison (1958a) and many others.

An attempt is made in this section to evaluate the urban pattern in the context of the rank-size relationship.

The concepts of the rank-size regularity (Zipf, 1941, 1949) and of the 'primate city' (Jefferson, 1939) were introduced almost the same time as a tool to describe the distribution of city sizes. The rank-size rule is explained mathematically as the following:

$$Pr = \frac{P_1}{r^q}$$

Where Pr is the population of the rth ranking city which equals the population of the largest city P_1 divided by rank r raised to an exponent q which generally has a value very close to unity. Stated in its simplest form the rule depicts s harmonic progression of cities within urban hierarchy. Thus if the largest city has 1 million population, the tenth city will have one-tenth or 100000 population. Thus an integrated system of cities will conform to the rank-size rule and if the observations are plotted on a double-logarithmic graph paper, the plotting will form an approximately straight line with a slope of -1. It is an emprically established rule though its interpretation varies from the opinon of G.K. Zipf who sees in it the reflection of unifying power to the opinion of H.A. Simon (1955) supported by B.J.L. Berry and W.L. Garrison (1958a) that it is a result of the law of entropy.

The index of primacy is the ratio of the population of the first city to that of the second city :

$$I = \frac{P_1}{P_2}$$

Where I is the index of primacy, P_1 is the population of the first city and P_2 is the population of the second city. This index is known as the "two-city index". Similar index using a large number of cities can also be constructed to measure the relation of the first city with other major cities of the region which are likely competitors of the first city and is called 'four-city index', which is given below:

$$I = \frac{P_1}{P_2 + P_3 + P_4}$$

Thus the index provides an objective basis for the ranking of towns according to high or low primacy, and thereby offers a way of assessing whether a primary city is 'disproportionately' large. Primacy will exist where a stratum of small towns is dominated by one or more large cities and the number of intermediate cities is less than the expected number under the rank-size rule.

Both measures have been used to describe the city-size distribution of the Chota Nagpur region. Table 4.10 shows the result of the application of the rank-size model to urban centres of the Chota Nagpur region. A comparison of the columns 3 and 5 will reveal that the expected and the actual size distribution are by no means the same. The deviation from the rank-size rule has been expressed as the per cent of population. The finding suggests that the hierarchy of urban settlements within the region does not confirm to the rank-size rule but the overall index of deviation is only 11.0 per cent which is small.

If individual places are considered for establishing the average discrepancy between the actual and expected population size, it will be noticed that deviation is less than 10 per cent in 8 towns (3 towns in 5000 - 9999 population size range and 5 towns in 20,000 - 49999 population size range); 11-30 per cent in 63 towns and more than 30 per cent in 14 towns. Urban settlements at the higher (9 towns with population above 45,000) and the lower (9 towns with population less than 5,500) levels have less population than expected size while intermediate towns have more than their expected population size. Therefore, we can say that towns of the Chota Nagpur region reveal approximation to the rank-size rule and this is supported by the index of primacy too. The 'two-city index' reveals that Jamshedpur (the first city) is twice (2.02) as large as Ranchi. The 'four-city index' presents roughly the same relations as the 'two-city index' (1.02). Thus it is clear that the first city is not 'disproportionately' larger than the next city and the city-size distribution does not reveal primacy.

FUNCTIONAL CHARACTERISTICS OF URBAN CENTRES

Urban centres differ among themselves in many respects. These variations may be observed through demographic, cultural and economic traits of towns. According to 1971 census, there were 85 towns in the Chota Nagpur region and the size of the urban population varied from 3,56,783 in Jamshedpur to 1740 in Chaitudih. At places, number of towns have grown in close proximity and their boundaries have merged giving an appearance of vast urban sprawl. These have been called urban agglomerations. Towns constituting urban agglomerations have not been treated separately while assigning them status as per their population size, but have been counted as a single unit. Distribution of towns and urban agglomeration in 1971 has been

TABLE 4.10

Chota Nagpur : Application of Rank - Size Model to Urban Centres (1971)

Town	Rank	Actual Population	Rec. Value of Rank	Expected Population	Exp: Actual Difference	Difference as Percentage of Actual	Difference as Percentage of Exp.
1	2	3	4	5	6	7	8
Jamshedpur	1	3,56,783	100,000	4,16,392	59,609	+ 16.7	+ 14.3
Ranchi	2	1,75,934	. 50000	2,08,196	32,262	+ 18.3	+ 15.5
Bokaro S City	3	94,007	. 33333	1,38,797	44,790	+ 47.6	+ 32.2
Dhanbad	4	79,838	. 25000	1,04,098	24,260	+ 30.4	+ 23.3
Jagannathnagar	5	55,663	. 20000	83,278	27,615	+ 49.6	+ 33.2
Hazaribagh	6	54,818	. 16667	69,399	14,581	+ 26.6	+ 21.0
Kerkend	7	51,314	. 14286	59,485	8,171	+ 15.9	+ 13.7
Sindri	8	46,385	. 12500	52,049	5,665	+ 12.2	+ 10.9
Jharia	9	45,236	. 11111	46,266	1,030	+ 2.3	+ 2.0
Jorapokhar	10	44,675	. 10000	41,639	3,036	- 6.8	- 7.3
Giridih	11	40,308	. 09091	37,854	2,454	- 6.1	- 6.5
Chaibasa	12	35,386	. 08333	34,699	687	- 1.9	- 2.0
Chakradharpur	13	34,967	. 07692	32,030	2,937	- 8.4	- 9.2
Tisra	14	33,891	. 07143	29,742	4,149	- 12.2	- 13.9
Jaridih Bazar	15	33,084	. 06667	27,759	5,325	- 16.1	- 19.2
Daltonganj	16	32,367	. 06250	26,024	6,343	- 19.6	- 24.4
Saunda	17	32,293	. 05882	24,494	7,799	- 24.1	- 31.8
Jhumri Tilaiya	18	29,097	. 05555	23,133	5,964	- 20.5	- 25.8
Adityapur	19	28,226	. 05263	21,915	6,311	- 22.4	- 28.8

Table 4.10 (contd.)

1	2	3	4	5	6	7	8
Bagbera	20	28,053	.05000	20,820	7,233	-25.8	-34.7
Jugsalai	21	27,364	.04762	19,828	7,536	-27.5	-38.0
Bhowrah	22	25,597	.04545	18,927	6,670	-26.1	-35.2
Doranda	23	23,954	.04348	18,104	5,850	-24.4	-32.3
Ramgarh Cantt	24	23,052	.04167	17,350	5,702	-24.7	-32.9
Bhuli	25	20,876	.04000	16,656	4,220	-20.2	-25.3
Gumia	26	20,884	.03846	16,015	4,869	-23.3	-30.4
Musabani	27	19,811	.03704	15,422	4,389	-22.1	-28.5
Katras	28	19,444	.03571	14,871	4,573	-23.5	-30.7
Loyabad	29	19,287	.03448	14,358	4,929	-25.6	-34.3
Kumardhubi	30	19,096	.03333	13,880	5,216	-27.3	-37.6
Ghatsila	31	18,351	.03226	13,432	4,919	-26.8	-36.6
Bhagatdih	32	17,465	.03125	13,012	4,453	-25.5	-34.2
Bermo	33	17,325	.03030	12,618	4,707	-27.2	-37.3
Lohardaga	34	17,087	.02941	12,247	4,840	-28.3	-39.5
Chatra	35	16,737	.02857	11,897	4,840	-28.9	-40.7
Jamadoba	36	16,646	.02778	11,566	5,080	-30.5	-43.9
Sijua	37	16,346	.02703	11,254	5,092	-31.1	-45.2
Gomoh	38	15,986	.02631	10,958	5,028	-31.4	-45.9
Kalimati	39	15,720	.02564	10,677	5,043	-32.1	-47.2
Garhwa	40	15,228	.02500	10,410	4,818	-31.6	-46.3
Gumla	41	15,131	.02439	10,156	4,975	-32.9	-49.0
Simdega	42	14,699	.02381	9,914	4,785	-32.5	-48.3
Patratu	43	14,502	.02325	9,683	4,819	-33.2	-49.8
Chas	44	13,152	.02273	9,463	3,689	-28.0	-39.0

Table 4.10 (contd.)

1	2	3	4	5	6	7	8
Chirkunda	45	12,945	.02222	9,253	3,692	- 28.5	- 39.9
Saram	46	12,800	.02174	9,052	3,748	- 29.3	- 41.4
Noamundi	47	11,992	.02128	8,859	3,133	- 26.1	- 35.4
Khunti	48	11,743	.02083	8,675	3,068	- 26.1	- 35.4
Bundu	49	11,153	.02041	8,498	2,655	- 23.8	- 31.2
Barki Saraiya	50	11,049	.02000	8,328	2,721	- 24.6	- 32.7
Kanke	51	10,994	.01961	8,164	2,830	- 25.7	- 34.7
Hussainabad	52	10,563	.01923	8,007	2,556	- 24.2	- 31.9
Maithon	53	10,163	.01887	7,856	2,307	- 22.7	- 29.4
Pathardih	54	9,906	.01852	7,711	2,195	- 22.2	- 28.5
Latehar	55	9,872	.01818	7,571	2,301	- 23.3	- 30.4
Kargali	56	9,538	.01786	7,435	2,103	- 22.0	- 28.3
Bokaro	57	9,374	.01754	7,305	2,069	- 22.1	- 28.3
Gua	58	9,347	.01724	7,179	2,168	- 23.2	- 30.2
Tenudam	59	9,037	.01695	7,057	1,980	- 21.9	- 28.1
Dugda	60	8,753	.01667	6,940	1,813	- 20.7	- 26.1
Chandrapura	61	8,544	.01639	6,826	1,718	- 20.1	- 25.2
Khelari	62	8,104	.01613	6,716	1,388	- 17.1	- 20.7
Sirka	63	7,936	.01587	6,609	1,327	- 26.7	- 20.1
Manoharpur	64	7,806	.01562	6,506	1,300	- 16.6	- 20.0
Barughutu	65	7,595	.01538	6,406	1,189	- 15.7	- 18.6
Domchanch	66	7,559	.01515	6,309	1,250	- 16.5	- 19.8
Kodarma	67	7,559	.01515	6,309	1,250	- 16.5	- 19.5
Jhinkpani	68	7,506	.01492	6,215	1,291	- 17.0	- 20.8
Barkakana	69	6,935	.01470	6,123	812	- 11.7	- 13.3

Table 4.10 (contd.)

1	2	3	4	5	6	7	8
Dumarkunda	70	6,889	.01449	6,035	854	− 12.4	− 14.1
Muri	71	6,712	.01428	5,948	764	− 11.4	− 12.8
Chakulia	72	6,646	.01408	5,865	781	− 11.7	− 13.3
Jadugora	73	7,558	.01389	5,783	775	− 11.8	− 13.4
Seraikela	74	6,290	.01370	5,704	586	− 9.3	− 10.3
Namkum	75	5,753	.01351	5,627	126	− 2.2	− 2.2
Panchet	76	5,425	.01333	5,552	127	+ 2.3	+ 2.3
Angarpathar	77	5,150	.01316	5,478	328	+ 6.4	+ 6.0
Sini	78	4,903	.01299	5,479	576	+ 11.7	+ 10.5
Kharsawan	79	4,765	.01282	5,338	573	+ 12.0	+ 10.7
Kiriburu	80	4,675	.01266	5,271	596	+ 12.7	+ 11.3
Barajamda	81	4,615	.01250	5,205	590	+ 12.8	+ 11.3
Kenduadih	82	4,220	.01234	5,141	921	+ 21.8	+ 17.9
Netarhat	83	2,527	.01219	5,078	2,551	+101.0	+ 50.2
Bera	84	2,349	.01205	5,017	2,668	+113.6	+ 53.2
Chaitudih	85	1,740	.01190	4,957	3,217	+184.9	+ 64.9
X	=	20,94,055	5.02905	20,94,154	4,60,059	2114.12	2286.10
X/N	=	24,635.94				24.9	26.9
N	=	85					

Deviation from the rank-size Rule $= \frac{230029.5}{2094055} \times 100 = 11.0$ percent.

shown in Fig 24. 1971 census recorded 4 urban agglomerations (25 towns) as class I cities (Population size - over 100,000), 1 urban agglomeration (4 towns) and 1 town as class II towns (50,000 - 99,999), 5 urban agglomerations (13 towns) and 5 towns as class III towns (20,000-49,999), 1 urban agglomeration (2 towns) and 15 towns as class IV towns (10,000-19,999), 14 towns as class V towns (5,000-9,999) and 6 towns having less than 5000 population as class VI towns. If population size of individual towns even those of constituting urban agglomerations are considered, the emerging picture is entirely different from the previous one. Only two urban centres of Jamshedpur and Ranchi qualify as class I cities, 5 as class II towns, 19 as class III towns, 27 as class IV towns, 24 as class V towns and 8 as class VI towns. The ratio of large, medium and small towns thus works out to be 1 : 12 : 29.5. However, the distribution pattern has changed in 1981 Census and there has been an increase in the number of towns in the size-classes of I, II and III; no change in class IV and decrease in the number of towns in classes V and VI. (Table 4.11). Although the impact of urban effect might be observed through the size of urban agglomeration, the pattern of growth of towns and variations in their characteristic features can be analysed when indiviual towns are studied.

As is evident from Fig 23, 29 towns are the new entrants in 1971 and two towns lost their urban status during 1961, but regained it during 1971. Variation in the population change during 1961-71 has been considerable among rest of 54 towns and cities (Table 4.12).

It is clear that growth rate has been faster in the initial phase of town's emergence. Later, stability comes and the growth rate slows down. Some of the centres particularly mining towns observe very high growth rate initially. Later, when the mines are gradually abandoned, negative change in population is a characteristic feature. Population growth rate is low (30 per cent and below) in majority of the urban centres (25); moderate (31-50 per cent) in 15 towns and high (51-70 per cent) to very high (above 70 per cent) in 3 and 7 towns respectively. Negative change has been experienced by four mining towns of Dumarkunda (-20.54 per cent), Angarpathar (-14.18 per cent), Chaitudih (-73.44 per cent) and Noamundi (-8.87 per cent). As is expected very high growth rate has been experienced by mining towns only.

Sex Ratio

Sex ratio expressed as proportion of females per 1000 males

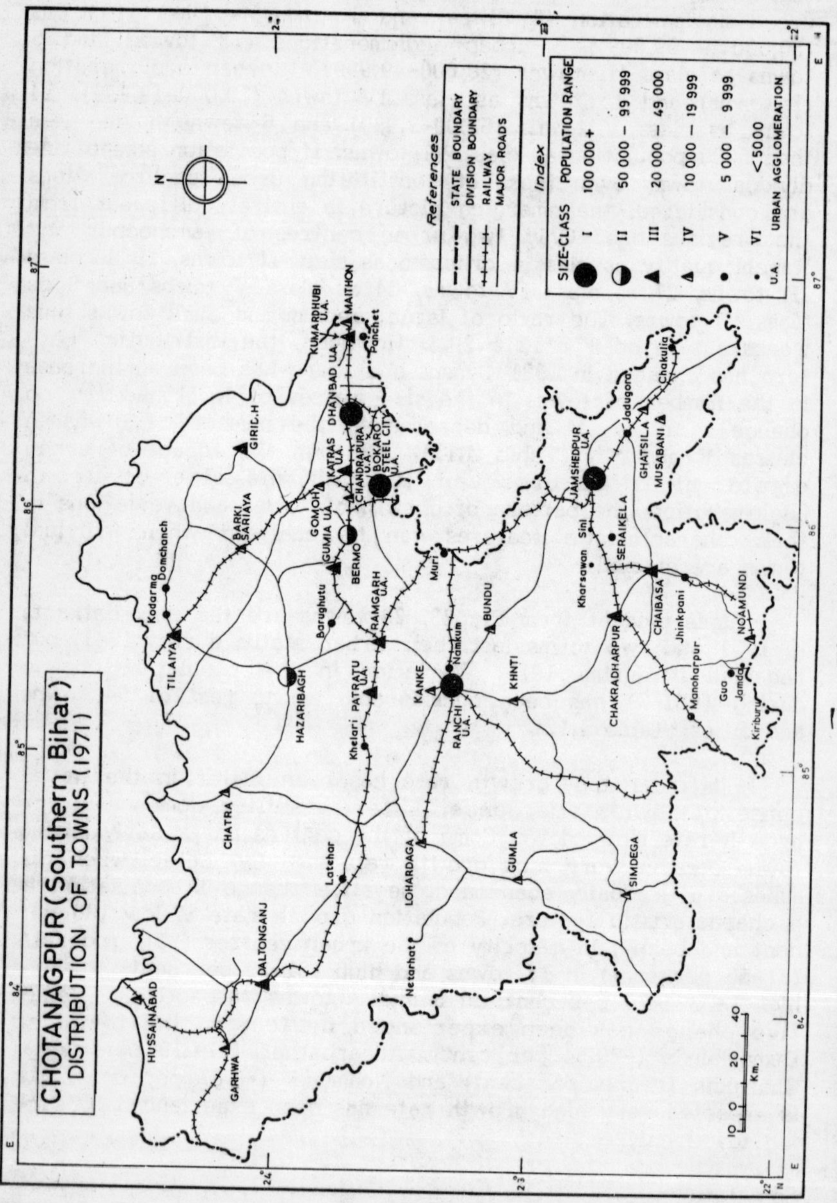
CHOTANAGPUR (Southern Bihar)
DISTRIBUTION OF TOWNS (1971)
References
STATE BOUNDARY
DIVISION BOUNDARY
RAILWAY
MAJOR ROADS
Index
SIZE-CLASS POPULATION RANGE
I 100 000 +
II 50 000 – 99 999
III 20 000 – 49 000
IV 10 000 – 19 999
V 5 000 – 9 999
VI <5000
U.A. URBAN AGGLOMERATION
HUSSAINABAD
GARHWA
DALTONGANJ
Latehar
CHATRA
TILAIYA
Kodarma
Domchanch
BARKI SARIAYA
GIRIDIH
HAZARIBAGH
Barughutu
GUMIA U.A.
GOMOH
BERMO
KATRAS U.A.
CHANDRAPURA U.A.
DHANBAD U.A.
KUMARDHUBI U.A.
MAITHON
Panchet
BOKARO STEEL CITY U.A.
RAMGARH U.A.
PATRATU U.A.
Khelari
KANKE
RANCHI U.A.
Namkum
Muri
BUNDU
KHUNTI
LOHARDAGA
Netarhat
GUMLA
SIMDEGA
CHAKRADHARPUR
CHAIBASA
Kharsawan
Sini
SERAIKELA
JAMSHEDPUR U.A.
GHATSILA
MUSABANI
Jadugora
Chakulia
Jhinkpani
NOAMUNDI
Manoharpur
Gua
Jamda
Kiriburu
10 0 20 40
Km.
84°
85°
86°
87°
22°
23°
24°
N
E

Fig. 24

TABLE 4.11

Chota Nagpur : Size of Urban Centres (1981)

CLASS I 100,000 +	CLASS II 50,000–99,999	CLASS III 20,000–49,999	CLASS IV 10,000–19,999	CLASS V 5,000–9,999	CLASS VI 5,000 & Less
1 Dhanbad	5 Saunda	15 Gumia	43 Khunti	70 Muri	85 Deorikalan
2 Jamshedpur	6 Hazaribagh	16 Chaibasa	44 Simdega	71 Bhojudih	86 Meghatuburu
3 Ranchi	7 Giridih	17 Chakradharpur	45 Chandrapura	72 Kiriburu	87 Netarhat
4 B.S. City	8 Daltonganj	18 Jhumri Tilaiya	46 Hussainabad	73 Nirsa	88 Tenu
	9 Kerkend	19 Musabani	47 Noamundi	74 Chakulia	89 Chaitudih
	10 Sindri	20 Ghatsila	48 Bundu	75 Seraikela	
	11 Jorapokhar	21 Lohardaga	49 Barki Saraiya	76 Panchet	
	12 Jharia	22 Chatra	50 Maithon	77 Chandaur	
	13 Mango	23 Gomoh	51 Khelari	78 Sini	
	14 Adityapur	24 Gumla	52 Gidi	79 Chiria	
		25 Garhwa	53 Latehar	80 Kharsawan	
		26 Itki	54 Barughutu	81 Malbera	
		27 Patratu	55 Jadugora	82 Kenduadih	
		28 Ramgarh	56 Gua	83 Angarpathar	
		29 Kumardhubi	57 Jhinkpani	84 Emlo	
		30 Tisri	58 Gadhra		
		31 Bhuli	59 Tenudam		
		32 Bhowrah	60 Sirka		
		33 Katras	61 Barkakana		
		34 Loyabad	62 Chirkunda		
		35 Jamadoba	63 Dumarkunda		
		36 Pathardih	64 Seraidhela		
		37 Bhagatdih	65 Chota Gobindpur		
		38 Sijua	66 Kanke		
		39 Bagbera	67 Bermo		
		40 Jugsalai	68 Bokaro		
		41 Chas	69 Kargali		
		42 Jaridih Bazar			

TABLE 4.12

Chota Nagpur : Decade Variation in Population for Urban Centres (1961–71)

NEGATIVE CHANGE (Percentage)	VERY LOW 15% & Less	LOW 16–30%	MODERATE 31–50%	HIGH 51–70%	VERY HIGH Above 70%
1 Dumarkunda (−20.54)	1 Hussainabad	1 Daltonganj	1 Hazaribagh	1 Loyabad	1 Bokaro
2 Angarpathar (−14.18)	2 Giridih	2 Garhwa	2 Jhumri Tilaiya	2 Sijua	2 Kerkend
3 Chaitudih (−73.44)	3 Ramgarh Cantt	3 Latehar	3 Chatra	3 Chaibasa	3 Jorapokhar
4 Noamundi (−8.87)	4 Jaridih Bazaar	4 Netarhat	4 Ranchi		4 Bhowrah
	5 Kargali	5 Bermo	5 Doranda		5 Tisra
	6 Sindri	6 Barki Saraiya	6 Khelari		6 Jamadoba
	7 Katras	7 Lohardaga	7 Muri		7 Musaban
	8 Jugsalai	8 Bundu	8 Khunti		
	9 Gua	9 Kumardhubi	9 Simdega		
	10 Chakradharpur	10 Maithon	10 Gumla		
	11 Jhinkpani	11 Panchet	11 Dhanbad		
	12 Seraikela	12 Jamshedpur	12 Jharia		
		13 Kharsawan	13 Chirkunda		
		14 Ghatsila	14 Gomoh		

is low in all urban centres of the region. An important reason seems to be male dominant migration towards urban centres. Some of the mining centres have excessively low porportion of females per 1000 males. Variations in the sex ratio ranges in between 513 for Angarpathar and 946 for Lohardaga (Table 4.13). Sex ratio is in between 501 and 600 in 8 towns, between 601 and 800 in 39 towns and between 801 and 950 in 38 towns.

TABLE 4.13

Chota Nagpur : Sex Ratio of Urban Centres (1971)

Proportion of Females per 1000 Males	Towns
501 - 600	Barughutu, Saunda, Loyabad, Kerkend, Bera, Tisra, Angarpathar and Chaitudih
601 - 800	Netarhat, Tenudam-cum-Kathara, Ramgarh Cantt, Sirka, Barkakana, Patratu, Bermo, Jaridih Bazar, Chandrapura, Kanke, Jagannathnagar, Namkum, Gumla, Dhanbad, Bhuli, Sijua, Kenduadih, Sindri, Jharia, Jorapokhar, Bhagatdih, Bhowrah, Pathardih, Jamadoba, Kumardhubi, Chirkunda, Adityapur, Chaibasa, Kiriburu, Sini, Dumarkunda, Boraro Steel City, Chas, Maithon, Gomoh, Jamshedpur, Chakulia, Musabani, and Jadugora.
801 - 950	Daltonganj, Hussainabad, Latehar, Garhwa, Hazaribagh, Jhumri Tilaiya, Kodarma, Domchanch, Barki Saraiya, Gumia, Saram, Chatra, Giridih, Kargali, Dugda, Ranchi, Doranda, Lohardaga, Khelari, Dugda, Muri, Khunti, Bundu, Simdega, Katras, Panchet, Jugsalai, Bagbera, Kalimati, Jhinkpani, Noamundi, Gua, Barajamda, Manoharpur, Chakradharpur, Seraikela, Kharsawan, Ghatsila.

Literacy Rate

Literacy rate is a good indicator of the quality of population. It is usually higher in urban areas than rural areas. While variations in the percentage of literacy among urban settlements are observed, only 24 per cent of urban population is literate in Saram but in Doranda 63 per cent of population is literate. There are only 23 towns in the region where more than 50 per cent of population is literate, of which 7 are in Ranchi, 5 in Dhanbad, 6 in Singhbhum, 4 in Hazaribagh and 1 in Palamau.

Workers to total population (participation ratio) is usually low in the urban centres of the region varying between 22 per cent (Hazaribagh) and 56 per cent (Angarpathar). Majority of urban centres (48) have less than 30 per cent of population employed. Worker's participation rate is in between 31 and 40 per cent in 28 towns and 41 and 50 per cent in 9 towns. Only one town has more than 50 per cent of population in the worker's category.

Participation Ratio for the Age-group 15-60 years

It describes the level of utilisation of the labour resources of an area and thus forms a link between the distribution of population and the distribution of employment. Low activity rate indicates concealed unemployment or reserves of potential labour. The rates are calculated by expressing the number of persons employed as a percentage of the total population of working age (aged 15 to 60 years) as against the worker's participation rate which expresses the number of persons employed as a percentage to total population irrespective of working age group. Urban agglomerations have been treated as single units because labour potential of the whole area will matter. Activity rates are low in majority of urban centres (28) and about half of the working age population is unemployed in these towns. Activity rates range between 51 and 60 per cent in 17 towns and 61 and 70 per cent in 7 towns (Table 4.14).

TABLE 4.14

Chota Nagpur : Activity Rates for the Urban Centres : 1971

Activity Rates (Percentage) size-range	Urban Centres
31 - 40	Hussainabad, Hazaribagh, Giridih, Gumla, Kanke
41 - 50	Daltonganj, Garhwa, Gumia U.A., Jhumri Tilaiya, Chatra, Barki Saraiya, Kodarma, Domchanch, Ranchi, Lohardaga, Simdega, Khunti, Muri, Gomoh, Maithon, Jamshedpur U.A., Chaibasa, Chakradharpur, Kharsawan, Seraikela, Jadugora, Chakulia, Ghatsila
51 - 60	Latehar, Netarhat, Bermo U.A, Ramgarh U.A., Chandrapura, U.A., Bundu, Khelari, Dhanbad U.A., Kumardhubi U.A., Katras U.A., Panchet, Musabani, Noamundi, Gua, Manoharpur, Jhinkpani, Sini
61 - 70	Patratu, Barughutu, Namkum, Bokaro U.A, Chaitudih, Kiriburu, Barajamda

Towns of comparatively recent origin have higher activity rates because more people in the working age group could get employment in the initial phase of town's emergence particularly mining and manufacturing towns. Employment opportunities have not been able to keep equal pace with the migration of population in the urban areas as such the backlog of unemployed persons has kept on increasing.

Employment Structure

It refers to distribution of workers in different occupations. Instead of the classification of occupations in nine categories as is followed in the Census of India publications, employment has been grouped in 3 major categories under the headings of agriculture, industry and servcie. Share of employment in these three categories varies significantly among urban centres. Employment in agriculture varies from 0.07 per cent (Gua) to 65 per cent (Latehar) of the total workers. Similar range of variation is observed for the industrial employment also, which is in between 0.13 (Latehar) and 94 (Angarpathar) percentages. As all urban centres perform some kind of service functions, employment in this category varies in between 6 per cent (Gua and Angarpathar) and 90 per cent (Maithon). In order to assess the magnitude of concentration of a particular economic activity in agricultural, industrial (separated into mining and manufacturing) and service activities, location quotients have been worked out for all towns (Fig 25). Mining activities are highly concentrated in few urban centres as is revealed by very high quotient values. Manufacturing towns are comparatively less specialised than mining but certainly more than service and agriculture. Location quotient values for service activities are usually high in a majority of towns highlighting importance of these towns as service centres for their hinterlands. Agricultural activity is highly dispersed and is inversely related with the industrial activity particularly mining.

Towns have been plotted on a coordinate graph on the basis of the percentage of workers in three economic activities (Fig 26). Three groups of towns have emerged which have been termed 'A', 'B', and 'C'. These reveal the importance of agricultural, industrial, and service activities respectively in these three groups. In general, mining, manufacturing and service activities constitute predominant functions of majority of towns in the region no doubt but one or two predominant functions of the town help to identify the pattern of their relationship with the hinterland as well as their growth prospects. In several towns (13) of the region, agricultural activities prodominate. These towns are distributed mostly in the forest

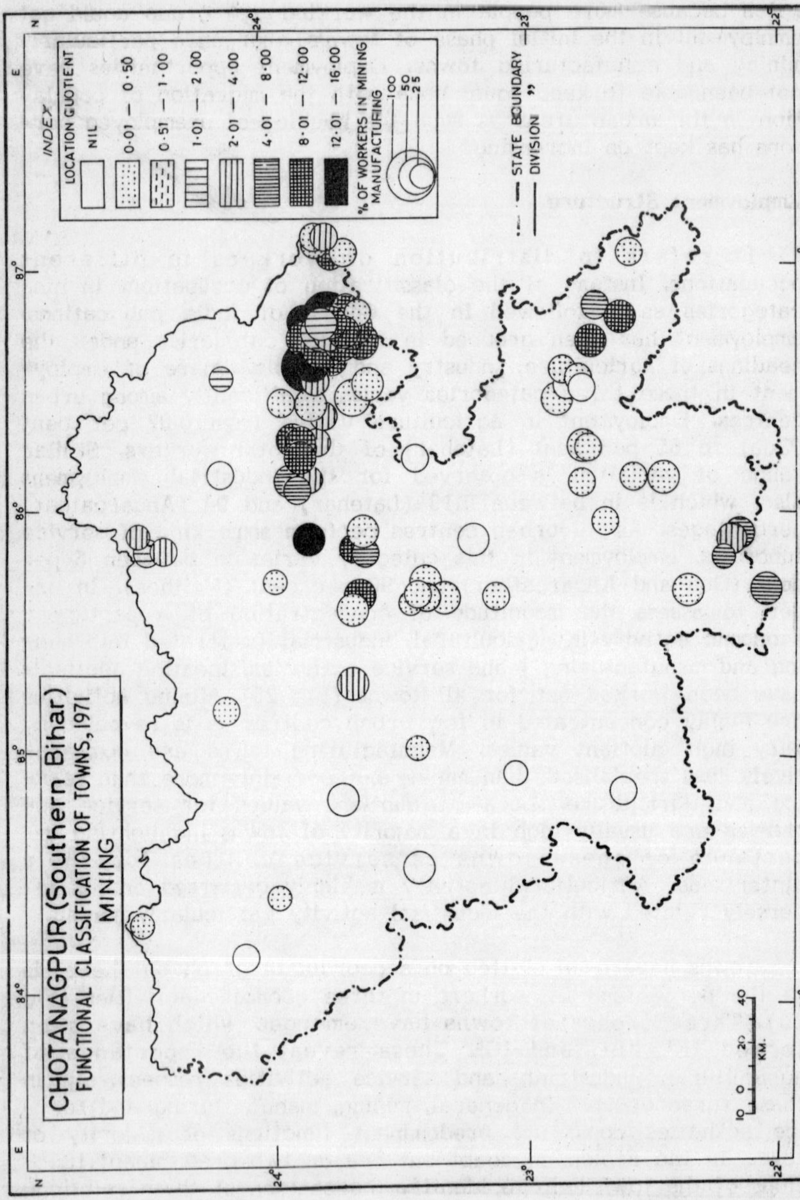

CHOTANAGPUR (Southern Bihar)
FUNCTIONAL CLASSIFICATION OF TOWNS, 1971
MINING
INDEX
LOCATION QUOTIENT
NIL
0·01 — 0·50
0·51 — 1·00
1·01 — 2·00
2·01 — 4·00
4·01 — 8·00
8·01 — 12·00
12·01 — 16·00
% OF WORKERS IN MINING MANUFACTURING
100
50
25
STATE BOUNDARY
DIVISION ,,
KM.
10 0 20 40
84°
85°
86°
87°
24°
23°
22°
N
E

Fig. 25 A

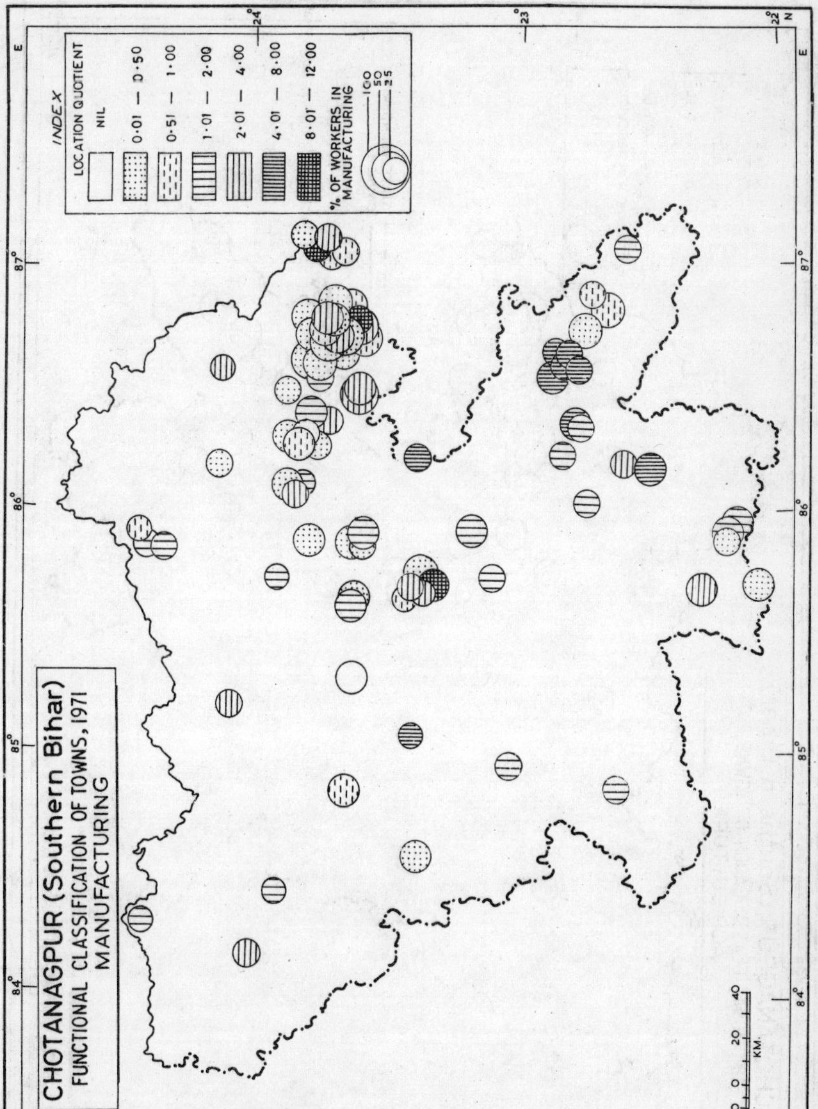
CHOTANAGPUR (Southern Bihar)
FUNCTIONAL CLASSIFICATION OF TOWNS, 1971
MANUFACTURING
INDEX
LOCATION QUOTIENT
NIL
0·01 — 0·50
0·51 — 1·00
1·01 — 2·00
2·01 — 4·00
4·01 — 8·00
8·01 — 12·00
% OF WORKERS IN MANUFACTURING
100
50
25
KM.
10 0 20 40
84°
85°
86°
87°
24°
23°
22°
N
E

Fig. 25 B

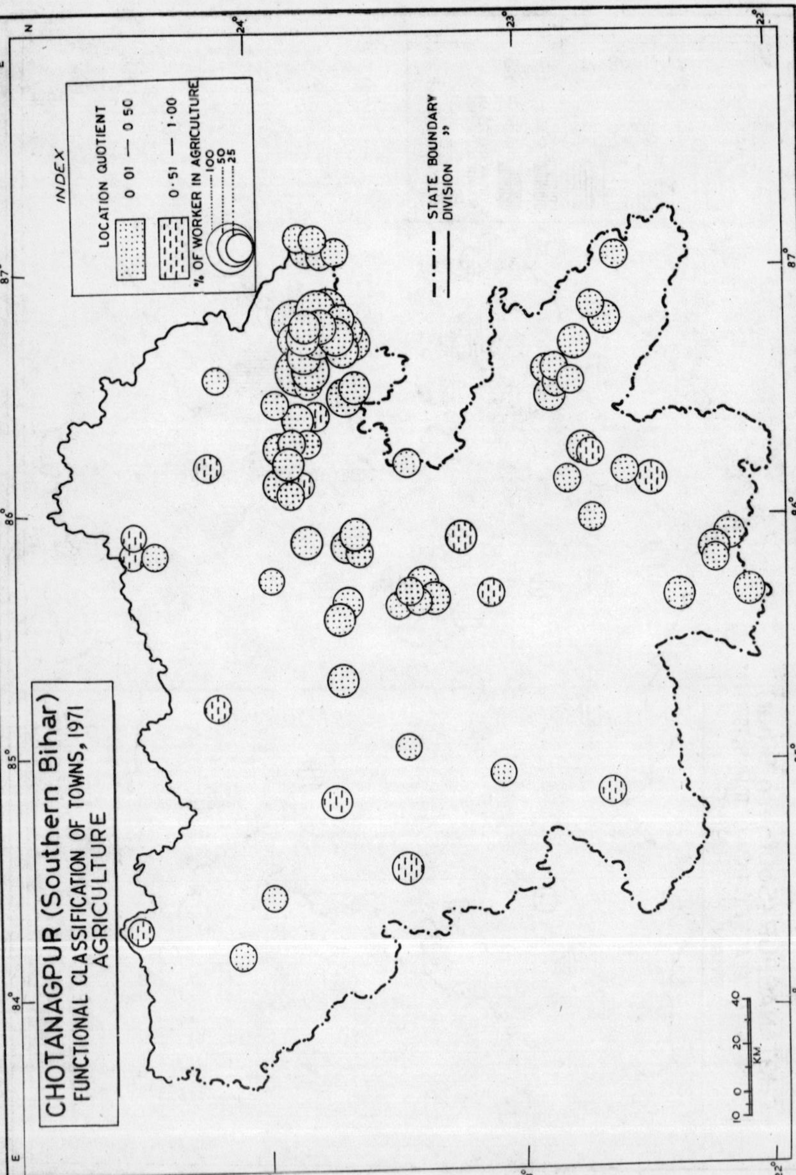
CHOTANAGPUR (Southern Bihar)
FUNCTIONAL CLASSIFICATION OF TOWNS, 1971
AGRICULTURE
INDEX
LOCATION QUOTIENT
0 01 — 0 50
0·51 — 1·00
% OF WORKER IN AGRICULTURE
100
50
25
STATE BOUNDARY
DIVISION ,,
10 0 20 40
KM.
84°
85°
86°
87°
24°
23°
22°
N
E

Fig. 25 C

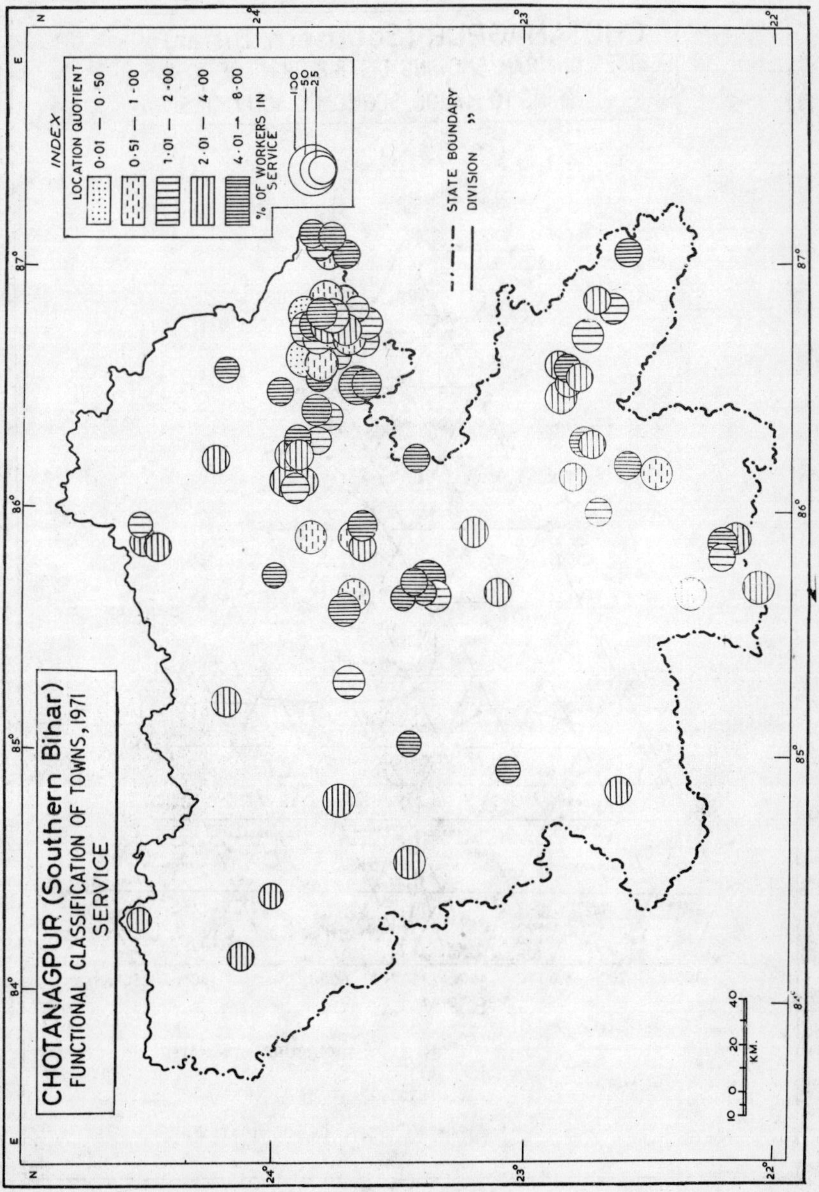
CHOTANAGPUR (Southern Bihar)
FUNCTIONAL CLASSIFICATION OF TOWNS, 1971
SERVICE
INDEX
LOCATION QUOTIENT
0·01 — 0·50
0·51 — 1·00
1·01 — 2·00
2·01 — 4·00
4·01 — 8·00
% OF WORKERS IN SERVICE
100
50
25
STATE BOUNDARY
DIVISION "
10 0 20 40
KM.
84°
85°
86°
87°
24°
23°
22°
N
E

Fig. 25 D

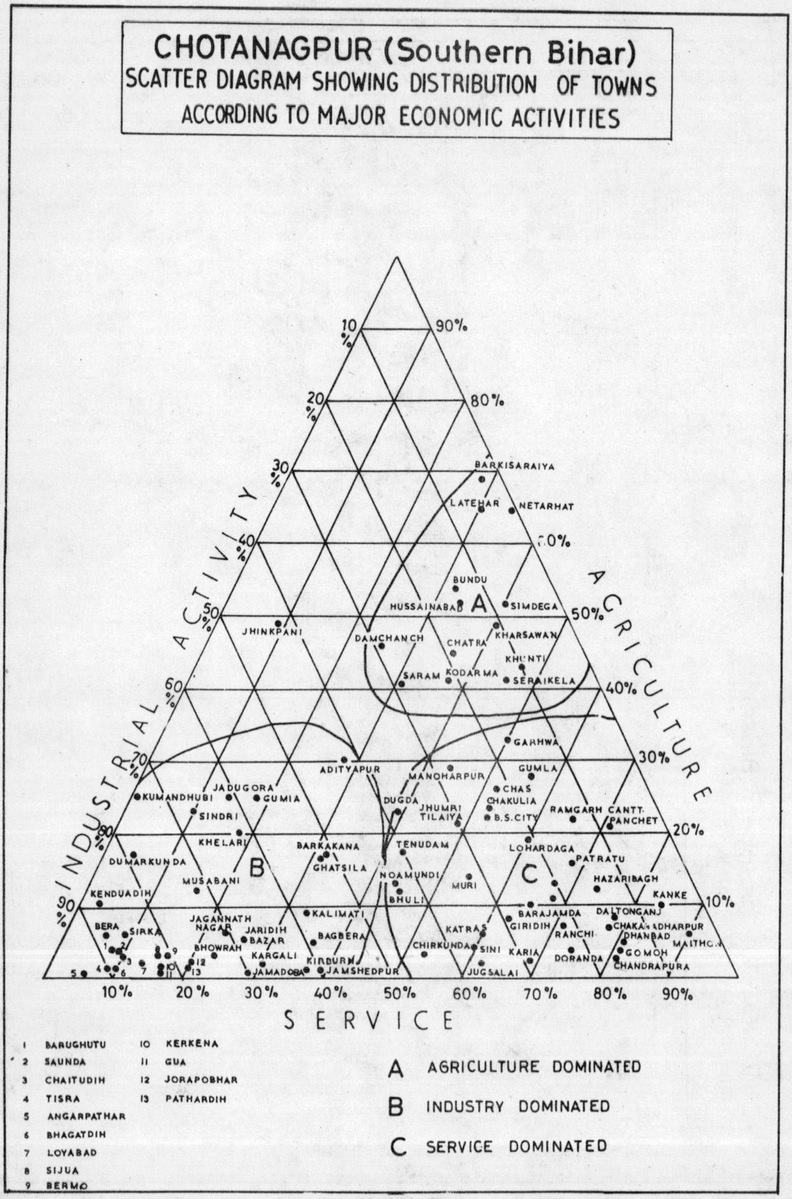
CHOTANAGPUR (Southern Bihar)
SCATTER DIAGRAM SHOWING DISTRIBUTION OF TOWNS
ACCORDING TO MAJOR ECONOMIC ACTIVITIES
INDUSTRIAL ACTIVITY
AGRICULTURE
SERVICE
10 %
20 %
30 %
40 %
50 %
60 %
70 %
80 %
90 %
90%
80%
50%
40%
30%
20%
10%
10%
20%
30%
40%
50%
60%
70%
80%
90%
BARKISARAIYA
LATEHAR
NETARHAT
BUNDU
HUSSAINABAD
SIMDEGA
JHINKPANI
DAMCHANCH
CHATRA
KHARSAWAN
KHUNTI
SARAM
KODARMA
SERAIKELA
GARHWA
ADITYAPUR
MANOHARPUR
GUMLA
KUMANDHUBI
JADUGORA
GUMIA
SINDRI
DUGDA
JHUMRI TILAIYA
CHAS
CHAKULIA
B.S.CITY
RAMGARH CANTT.
PANCHET
KHELARI
BARKAKANA
GHATSILA
TENUDAM
LOHARDAGA
PATRATU
DUMARKUNDA
MUSABANI
NOAMUNDI
BHULI
MURI
HAZARIBAGH
KENDUADIH
KANKE
BERA
SIRKA
JAGANNATH NAGAR
KALIMATI
JARIDIH BAZAR
BHOWRAH
KARGALI
BAGBERA
KIRBURN
JAMADOBA
JAMSHEDPUR
CHIRKUNDA
KATRAS
SINI
JUGSALAI
BARAJAMDA
GIRIDIH
KARIA
RANCHI
DORANDA
DALTONGANJ
CHAKARADHARPUR
DHANBAD
GOMOH
CHANDRAPURA
MAITHON
A
B
C
1 BARUGHUTU
2 SAUNDA
3 CHAITUDIH
4 TISRA
5 ANGARPATHAR
6 BHAGATDIH
7 LOYABAD
8 SIJUA
9 BERMO
10 KERKENA
11 GUA
12 JORAPOBHAR
13 PATHARDIH
A AGRICULTURE DOMINATED
B INDUSTRY DOMINATED
C SERVICE DOMINATED

Fig. 26

belts of Palamau, Hazaribagh, Ranchi and Singhbhum districts and have developed as service centres for their hinterlands. But majority of people are still attached to agriculture.

The second group of towns with industrial activity as the predominant function includes 35 towns of the region. These towns are distributed mainly in the eastern half of the region forming small clusters. Of 35 towns, 8 towns are in Hazaribagh, 16 towns are in Dhanbad, 2 in Ranchi and 9 in Singhbhum. Majority of these towns have developed basically as mining centres with associated manufacturing activities. In fact, Jamshedpur, Sindri, Kalimati and Kumardhubi are the only 4 towns in this category where manufacturing is much more important than mining.

In the third category of towns, with service as the predominant function, there are 37 towns. Of these towns, 2 are in Palamau, 8 in Hazaribagh, 10 in Dhanbad, 8 in Ranchi and 9 in Singhbhum. These centres are distributed more uniformly and seem to have grown primarily as the service centres.

To conclude the process of urbanisation in the region is closely associated with the industrial development as (a) post-independence period has witnessed a faster rate of growth than that of pre-independence period; and (b) concentration of towns and urban population is high in the mining and manufacturing areas. Inherent weakness of the process of industrialisation in terms of highly localised and foot-loose character of heavy and basic industries on the one hand and low extent of diversification of small industries on the other have been reflected in the process of urbanisation too. As a result, the rate of urbanisation has been slow. Spatial and temporal variations in the pattern of urbanisation are sharp and present a higly polarised development towards east. Besides the concentration of towns in few areas of the Chota Nagpur their distribution among different size-classes is also disproportionate, and in general, higher and lower order urban settlements are few. Functionally, majority of towns are service centres for their undeveloped rural hinterland. Thus the region is marked by the absence of well-structured spatial organisation of urban settlements which reflects poor integration of the industrial-urban economy with the rural economy.

FIVE

Settlements, Nodality and Patterns of Spatial Organisation

Settlement system is of special importance in regional development studies because it forms the framework through which the economy of a region gets organised spatially. The emergence of settlements and their development is a general historical phenomenon but they are regulated by their socio-economic basis which can be rural, semi-rural and non-rural.

Rural forms of activity depend primarily on land as a means of production and is, therefore, distributed contiguously. Settlements developed on such a landscape have a dispersed character. Semi-rural activities like mining centre around locations of mineral resources give rise to cluster-like settlements. Non-rural activities depend primarily on accumulation of manpower, availability of funds and concentration of consumers. Except for the geographical location, they are hardly influenced by the local properties of the territory. As such these activities tend to concentrate at favourable geographical locations.

The process of concentration starts usually with economic activities getting more and more complex and specialised. The hinterland of urban settlements is mainly the scene of rural activities although this dichotomy is not conducive for a developing country like India. As a result of the steady communication in the sphere of production and servicing between urban and rural settlements, there develops an integral regional system of settlements.

The Chota Nagpur region is predominantly a rugged hilly country region and is known for its forest and mineral resources. The settlement structure and distributional pattern is, therefore, greatly influenced by the terrain and the nature of productive forces. The rural settlements - generally small - are dotted along the river or scattered in the hilly interiors. As a consequence of the process of urbanisation and industrialisation based mainly on forestry and mineral wealth the larger urban and rural settlements have tended to form axis of growth with little impact on the country side.

The spatial distribution of the settlements in Chota Nagpur also reflects the socio-economic organisation in its regional environment. An examination of the spatial pattern of central places, mainly nucleated settlements with certain central facilities and services in an interlocking spatial system reveals the relationship between the economic functions and the hierarchical levels of development.

SETTLEMENT STRUCTURE AND SPATIAL PATTERN OF DISTRIBUTION BY POPULATION SIZE

The population of the region is distributed among 18,901 rural settlements and 85 urban centres (1971). However, the number of towns according to 1981 Census has increased to 89. The frequency distribution of the settlements within the region at the district level is shown in Table 5.1.

From the table it is clear that the population of the region is distributed among different size-categories of settlements unevenly. Small size settlements (less than 500 population) are more than two-third of the total number of settlements (about 68 per cent) in the region but they contain only one-fourth of the total population (27 per cent). Medium size settlements (500-1999 population size) constitute nearly 30 per cent of the total settlements in the region and have 44 per cent of the total population. Large settlements (2000 + population) are very few and they constitute 2 per cent of the total settlements but the concentration of population is very high in these settlements (29 per cent) and it is, in fact, more than the percentage of popu- lation contained by the small size settlements. This is partly due to the urban centres and their relatively large size. Distribution of small, medium and large settlements within the region varies significantly because of the differences in the toporaphy and land use.

Hilly and forested terrain of the region has widely scattered small size settlements. Palamau, Hazaribagh and Singhbhum districts, therefore, have 70-74 per cent of settlements under less than 500 population size category. Ranchi and Dhanbad have comparatively large plain areas and, therefore, the percentages of medium and large size settlements are higher (42-43 per cent). But a closer look at the distribution pattern of settlements in Ranchi and Dhanbad reveals variation even between them. Whereas Ranchi has comparatively higher percentage of small and medium size settlements, Dhanbad has compara-

TABLE 5.1

Chota Nagpur : Frequency Distribution of Settlements by Population Size and Their Population (1971)

DISTRICT/ REGION	1 - 199 No. of Settlements.	1 - 199 Population	200 - 499 No. of Settlements.	200 - 499 Population	500 - 999 No. of Settlements.	500 - 999 Population	1000 - 1999 No. of Settlements Rural	1000 - 1999 No. of Settlements Urban	1000 - 1999 No. of Settlements Total	Total Population
1	2	3	4	5	6	7	8	9	10	11
Palamau	1082	111374	1161	381905	677	469008	254	-	254	345044
%	33.57	7.40	36.02	25.38	21.00	31.18			7.88	22.94
Hazaribagh	2524	249275	2044	657620	988	687977	436	-	436	589204
%	41.02	8.26	33.22	21.77	16.06	22.78			7.09	19.51
Ranchi	657	85178	1573	530821	1058	737055	448	-	448	601727
%	17.07	3.26	40.88	20.33	27.50	28.22			11.64	23.04
Dhanbad	361	39679	433	143667	343	240595	179	1	180	247516
%	25.95	2.70	31.13	9.80	24.66	16.41			12.94	16.88
Singhbhum	1354	152406	1795	599987	930	639888	244	-	244	324323
%	30.98	6.25	41.06	24.61	21.28	26.25			5.58	13.30
Chota Nagpur	5978	637912	7006	2314000	3996	2774523	1561	1	1562	2107814
%	31.49	5.78	36.90	20.96	21.05	25.13			8.23	19.09

Table 5.1 Continued.

DISTRICT/ REGION	2000 - 4999 No. of Settlements Rural	Urban	Total	Total Popu-Lation	5000 + No. of Settlements Rural	Urban	Total	Total Popu-Lation	TOTAL No. of Settlements Rural	Urban	Total	Total Popu-Lation
1	12	13	14	15	16	17	18	19	20	21	22	23
Palamau	43	1	44	123155	1	4	5	73864	3218	5	3223	1504350
%			1.37	8.19			0.16	4.91			100.00	100.00
Hazaribagh	124	-	124	348028	15	22	37	488110	6131	22	6153	3020214
%			2.01	11.52			0.60	16.16			100.00	100.00
Ranchi	94	-	94	262412	6	12	18	394252	3836	12	3848	2611445
%			2.44	10.05			0.47	15.10			100.00	100.00
Dhanbad	45	2	47	137234	4	23	27	657726	1365	26	1391	1466417
%			3.38	9.36			1.94	44.85			100.00	100.00
Singhbhum	26	4	30	88399	2	16	18	632796	4351	20	4371	2437799
%			0.69	3.63			0.41	25.96			100.00	100.00
Chota Nagpur	332	7	339	959228	28	77	105	2246748	18901	85	18986	11040225
%			1.78	8.69			0.55	20.35			100.00	100 00

tively higher percentage of large settlements.

Variations in the distribution of population among different size categories of settlements in different districts of the region are more conspicuous. Considering the large proportion of small size settlements in all districts, the proportion of population contained by them is very low. Ranchi and Dhanbad have almost the same percentage of settlements under small size category. However, the percentage of population contained by Dhanbad in that group is almost half of the percentage contained by Ranchi. Similarly, under medium size settlement category, variations are sharp in the population concentration. Except Dhanbad, all other districts of the region contain a higher percentage of population in comparison to the percentage of settlements in this category. In fact, all districts except Dhanbad have the highest percentage of population in this category. So far as percentage distribution of large settlements and the percentage of population contained by them are concerned, Dhanbad has the highest percentage in both of them.

A settlement grows in size when it possesses certain advantages which attract a large number of population. There are extensive and contiguous areas of small settlements which inhibit the process of spatial integration in the process of development. In order to bring out the characteristics of the distributional pattern of settlements by population size, the data are mapped and analysed using Block as the unit of study (Fig 31). The emerging patterns and their interpretation is based on the analysis of landform and land use characteristics brought out in Figs. 2, 4-6. The main findings are summarised below:

(a) Most parts of Palamau, Ranchi and Singhbhum districts (38 blocks) do not have any large settlement and are characterised by small settlements as is common in hilly and forested terrain.

(b) Nearly 56 per cent of the Blocks do not have more than 5 per cent of settlements in the size category of over 500 population. These areas are mostly forested and agriculturally less productive.

(c) In 19 Blocks, only 5-10 percent of their settlements have more than 2000 population. These are sporadic in their distribution having good agricultural lands, or being close to mineral and industrial activities.

(d) Only 10 Blocks of the region have high to very high percentage of large settlements. In fact, these areas are restricted mostly to the mining-manufacturing belts of Dhanbad, Giridih, Hazaribagh and Ranchi.

On the basis of the above observations, one can conclude that the distribution of settlements in the region closely conforms to the topography and land use of the area. Agriultural areas have small and isolated settlements whereas relatively larger settlements have grown close to relatively small pockets of industiral urban activities. The Damodar basin with the mining and manufacturing activities seems to be the main belt having large settlements.

DISTRIBUTION OF INFRASTRUCTURE, SOCIAL FACILITIES AND AMENITIES IN CHOTA NAGPUR

While every settlement acquires over a period of time certain types and levels of social facilities and amenities corresponding to its size and situation, there are certain facilities and amenities which are non-ubiquitous in nature. Settlements preforming such non-ubiquitous functions, therefore, serve not only local people but also those of adjoining settlements. These kinds of services and functions are known as central functions and places performing them are hence called the central places or nodal centres. The area which is served by a particular nodal settlement is called the hinterland or the tributary area. Space relations develop between the nodal settlements and the other settlements of hinterland (Deshpande, et. al. 1979). With the increasing number of functions, the size of the tributary area of the nodal settlements are organised functionally in space around different sizes of nodes or central places giving rise to hierarchical pattern (Wanmali, 1970). The central place theory of Christaller and its modified form by Losch provide the basis to understand and interprete the pattern of functional organisation particularly of agricultural regions. Even in those areas where criteria of homogenity in physical landscape, resource base or in purchasing power are absent, the geometrical patterns may be distorted but some kind of functional hierarchy and spatial regularity of settlements may be observed (Bhat, et. al. 1976).

The occurrence of certain types and levels of social facilities and amenities is influenced to a great extent by the population size of the settlement, its growth and situation (Deshpande, et. al. 1979). An understanding of the emergence of central places in a particular region, therefore, requires an analytical study of the relationship between population size of the settlements and the types of social facilities and amenities and their spatial pattern of distribution in the region. As such, the existing spatial pattern of the infrastructure, social facilities and amentities for the six size-classes of rural settlements of the region have been analysed. Criteria for the selection of these services and amenities have been that (i) they represent different kinds of major facilities and services; and (ii) the data is available for all settlements of the region.

SPATIAL PATTERN OF RURAL INFRASTRUCTURE

Roads and Railways

The region is comparatively better served by roads than railways (Table 5.2). Roads in the region run avoiding the rugged terrain. Footpaths usually connect the scattered small settlements in the hilly forested parts particularly the 'Pat' region (Table 5.2).

TABLE 5.2
Chota Nagpur: Distribution of Roads and Railways

DISTRICTS	Length of Road in Kms per 100 Sq. Km. of Area	Length of Railways in Kms per 100 Sq. Km of Area
Palamau	7.5	2.0
Ranchi	11.0	1.2
Hazaribagh	13.7	2.1
Giridih	14.9	2.6
Singhbhum	14.6	2.6
Dhanbad	33.1	16.4

As is evident from the above table, road and railway lengths vary significantly from one district to another. Palamau with 7.5 Kms of road per 100 Sq Km of the area has the poorest accessibility. Ranchi, Hazaribagh, Giridih and Singhbhum have 11 to 15 Kms of road length per 100 sq km. of area which is also quite low from accessibility point of view. Dhanbad is the only district in the region which is better placed in terms of accessibility by roads as well as railways. Railway length varies from 1.2 Km to 2.6 Km per 100 sq. km. of area in all other districts which no doubt is very low.

On account of the rugged terrain, railways and road lines seem to converge in the lower Damodar basin and hence density of railway lines is the highest in that part. Besides main artery lines, there are few truncated lines which join the mining centres. For example, the railway line from Lohardaga to

Ranchi, Gua to Jamda, Badampahar in Orissa to Jamshedpur, Giridih to Madhupur in Santal Parganas. The trunk routes and their spatial arrangement are influenced to some extent by the exogenous forces, for example, the pull exerted by the industrial belt of West Bengal and other parts of India, which depend on the industrial produce of this region.

Educational Facilities (Fig 27)

Included in this category are the primary schools, middle schools, high schools and other institutions like training centres and colleges. Even the primary school facility is not ubiquitous. Thus out of 18901 rural settlements only 42 per cent of them have primary schools, 7 per cent have middle schools, and only 2 per cent have high schools. Among higher order facilities only 50 settlements have other institutions (Table 5.3). Situation is more or less similar in all districts though there are slight variations among districts. For example, only 34 per cent of the total settlements in Hazaribagh have primary schools whereas in Ranchi 53 per cent of the settlements have this facility. But the variation is less among the districts with regard to the percentage of settlements having middle schools, high schools and colleges and other institutions. For example, the percentage of settlements having middle school facilities varies between 5 per cent in Hazaribagh and 10 per cent in Ranchi and Dhanbad. Number of settlements having high schools constitute only 1 per cent of total settlements in Palamau and Hazaribagh and 3 per cent in Dhanbad. The percentage of settlements with college or any other institutional facility varies between 0.2 and 0.4 per cent respectively for Singhbhum and Palamau.

Variations in the distribution of educational facilities are observed more clearly at the Block level (Fig 27). Distribution of each type of educational amenity has been taken separately with primary school as the lowest order of educational amenity. At least 20 per cent of the settlements in each Block have primary schools. Ranchi and Dhanabad emerge better in respect of this facility as only 3 Blocks in Ranchi and 1 in Dhanbad have 20-39 per cent of settlements with primary schools which is lower than the average (42 per cent) for the Chota Nagpur region. Singhbhum and Palamau rank next in the number of Blocks having higher or equal value to the average for the Chota Nagpur. Hazaribagh and Giridih with more than 50 per cent of Blocks (25 out of 42 blocks) have lower value than the average of 42 per cent for the Chota Nagpur from the third category.

As the order of the educational amenity increases, its distribution becomes more and more non-ubiquitous which is evident from the Figs 27a-d. Whereas highest percentage of settlements having primary school is 84.6 per cent, it decreases to 40 per cent in the case of middle and high schools and 20 per cent in the case of colleges and other institutions.

TABLE 5.3

Chota Nagpur : Educational Facilities in the Rural Settlements (1971)

(Figures in brackets are percentages to total number of settlements)

DISTRICT/ REGION	Total Rural Settlements	No. of Settlements Having: Primary Schools	Middle Schools	High Schools	Colleges
Palamau	3218	1328 (41)	220 (7)	33 (1)	12 (0.4)
Hazaribagh	6131	2098 (34)	301 (5)	80 (1)	14 (0.3)
Ranchi	3836	2050 (53)	368 (10)	89 (2)	12 (0.3)
Dhanbad	1365	687 (50)	134 (10)	36 (3)	4 (0.3)
Singhbhum	4351	1726 (40)	296 (7)	68 (2)	8 (0.2)
Chota Nagpur	18901	7883 (42)	1319 (7)	306 (2)	50 (0.3)

Ranchi and Dhanbad have comparatively higher percentage of settlements with middle school facilities than other districts of the region. Leaving only three Blocks in Ranchi, all other Blocks of these two districts have at least 5 per cent of settlements with middle schools facilities. Blocks with more than 20 per cent of settlements with these facilities are also located only in these two districts (Jharia in Dhanbad with 40 per cent, and Kurdeg and Kolebira in Ranchi with 24.4 per cent and 26.4 per cent respectively). Bermo in Giridih is the only Block in the region where middle school facilities are nil. On the whole, only 10 per cent of the settlements of the region have this facility.

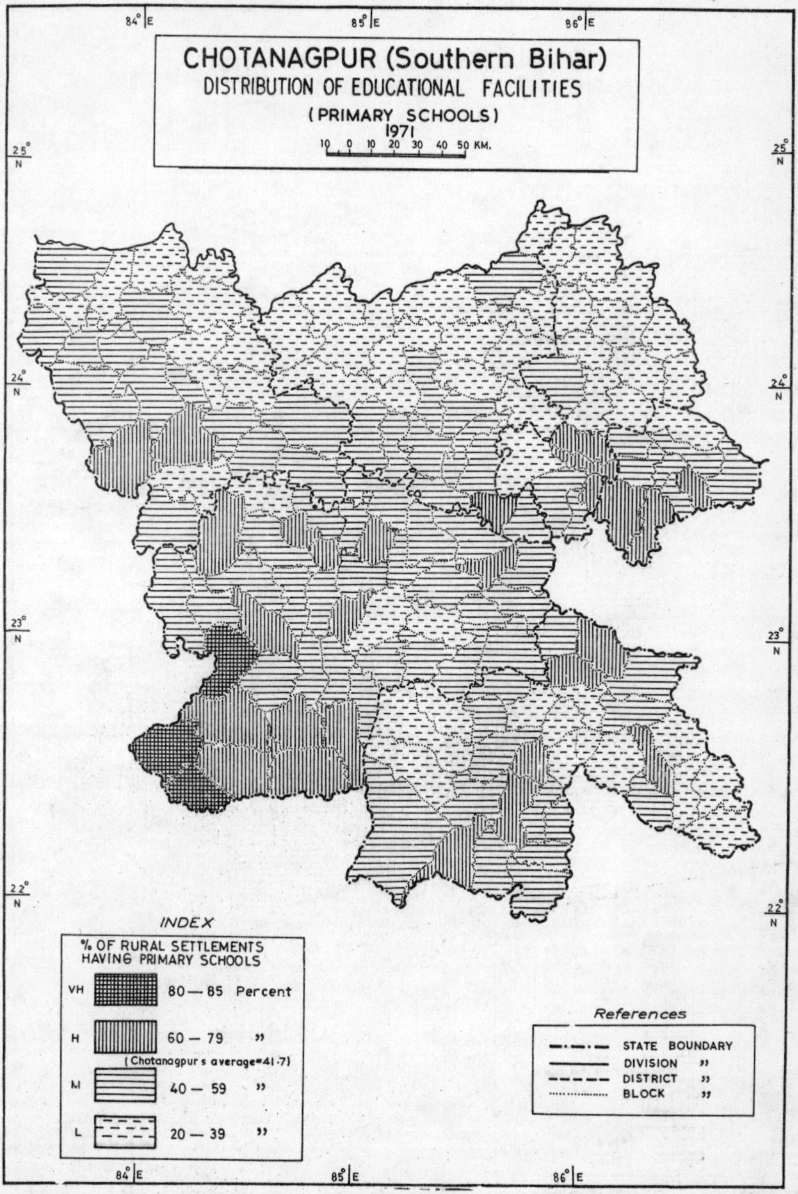
CHOTANAGPUR (Southern Bihar)
DISTRIBUTION OF EDUCATIONAL FACILITIES
(PRIMARY SCHOOLS)
1971
10 0 10 20 30 40 50 KM.
84° E
85° E
86° E
25° N
24° N
23° N
22° N
INDEX
% OF RURAL SETTLEMENTS HAVING PRIMARY SCHOOLS
VH 80 — 85 Percent
H 60 — 79 "
(Chotanagpur s average=41·7)
M 40 — 59 "
L 20 — 39 "
References
STATE BOUNDARY
DIVISION "
DISTRICT "
BLOCK "

Fig. 27 A

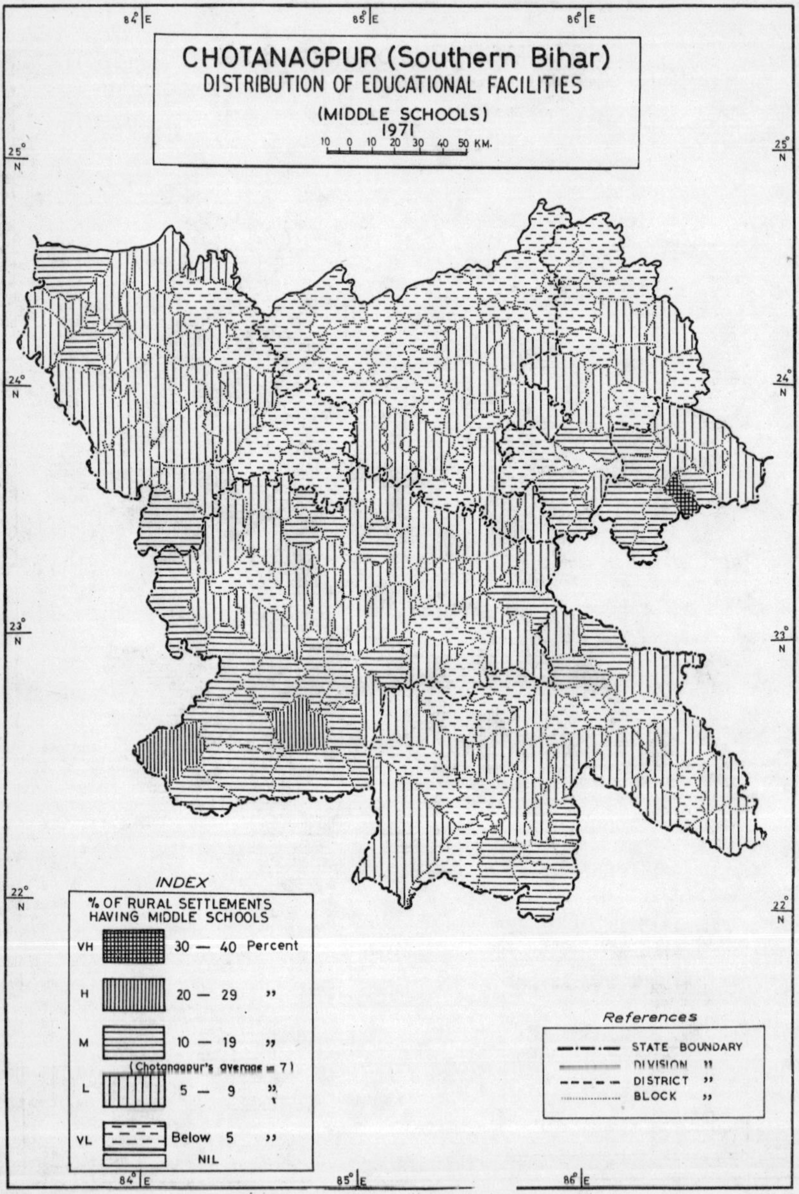

CHOTANAGPUR (Southern Bihar)
DISTRIBUTION OF EDUCATIONAL FACILITIES
(MIDDLE SCHOOLS)
1971
10 0 10 20 30 40 50 KM.
84° E
85° E
86° E
25° N
24° N
23° N
22° N
INDEX
% OF RURAL SETTLEMENTS HAVING MIDDLE SCHOOLS
VH 30 — 40 Percent
H 20 — 29 ,,
M 10 — 19 ,,
(Chotanagpur's average = 7)
L 5 — 9 ,,
VL Below 5 ,,
NIL
References
STATE BOUNDARY
DIVISION ,,
DISTRICT ,,
BLOCK ,,

Fig. 27 B

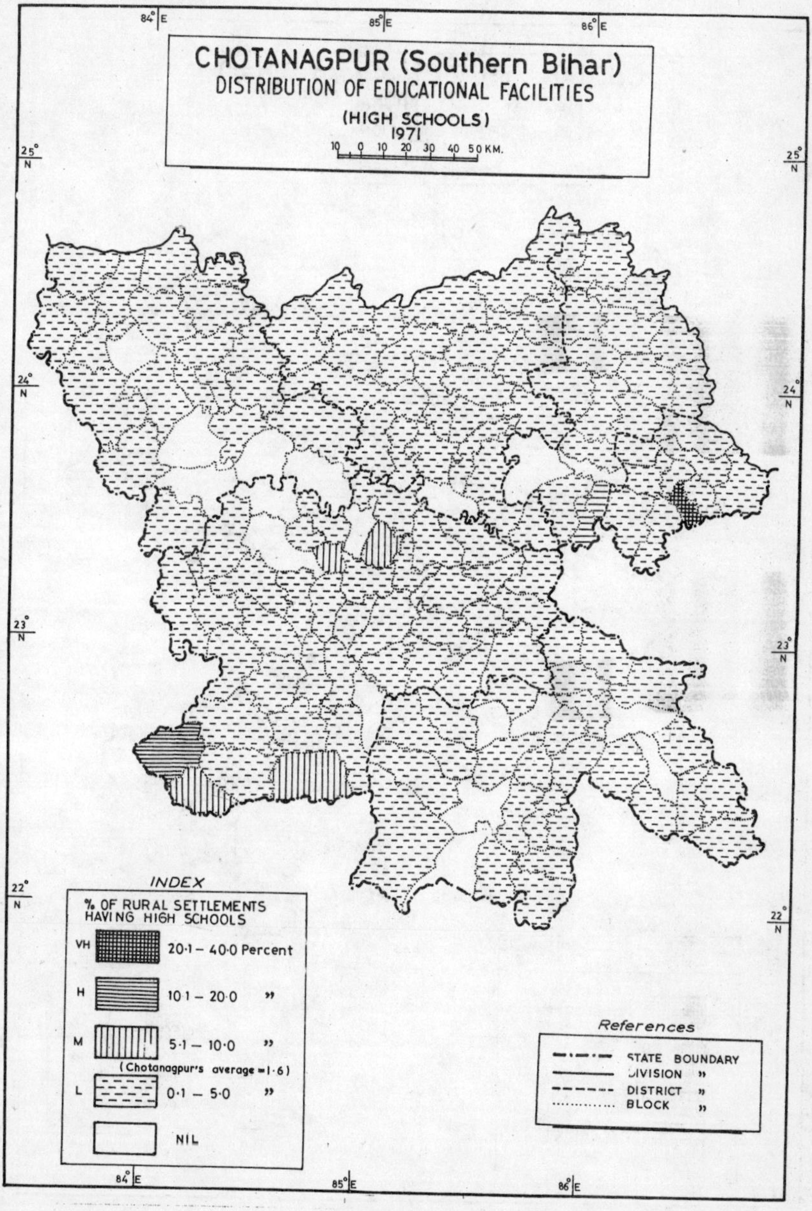

CHOTANAGPUR (Southern Bihar)
DISTRIBUTION OF EDUCATIONAL FACILITIES
(HIGH SCHOOLS)
1971
10 0 10 20 30 40 50 KM.
84° E
85° E
86° E
25° N
24° N
23° N
22° N
INDEX
% OF RURAL SETTLEMENTS HAVING HIGH SCHOOLS
VH 20·1 – 40·0 Percent
H 10·1 – 20·0 "
M 5·1 – 10·0 "
(Chotanagpur's average = 1·6)
L 0·1 – 5·0 "
NIL
References
STATE BOUNDARY
DIVISION "
DISTRICT "
BLOCK "

Fig. 27 C

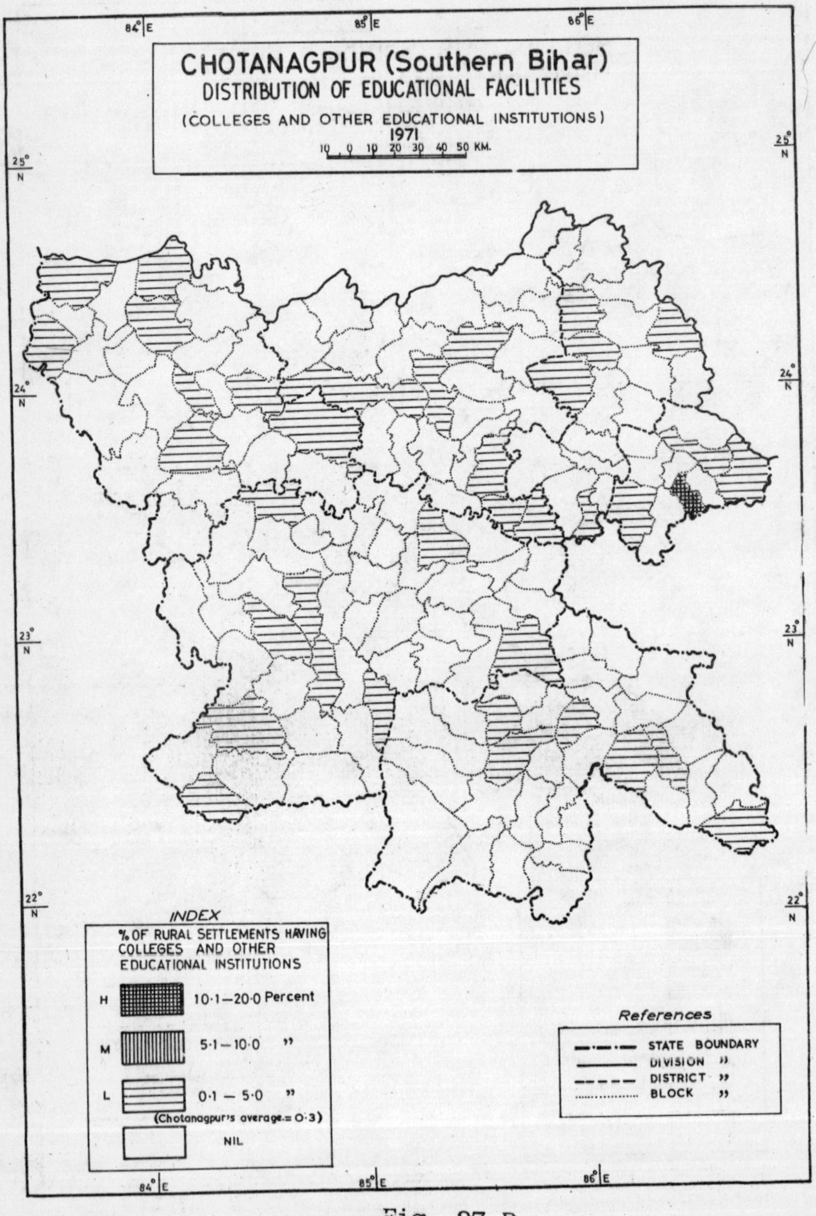
CHOTANAGPUR (Southern Bihar)
DISTRIBUTION OF EDUCATIONAL FACILITIES
(COLLEGES AND OTHER EDUCATIONAL INSTITUTIONS)
1971
10 0 10 20 30 40 50 KM.
84° E
85° E
86° E
25° N
24° N
23° N
22° N
INDEX
% OF RURAL SETTLEMENTS HAVING COLLEGES AND OTHER EDUCATIONAL INSTITUTIONS
H 10·1—20·0 Percent
M 5·1—10·0 "
L 0·1 — 5·0 "
(Chotanagpur's average = 0·3)
NIL
References
STATE BOUNDARY
DIVISION "
DISTRICT "
BLOCK "

Fig. 27 D

High Schools in the region are very few and there are extensive areas without this facility. In fact, settlements having high school cater mostly to the demand of the local population. Only 4 Blocks in Ranchi and 2 in Giridih have 5 - 10 per cent of settlements with high schools. Kurdeg in Ranchi and Jharia in Dhanbad have 13.3 per cent and 40 per cent of settlements with this facility respectively. None of the Blocks in Palamau, Hazaribagh and Singhbhum districts have more than 5 per cent of settlements with this facility. Distribution of colleges and other institutions at the Block level shows that nearly 74 per cent of Blocks do not have any college or other institution. Except Jharia, remaining Blocks have less than 5 per cent of their settlements with this facility.

An important observation of the distributional pattern of these facilities is that higher order amenities are less ubiquitous in their distribution. As such primary schools being lowest in the order of educational facilities are distributed relatively widely.

Table 5.4 shows the distribution of educational facilities in settlements of different size categories at the district level. It is clear from the analysis of this table that with the increase in the size of the settlements the order as well as the number of these amenities also increase.

Medical Facilities (Fig 28)

Medical facilities in the region include hospitals and dispensaries, family welfare centres, and health centres. On the whole these facilities are meagre as not more than 2.8 per cent of the settlments in the whole region have these facilities (Table 5.5). Even among large settlements only few have some kind of medical facility. In fact, there is little relationship between the nature of medical facility and the population size of the rural settlement. (Table 5.6).

Even at this low level of existing facility there are marked intra-district variations. In Palamau less than 2 per cent of settlements have dispensaries whereas in Dhanbad little over than 7 per cent of the settlements have dispensaries. Similar trends are seen in the distributional pattern of family welfare centres and health centres. Even after taking all facilities together the percentage of settlements having medical facilities is not more than 11.

Figure 28 shows the distribution of medical facilities at the Block level. Each kind of medical facility has been taken

TABLE 5.4

Chota Nagpur : Distribution of Educational Facilities in Different Size Range of Settlements (1971)

(Figures in Brackets are Percentages to total number of Settlements)

DISTRICT/ REGION	Population size	Total Rural Settle- ments	Rural Settlements Having			Others
			Primary Schools	Middle Schools	High Schools	
1	2	3	4	5	6	7
PALAMAU	1 - 199	1082	126 (11.6)	6 (0.6)	2 (0.2)	1 (0.1)
	200 - 499	1161	521 (44.9)	42 (3.6)	1 (0.1)	1 (0.1)
	500 - 999	677	469 (69.3)	63 (9.3)	5 (0.7)	4 (0.6)
	1000 - 1999	254	182 (71.7)	82 (32.3)	15 (5.9)	3 (1.2)
	2000 - 4999	43	29 (67.4)	26 (60.5)	9 (20.9)	3 (7.0)
	5000 +	1	1 (100.00)	1 (100.00)	1 (100.00)	-
HAZARIBAGH	1 - 199	2524	215 (8.5)	17 (0.7)	4 (0.2)	-
	200 - 499	2044	733 (35.9)	48 (2.3)	14 (0.7)	4 (0.2)
	500 - 999	986	697 (70.7)	74 (7.5)	15 (1.5)	3 (0.3)
	1000 - 1999	436	344 (78.9)	81 (18.6)	22 (5.0)	4 (0.9)
	2000 - 4999	124	89 (71.8)	70 (56.5)	20 (16.1)	1 (0.8)
	5000 +	15	14 (93.3)	11 (73.3)	5 (33.3)	2 (13.3)
RANCHI	1 - 199	657	85 (12.9)	9 (1.4)	1 (0.1)	2 (0.3)
	200 - 499	1573	701 (44.6)	62 (3.9)	10 (0.6)	1 (0.1)
	500 - 999	1058	810 (76.6)	103 (9.7)	22 (2.1)	2 (0.2)
	1000 - 1999	448	366 (81.7)	132 (29.5)	31 (6.9)	4 (0.9)
	2000 - 4999	94	82 (87.2)	57 (60.6)	20 (21.3)	3 (3.2)

Table 5.4 (contd.)

1	2	3	4	5	6	7
	5000 +	6	6 (100.0)	5 (83.3)	5 (83.3)	-
DHANBAD	1 - 199	361	61 (16.9)	7 (1.9)	2 (0.6)	-
	200 - 499	433	197 (45.5)	22 (5.1)	4 (0.9)	-
	500 - 999	343	260 (75.8)	35 (10.2)	7 (2.0)	1 (0.3)
	1000 - 1999	179	131 (73.2)	44 (24.6)	12 (6.7)	2 (1.1)
	2000 - 4999	45	36 (80.0)	22 (48.9)	8 (17.8)	-
	5000 +	4	2 (50.0)	4 (100.0)	3 (75.0)	1 (25.0)
SINGHBHUM	1 - 199	1354	127 (9.4)	19 (1.4)	5 (0.4)	3 (0.2)
	200 - 499	1795	734 (40.9)	83 (4.6)	18 (1.0)	-
	500 - 999	930	673 (72.4)	102 (11.0)	20 (2.1)	3 (0.3)
	1000 - 1999	244	174 (71.3)	71 (29.1)	15 (6.1)	-
	2000 - 4999	26	16 (61.5)	21 (80.8)	10 (38.5)	2 (7.7)
	5000 +	2	2 (100.0)	-	-	-
CHOTA NAGPUR	1 - 199	5978	614 (10.3)	58 (1.0)	14 (0.2)	6 (0.1)
	200 - 499	7006	2886 (41.2)	257 (3.7)	47 (0.7)	6 (0.1)
	500 - 999	3996	2909 (72.8)	377 (9.4)	69 (1.7)	13 (0.3)
	1000 - 1999	1561	1197 (76.7)	410 (26.3)	95 (6.1)	13 (0.8)
	2000 - 4999	332	252 (75.9)	196 (59.0)	67 (20.2)	9 (2.7)
	5000 +	28	25 (89.3)	21 (75.0)	14 (50.0)	3 (10.7)

TABLE 5.5

Chota Nagpur : Medical Facilities in the Rural Settlements (1971)

(Figures in brackets are percentages to total Number of settlements)

DISTRICT/ REGION	Total Rural Settle-ments	Settlements Having		
		Hospitals/ Dispensaries	Family Welfare Centres	Health Centres
Palamau	3218	56 (1.7)	14 (0.4)	73 (2.3)
Hazaribagh	6131	150 (2.5)	34 (0.6)	112 (1.8)
Ranchi	3836	111 (2.9)	29 (0.8)	114 (3.0)
Dhanbad	1365	99 (7.3)	21 (1.5)	20 (1.5)
Singhbhum	4351	111 (2.6)	15 (0.3)	81 (1.9)
Chota Nagpur	18901	527 (2.8)	113 (0.6)	400 (2.1)

separately. It is clear from Fig. 28 (c) that large number of Blocks in the region have less than 5 per cent of settlements with hospitals or dispensaries. Dhanbad is comparatively better placed in this respect as out of 10 Blocks only 2 have less than 5 per cent, 5 with 5-10 per cent and 3 with 10-20 per cent of settlements with dispensaries. 9 Blocks in Ranchi, 2 in Palamau, 3 in Hazaribagh, 2 in Giridih and 4 in Singhbhum have 5-10 percent of settlements with this facility. Only 1 Block in Ranchi has 11.5 percent of settlements with this facility. Family Welfare Centres are absent in a large number of Blocks (77) except Dhanbad. (Fig 28 b). Almost the same number of Blocks (73) have less than 5 percent of settlements with family welfare centres. Only two Blocks (1 in Giridih i.e. Peterbar with 6.2 per cent and 1 in Dhanbad i.e. Jharia with 20 per cent) have more than 5 per cent of settlements with this facility (Fig. 28 b). Health Centres are comparatively more uniformly distributed than family welfare centres as majority of Blocks have at least some percentage of settlements with this facility. Blocks with 5-10 per cent of settlements having health centres are only 11 in

TABLE 5.6

Chota Nagpur : Distribution of Medical Facilities in the Rural Settlements by Population Size (1971)

(Figures in brackets are percentages to total number of settlements in particular size-category)

DISTRICT/ REGION	Population size	Total Rural Settle-ments	Settlements Having: Hospitals/ Dispensaries	Family Welfare Centres	Health Centres
1	2	3	4	5	6
PALAMAU	1 - 199	1082	3 (0.3)	1 (0.1)	5 (0.5)
	200 - 499	1161	12 (1.0)	-	14 (1.2)
	500 - 999	677	13 (1.9)	2 (0.3)	19 (2.8)
	1000 - 1999	254	18 (7.1)	6 (2.4)	27 (10.6)
	2000 - 4999	43	9 (20.9)	5 (11.6)	8 (18.6)
	5000 +	1	1 (100.0)	-	-
HAZARIBAGH	1 - 199	2524	10 (0.4)	-	5 (0.2)
	200 - 499	2044	37 (1.8)	6 (0.3)	36 (1.8)
	500 - 999	986	30 (3.0)	3 (0.3)	32 (3.2)
	1000 - 1999	436	38 (8.7)	15 (3.4)	24 (5.5)
	2000 - 4999	124	30 (24.2)	8 (6.4)	11 (8.9)
	5000 +	15	5 (33.3)	2 (13.3)	4 (26.7)
RANCHI	1 - 199	657	-	-	6 (0.9)
	200 - 499	1573	18 (1.1)	1 (0.1)	17 (1.1)
	500 - 999	1058	33 (3.1)	9 (0.9)	37 (3.5)
	1000 - 1999	448	41 (9.2)	12 (2.7)	39 (8.7)

Table 5.6 (contd.)

1	2	3	4	5	6
	2000 - 4999	94	16 (17.0)	7 (7.4)	15 (16.0)
	5000 +	6	3 (50.0)	-	-
DHANBAD	1 - 199	361	5 (1.4)	-	1 (0.3)
	200 - 499	433	17 (3.9)	1 (0.2)	4 (0.9)
	500 - 999	343	24 (7.0)	6 (1.7)	9 (2.6)
	1000 - 1999	179	34 (19.0)	7 (3.9)	6 (3.3)
	2000 - 4999	45	15 (33.3)	4 (8.9)	-
	5000 +	4	4 (100.0)	3 (75.0)	-
SINGHBHUM	1 - 199	1354	9 (0.7)	-	6 (0.4)
	200 - 499	1795	38 (2.1)	7 (0.4)	24 (1.3)
	500 - 999	930	31 (3.3)	4 (0.4)	25 (2.7)
	1000 - 1999	244	21 (8.6)	3 (1.2)	22 (9.0)
	2000 - 4999	26	12 (46.1)	1 (3.8)	4 (15.4)
	5000 +	2	-	-	-
CHOTA NAGPUR	1 - 199	5978	27 (0.5)	1 (0.01)	23 (0.4)
	200 - 499	7006	122 (1.7)	15 (0.2)	95 (1.4)
	500 - 999	3996	131 (3.3)	24 (0.6)	122 (3.1)
	1000 - 1999	1561	152 (9.7)	43 (2.8)	118 (7.6)
	2000 - 4999	332	82 (24.7)	25 (7.5)	38 (11.4)
	5000 +	28	13 (46.4)	5 (17.9)	4 (14.3)

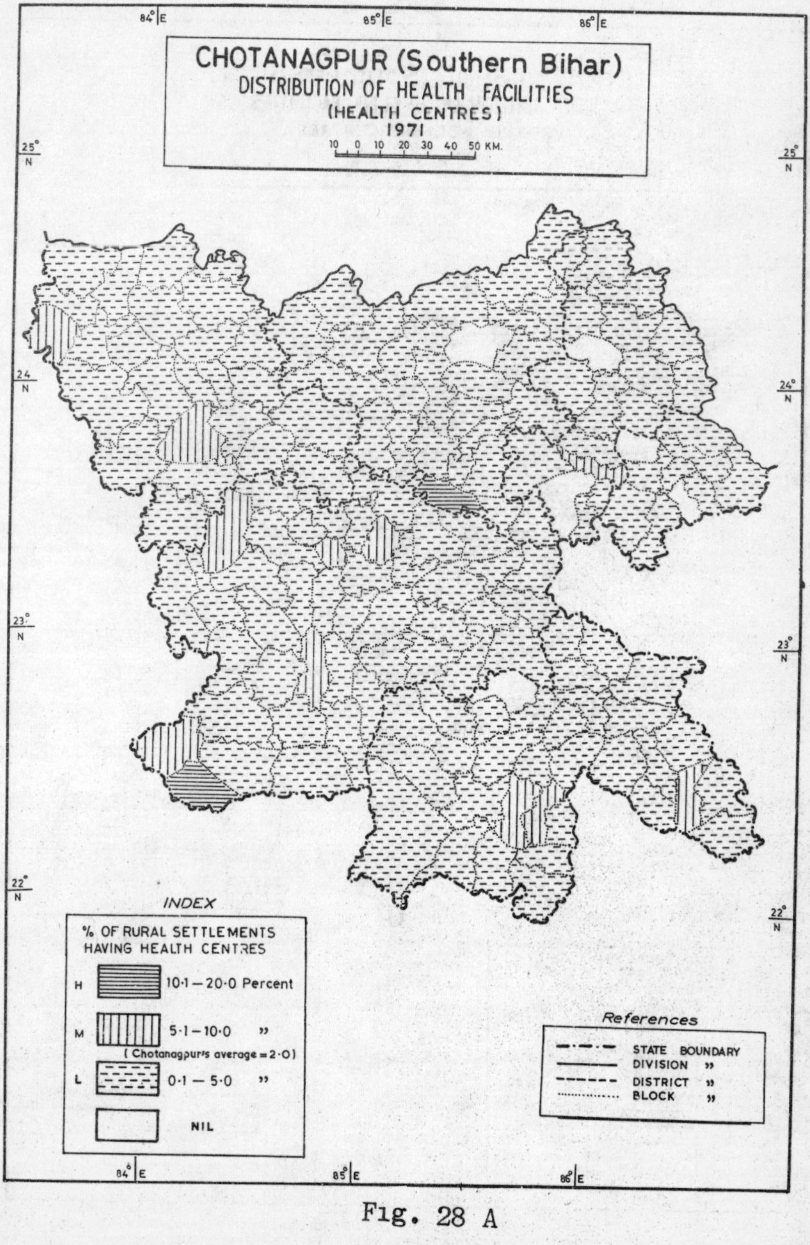
84° E
85° E
86° E
25° N
24° N
23° N
22° N
CHOTANAGPUR (Southern Bihar)
DISTRIBUTION OF HEALTH FACILITIES
(HEALTH CENTRES)
1971
10 0 10 20 30 40 50 KM.
INDEX
% OF RURAL SETTLEMENTS HAVING HEALTH CENTRES
H 10·1 — 20·0 Percent
M 5·1 — 10·0 "
(Chotanagpur's average = 2·0)
L 0·1 — 5·0 "
NIL
References
STATE BOUNDARY
DIVISION "
DISTRICT "
BLOCK "

Fig. 28 A

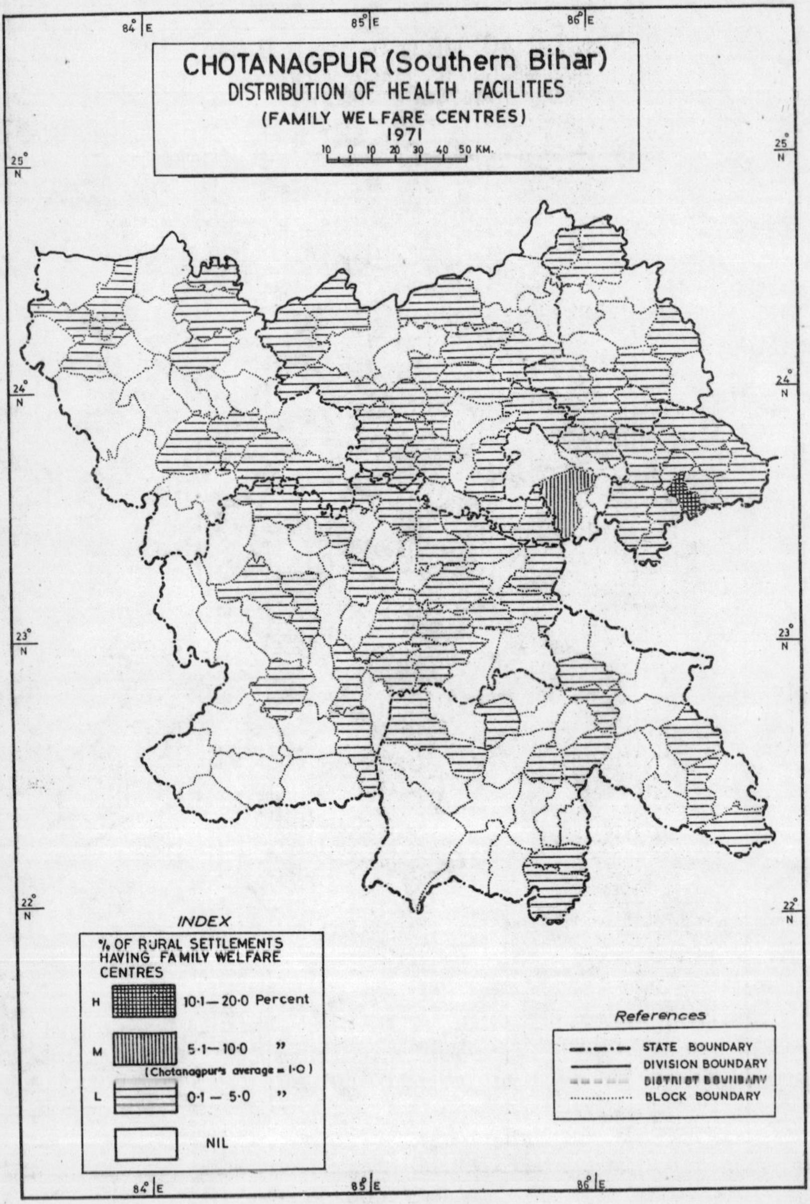
CHOTANAGPUR (Southern Bihar)
DISTRIBUTION OF HEALTH FACILITIES
(FAMILY WELFARE CENTRES)
1971
10 0 10 20 30 40 50 KM.
84° E
85° E
86° E
25° N
24° N
23° N
22° N
INDEX
% OF RURAL SETTLEMENTS HAVING FAMILY WELFARE CENTRES
H 10·1—20·0 Percent
M 5·1—10·0 "
(Chotanagpur's average = 1·0)
L 0·1 — 5·0 "
NIL
References
STATE BOUNDARY
DIVISION BOUNDARY
DISTRICT BOUNDARY
BLOCK BOUNDARY

Fig. 28 B

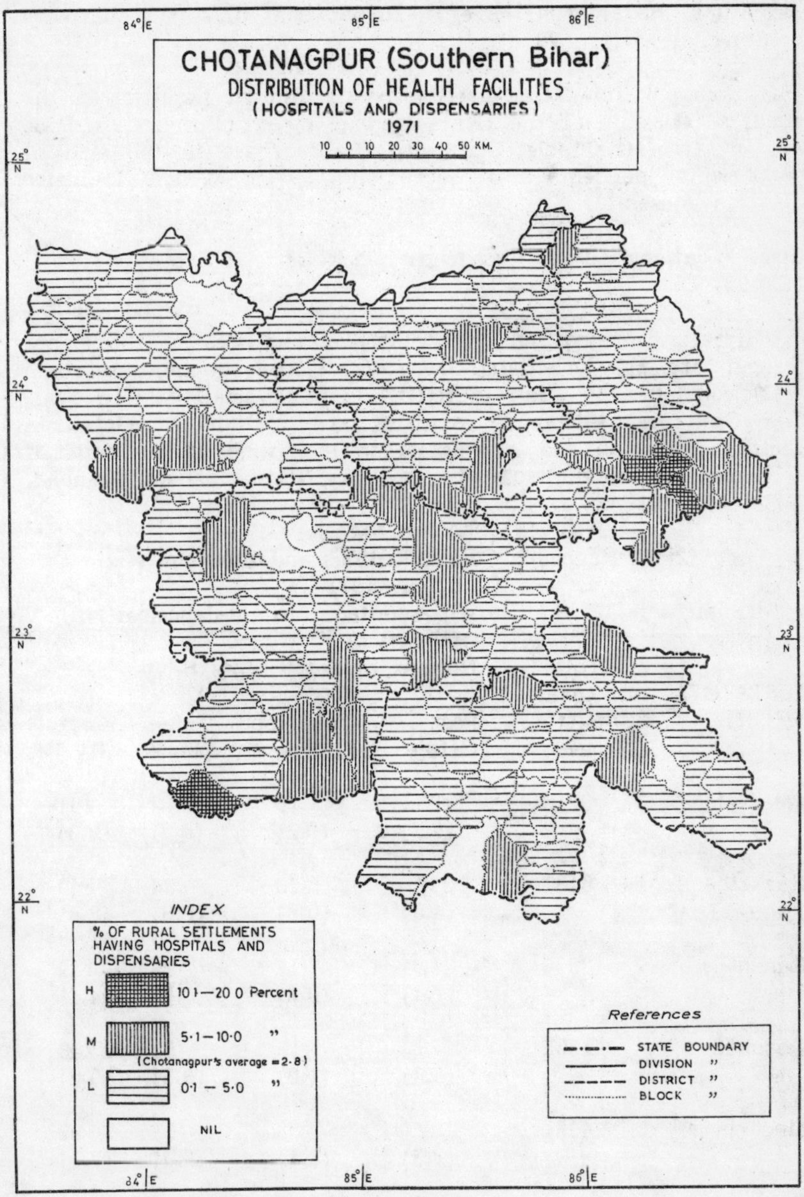
CHOTANAGPUR (Southern Bihar)
DISTRIBUTION OF HEALTH FACILITIES
(HOSPITALS AND DISPENSARIES)
1971
10 0 10 20 30 40 50 KM.
84° E
85° E
86° E
25° N
24° N
23° N
22° N
INDEX
% OF RURAL SETTLEMENTS HAVING HOSPITALS AND DISPENSARIES
H 10·1—20·0 Percent
M 5·1—10·0 "
(Chotanagpur's average = 2·8)
L 0·1 — 5·0 "
NIL
References
STATE BOUNDARY
DIVISION "
DISTRICT "
BLOCK "

Fig. 28 C

the region, of which 2 are in Palamau, 5 in Ranchi, 1 in Giridih and 3 in Singhbhum. Only two Blocks (Bolba in Ranchi and Patratu in Hazaribagh) have 10-20 per cent of settlements with health centres (Fig 28 a).

Table 5.6 shows the distribution of medical facilities in the rural settlements of the Chota Nagpur by population size. It is evident from the table that with the increase in the size of settlements, percentage of settlements having medical facilities also increases.

Communications - Post, Telegraph and Telephone Facilities (Fig.29)

The post, telegraph and telephone facilities in the Chota Nagpur are also unsatisfactory (Fig. 29). Percentage of rural settlements having such facilities is very small (Table 5.7). Telegraph and telephone facilities are further restricted in their distribution and are found in less than 1 per cent of settlements in all districts of the Chota Nagpur except Dhanbad.

TABLE 5.7

Chota Nagpur : Communications and Electricity Facilities, 1971

(Figures in brackets are percentages to total number of settlements)

DISTRICT/ REGION	Total Rural Settle ments	Number of Settlements Having			
		Post Office	Telegraph Office	Tele-phone	Electri-city
Palamau	3218	183 (5.7)	6 (0.2)	8 (0.3)	291 (9.0)
Hazaribagh	6131	297 (4.8)	20 (0.3)	34 (0.6)	540 (8.8)
Ranchi	3836	283 (7.4)	11 (0.3)	22 (0.6)	159 (4.1)
Dhanbad	1365	78 (5.7)	13 (1.0)	52 (3.8)	268 (19.6)
Singhbhum	4351	142 (3.3)	5 (0.1)	13 (0.3)	92 (2.1)
Chota Nagpur	18901	983 (5.2)	55 (0.3)	129 (0.7)	1350 (7.1)

Distribution of post offices (Fig 29 a) reveals that large number of Blocks in the region have very low to low distribution of post offices. Only two Blocks in the region (Kurdeg in Ranchi and Jharia in Dhanbad) are better placed in this respect. Telegraph facilities are almost negligible as the major part of the region does not have this facility (Fig 29 b). Even in the Blocks where some settlements have this facility, they do not constitute more than 5 per cent of the total settlements of the Block. Telephones, of course, are more widely distributed than telegraph facilities (Fig 29 c) but the number of Blocks with settlements without telephone facility is quite large. Dhanbad is the only district where all the Blocks have at least some per centage of settlements with telephone facility. In the whole region, only three Blocks (2 in Dhanbad i.e. Dhanbad and Jharia and 1 in Giridih, i.e Bermo) have a higher per centage (10-20 percent) of settlements having this facility.

Electricity (Fig 30)

Despite region's rapid industrial and urban growth, 93 per cent villages of the region are without electricity, and such areas are extensive (Fig 30). Villages which are electrified are mostly in and around the mining and industrial belt of the Damodar basin, particularly in Dhanbad district. Several blocks in Ranchi, Palamau and Singhbhum are without electricity. If a line is drawn diagonally from north-west part of Palamau to south-east part of Singhbhum, majority of the areas without electricity will fall to the west of it, and this is an area which is devoid of any industrial activity.

LARGE SETTLEMENTS AS POTENTIAL NODAL CENTRES - EVALUATION OF EXISTING FACILITIES AND AMENITIES

Earlier discussions suggest that distribution of different social amenities and facilities in the region is uneven and tends to concentrate in a limited number of settlements. Table 5.9 gives the distribution of each kind of social amenity in three size classes—large (+2000 population); medium (500 - 1999 Population); and small (less than 500 population) of rural settlements for each district as well as the Chota Nagpur region.

An analysis of the table brings out certain facts relating to spatial distribution and centrality of different services and facilities.

(a) For each kind of social amenity, the percentage of settlements having that particular amenity usually decreases sharply from the large to medium and to small sizes of

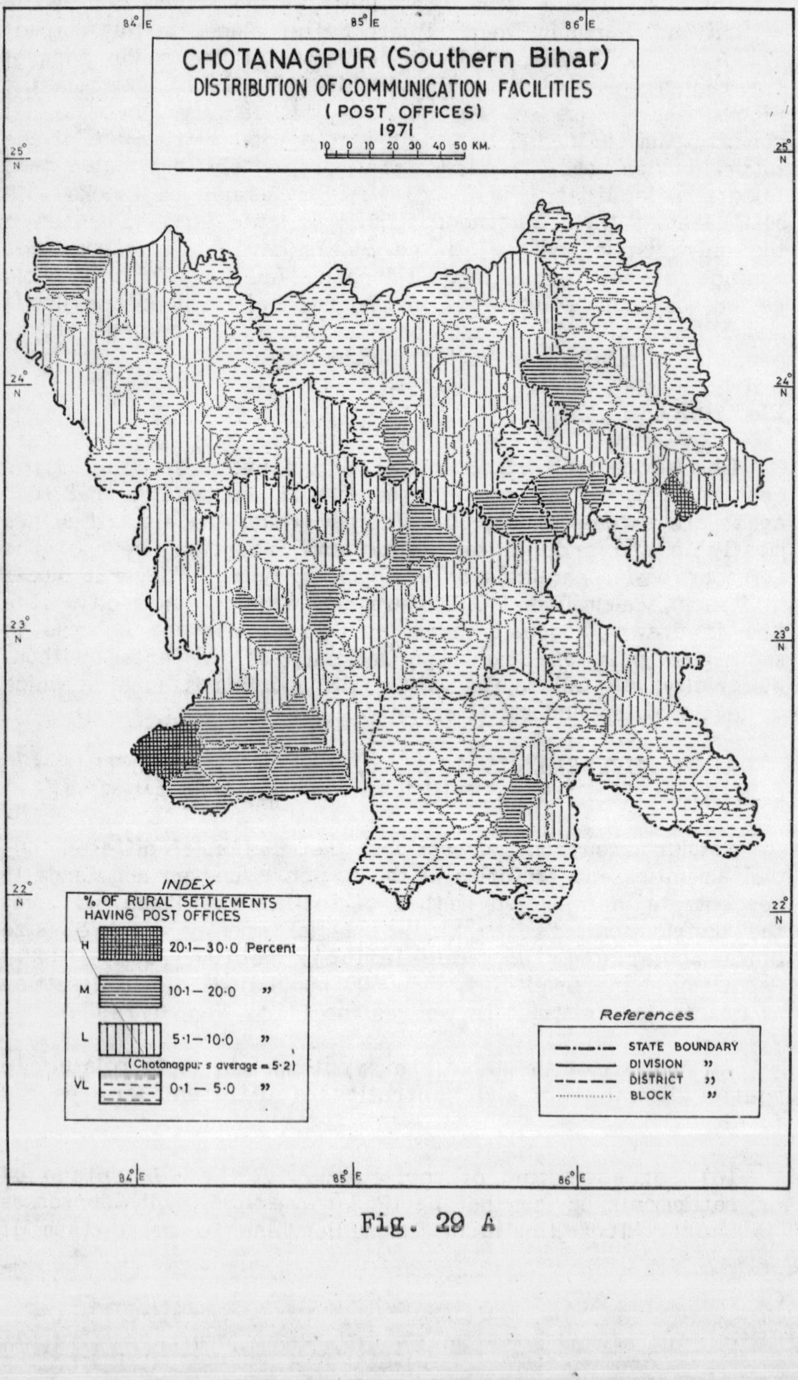
CHOTANAGPUR (Southern Bihar)
DISTRIBUTION OF COMMUNICATION FACILITIES
(POST OFFICES)
1971
10 0 10 20 30 40 50 KM.
84° E
85° E
86° E
25° N
24° N
23° N
22° N
INDEX
% OF RURAL SETTLEMENTS HAVING POST OFFICES
H 20·1—30·0 Percent
M 10·1— 20·0 "
L 5·1—10·0 "
(Chotanagpur's average = 5·2)
VL 0·1 — 5·0 "
References
STATE BOUNDARY
DIVISION "
DISTRICT "
BLOCK "

Fig. 29 A

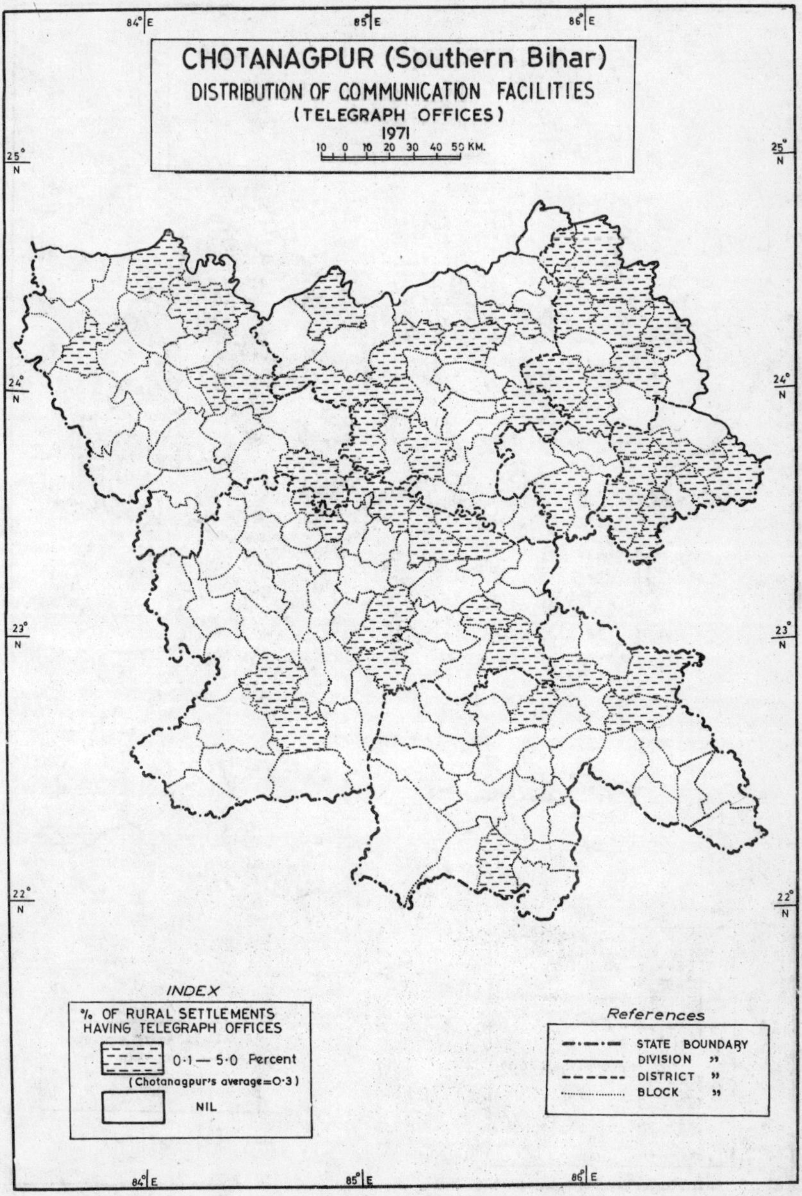
84° E
85° E
86° E
CHOTANAGPUR (Southern Bihar)
DISTRIBUTION OF COMMUNICATION FACILITIES
(TELEGRAPH OFFICES)
1971
10 0 10 20 30 40 50 KM.
25° N
24° N
23° N
22° N
INDEX
% OF RURAL SETTLEMENTS HAVING TELEGRAPH OFFICES
0·1 — 5·0 Percent
(Chotanagpur's average=0·3)
NIL
References
STATE BOUNDARY
DIVISION "
DISTRICT "
BLOCK "

Fig. 29 B

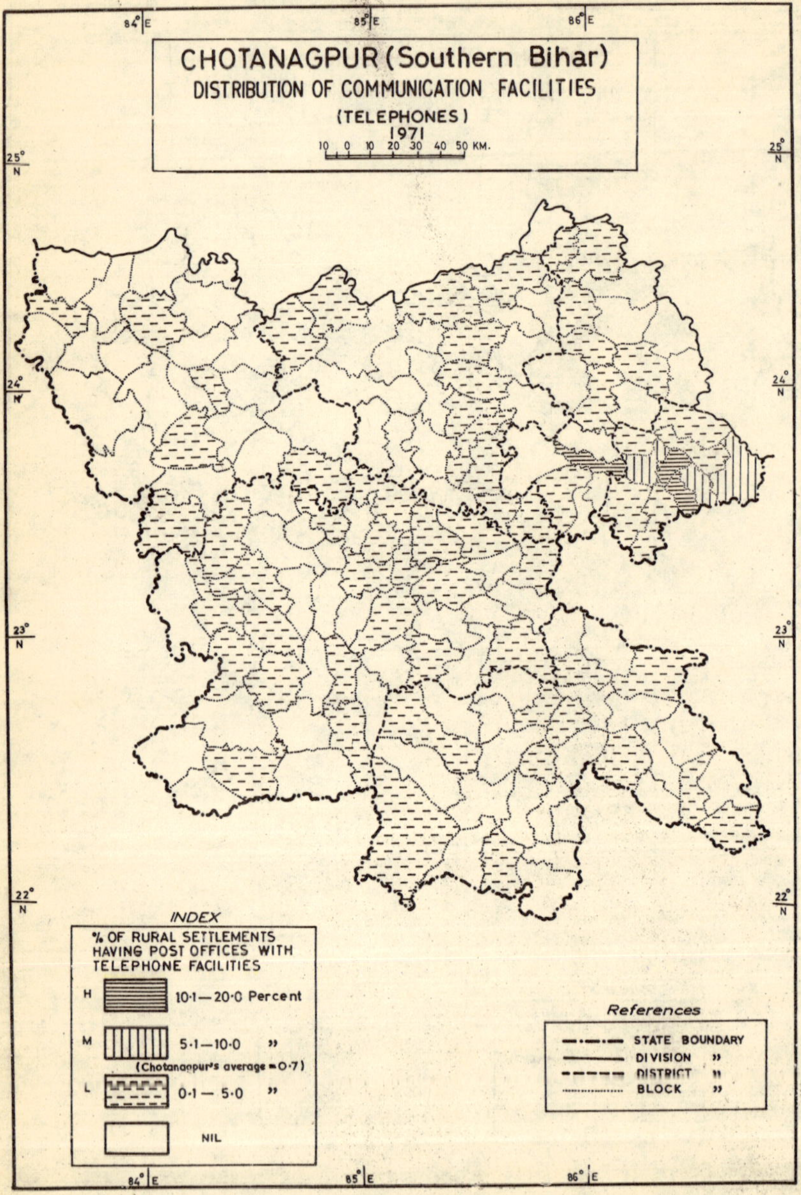
CHOTANAGPUR (Southern Bihar)
DISTRIBUTION OF COMMUNICATION FACILITIES
(TELEPHONES)
1971
10 0 10 20 30 40 50 KM.
84° E
85° E
86° E
25° N
24° N
23° N
22° N
INDEX
% OF RURAL SETTLEMENTS HAVING POST OFFICES WITH TELEPHONE FACILITIES
H 10·1—20·0 Percent
M 5·1—10·0 "
(Chotanagpur's average = 0·7)
L 0·1 — 5·0 "
NIL
References
STATE BOUNDARY
DIVISION "
DISTRICT "
BLOCK "

Fig. 29 C

TABLE 5.8

Chota Nagpur : Distribution of Post Offices, Telegraph Offices, Telephone and Electricity Facilities in the Rural Settlements by Population Size, 1971

DISTRICT/ REGION	Population size	Total Rural Settlements	Number of Settlements Having: Post Office	Telegraph Office	Telephone	Electricity
1	2	3	4	5	6	7
PALAMAU	1 - 199	1082	7 (0.6)	-	-	58 (5.4)
	200 - 499	1161	22 (1.9)	-	-	85 (7.3)
	500 - 999	677	58 (8.6)	-	1 (0.1)	81 (12.0)
	1000 - 1999	254	70 (27.6)	2 (0.8)	5 (2.0)	48 (18.9)
	2000 - 4999	43	25 (58.1)	4 (9.3)	2 (4.7)	18 (41.9)
	5000 +	1	1 (100.0)	-	-	1 (100.0)
HAZARIBAGH	1 - 199	2524	12 (0.5)	-	2 (0.1)	82 (3.2)
	200 - 499	2044	44 (2.1)	1 (0.05)	2 (0.1)	143 (7.0)
	500 - 999	986	74 (7.5)	5 (0.5)	5 (0.5)	110 (11.2)
	1000 - 1999	436	92 (21.1)	6 (1.4)	9 (2.1)	119 (27.3)
	2000 - 4999	124	62 (50.0)	8 (6.4)	14 (11.3)	74 (60.0)
	5000 +	15	13 (86.7)	-	2 (13.3)	12 (80.0)
RANCHI	1 - 199	657	6 (0.9)	-	-	4 (0.6)
	200 - 499	1573	42 (2.7)	2 (0.1)	-	32 (2.0)
	500 - 999	1058	75 (7.1)	1 (0.1)	5 (0.5)	48 (4.5)
	1000 - 1999	448	103 (23.0)	4 (0.9)	8 (1.8)	49 (10.9)
	2000 - 4999	94	53 (56.4)	3 (3.2)	7 (7.5)	23 (24.5)

Table 5.8 (contd.)

1	2	3	4	5	6	7
	5000 +	6	4 (66.7)	1 (16.7)	2 (33.3)	3 (50.0)
DHANBAD	1 - 199	361	2 (0.6)	1 (0.3)	3 (0.8)	27 (7.5)
	200 - 499	433	19 (4.4)	-	6 (1.4)	62 (14.3)
	500 - 999	343	18 (5.2)	-	17 (5.0)	83 (24.2)
	1000 - 1999	179	22 (12.3)	7 (3.9)	17 (9.5)	62 (34.6)
	2000 - 4999	45	16 (35.6)	4 (8.9)	6 (13.3)	30 (66.7)
	5000 +	4	1 (25.0)	1 (25.0)	3 (75.0)	4 (100.0)
SINGHBHUM	1 - 199	1354	9 (0.7)	-	1 (0.1)	11 (0.8)
	200 - 499	1795	22 (1.2)	-	2 (0.1)	25 (1.4)
	500 - 999	930	57 (6.1)	-	3 (0.3)	22 (2.4)
	1000 - 1999	244	40 (16.4)	2 (0.8)	2 (0.8)	26 (10.7)
	2000 - 4999	26	14 (53.8)	3 (11.5)	5 (19.2)	7 (26.9)
	5000 +	2	-	-	-	1 (50.0)
CHOTA NAGPUR	1 - 199	5978	36 (0.6)	1 (0.02)	6 (0.1)	182 (3.0)
	200 - 499	7006	149 (2.1)	3 (0.04)	10 (0.01)	347 (5.0)
	500 - 999	3996	282 (7.1)	6 (0.2)	31 (0.8)	344 (8.6)
	1000 - 1999	1561	327 (20.9)	21 (1.3)	41 (2.6)	304 (19.5)
	2000 - 4999	332	170 (51.2)	22 (6.6)	34 (10.2)	152 (45.8)
	5000 +	28	19 (67.9)	2 (7.1)	7 (25.0)	21 (75.0)

TABLE 5.9

Chota Nagpur : Distribution of Social Amenities in three Size-Classes of Rural Settlements : 1971

DISTRICT/ REGION	SIZE CLASS	NO. OF SETTLE MENTS	PERCENTAGE OF SETTLEMENTS HAVING										
			Primary School	Middle School	High School	Colleges	Hos-pital/ Dispen sary	Family Welfare Centre	Health Centre	Post Office	Tele-graph Office	Tele-phone	Electri-city
1	2	3	4	5	6	7	8	9	10	11	12	13	14
PALAMAU	Large	44	68.2	61.4	22.7	6.8	22.7	11.4	18.2	59.1	9.1	4.5	43.2
	Medium	931	69.9	15.6	2.1	0.8	3.3	0.9	4.9	13.7	0.2	0.6	13.9
	Small	2243	28.8	2.1	0.1	0.1	0.7	0.04	0.8	1.3	-	-	6.4
HAZARIBAGH	Large	139	74.1	58.3	18.0	2.2	25.2	7.2	10.8	54.0	5.8	11.5	61.9
	Medium.	1422	73.2	10.9	2.6	0.5	4.8	1.3	3.9	11.7	0.8	1.6	16.1
	Small	4568	20.8	1.4	0.4	0.1	1.0	0.1	0.9	1.2	0.02	0.1	4.9
RANCHI	Large	100	88.0	63.0	25.0	3.0	19.0	7.0	15.0	57.0	4.0	9.0	26.0
	Medium	1506	78.1	15.6	3.5	0.4	4.9	1.4	5.1	11.8	0.3	0.9	6.4
	Small	2230	35.2	3.2	0.5	0.1	0.8	0.04	1.0	2.2	0.08	-	1.6
DHANBAD	Large	49	77.6	53.1	22.5	2.0	38.8	14.3	-	34.7	10.2	18.4	69.4
	Medium	522	74.9	1.5	3.6	0.6	11.1	2.5	2.9	7.7	1.3	6.5	27.8
	Small	794	32.5	3.6	0.8	-	2.8	0.1	0.6	2.6	0.1	1.1	11.2
SINGHBHUM	Large	28	64.3	75.0	35.7	7.1	42.9	3.6	14.3	50.0	10.7	17.9	2.9
	Medium	1174	72.1	14.7	3.0	0.3	4.4	0.6	4.0	8.3	0.2	0.4	4.1
	Small	3149	73.3	8.7	2.0	0.3	4.0	0.6	2.6	2.6	-	0.3	3.1
CHOTA NAGPUR	Large	360	76.9	60.3	22.5	3.3	26.4	8.3	11.7	52.5	6.7	11.4	48.1
	Medium	5557	73.9	14.2	2.9	0.4	5.1	1.2	2.8	11.0	0.5	1.3	11.7
	Small	12984	27.0	2.4	0.5	0.1	1.1	0.1	0.9	1.4	0.03	0.1	4.1

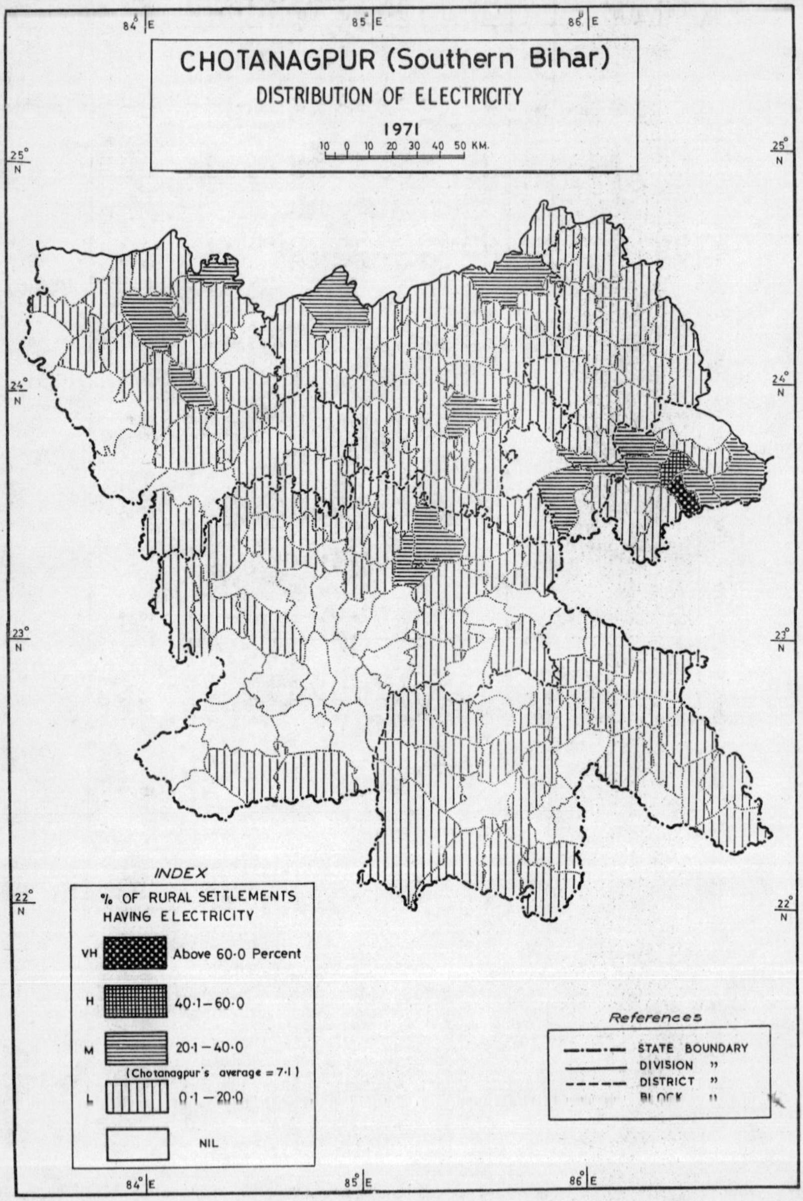
CHOTANAGPUR (Southern Bihar)
DISTRIBUTION OF ELECTRICITY
1971
10 0 10 20 30 40 50 KM.
84° E
85° E
86° E
25° N
24° N
23° N
22° N
INDEX
% OF RURAL SETTLEMENTS HAVING ELECTRICITY
VH Above 60·0 Percent
H 40·1 – 60·0
M 20·1 – 40·0
(Chotanagpur's average = 7·1)
L 0·1 – 20·0
NIL
References
STATE BOUNDARY
DIVISION "
DISTRICT "
BLOCK "

Fig. 30

settlements.

(b) Except for primary schools, every other kind of social amenity is distributed very sparsely within the region.

Provision of these amenities is guided mainly by concentration of population, although there are often anomalous cases which reflect the influence of administrative and political considerations. Higher percentage of large settlements (over 2000 population) have these facilities. Because of locational advantages and demand factor, some of the settlements have a clustering of different kinds of amenities. It makes these settlements more attractive for further concentration as location of other public utilities and functions are also economically viable at those places. Non-central places of the hinterland being served by these service centres get linked with them. Some of the service centres which are more accessible or have more number of facilities grow as nodes of higher order catering to the needs of different service centres besides their own customers. This is the basis for the emergence of a system of nodal centres in the initial stage of the spatial development process.

As large settlements are economically more viable to develop as service centres and have more chances to grow as model centres in future, an attempt is made to evaluate the existing facilities and amenities of each large rural settlement of the region which would help in identifying service centres. With proper planning these centres can help tremendously in the socio-economic development of the area.

There are 360 large settlements within the region, of which 44 are in Palamau, 139 in Hazaribagh and Giridih, 100 in Ranchi, 49 in Dhanbad and 28 in Singhbhum. Considering the size of Dhanbad district, number of large settlements is comparatively very high. Palamau and Singhbhum districts, on the other hand, have fewer number of large settlements in comparison to their sizes. Fig 31 shows the Blockwise distribution of large settlements. It is apparent from the map that 38 Blocks of the region do not have even single large rural settlement. But for four Blocks in the eastern part of the region, all the Blocks in this category lie to the west of the line drawn diagonally in north-west to south-east direction. Land-use and population distribution maps show that these Blocks are generally forested and hilly which do not permit growth of large settlements. Distributional pattern of large settlements further reveals that the next category is formed by those Blocks where large settlements form less than 5 per cent share of the total settlements. Eightyfive Blocks come under this category which are most widely

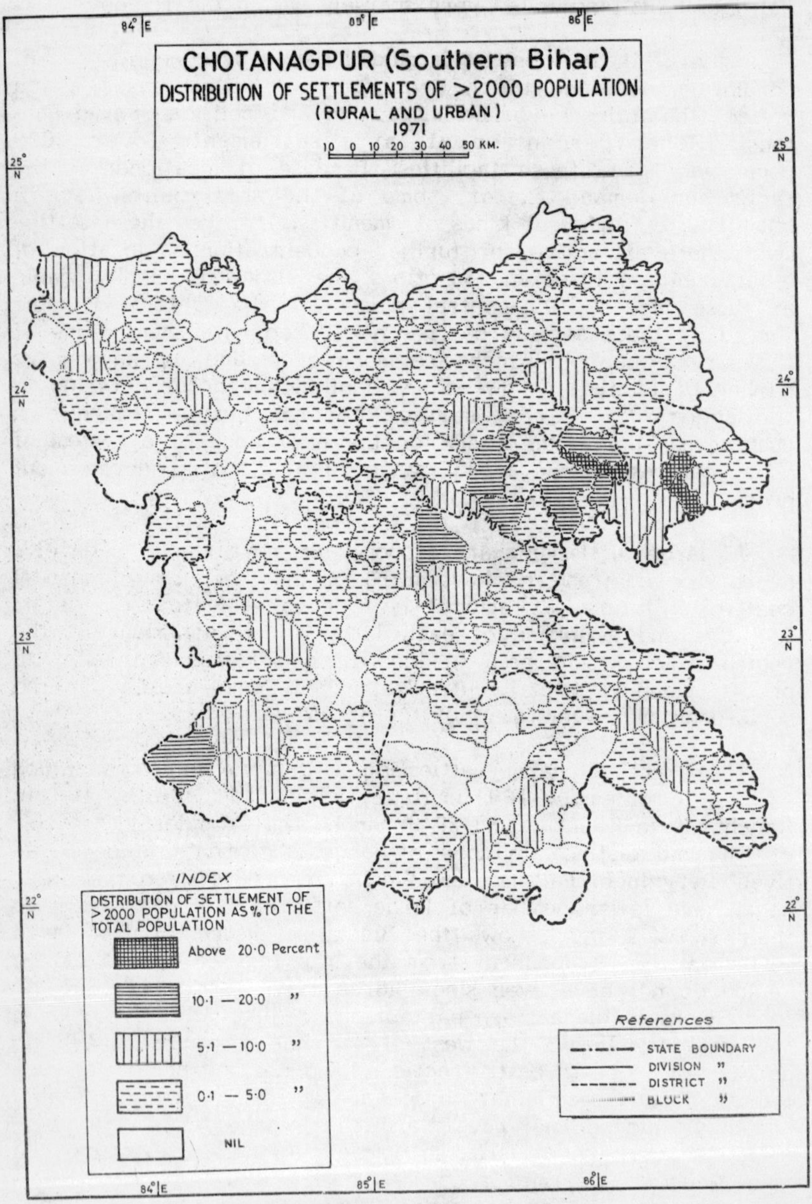
CHOTANAGPUR (Southern Bihar)
DISTRIBUTION OF SETTLEMENTS OF >2000 POPULATION
(RURAL AND URBAN)
1971
10 0 10 20 30 40 50 KM.
84° E
85° E
86° E
25° N
24° N
23° N
22° N
INDEX
DISTRIBUTION OF SETTLEMENT OF >2000 POPULATION AS % TO THE TOTAL POPULATION
Above 20·0 Percent
10·1 — 20·0 "
5·1 — 10·0 "
0·1 — 5·0 "
NIL
References
STATE BOUNDARY
DIVISION "
DISTRICT "
BLOCK "

Fig. 31

distributed in the region. In the next higher category, there are 19 Blocks where 5-10 per cent of settlements are large sized, i.e concentration is of medium scale. Distribution of these Blocks is restricted to five areas only. These may be identified as the following:

(a) An elogated area from north-western to central part of Palamau comprising of three Blocks - Bhawnathpur, Meral and Daltonganj which lie is close proximity;

(b) a semi-circular belt running through Namkum and Ratu (Ranchi); Patratu and Hazaribagh (Hazaribagh); Bagodar (Giridih); Baghmara, Chas, Chandankiyari and Baliapur (Dhanbad):

(c) Gumla, Simdega and Thethaitangar to the south-west part of Ranchi district;

(d) Barajamda, and Jhinkpani Blocks in southern Singhbhum; and

(e) Golmuri and Musabani in eastern Singhbhum.

Seven of the Blocks where large size settlements form 10-20 per cent of the total number of settlements are in the next category. None of these Blocks are in Singhbhum, Palamau and Dhanbad districts. Even in Ranchi, Hazaribagh and Giridih, their distribution is restricted to two areas. Kurdeg Block in Ranchi forms an isolated patch within the above mentioned value range, but it is in fact a part of the Gumla-Simdega-Thethaitangar group though of slightly higher value. The other area is almost a contiguous belt comprising Kanke in Ranchi district ; Mandu and Ramgarh in Hazaribagh district; and Peterbar, Nawadih and Jaridih in Giridih district. These Blocks also form part of the semi-circular belt which has been described earlier. Concentration of large settlements is comparatively very high in only three Blocks where they comprise more than 20 per cent share of the total settlements. Variations in the value among three Blocks are great as it is about 23 per cent in Dhanbad, 35 in Bermo and 77 per cent in Jharia. These Blocks are also located in a semi-circular belt.

It is thus clear that five areas as mentioned earlier with reference to the medium concentration of large settlements, emerge out distinctly. Of these, three areas—northwest - central Palamau, southern and eastern Singhbhum have only medium concentration of large settlements; southwest Ranchi has medium to high concentration and the semi-ciruclar belt of

Ranchi, Hazaribagh, Giridih and Dhanbad have medium to very high concentration which is a fast developing mining and manufacturing area of the region. Due to variations in the distribution pattern of large rural settlements, area served by one large rural settlement also varies significantly. Areas with higher concentration of large rural settlements have a small area to be served by one large settlement. But forest and hilly belts have few large rural settlements and, therefore, size of area to be served by a large settlement also increases (Fig. 32).

To assess the growth potential of the large settlements in terms of centrality is difficult because it depends upon several factors. Some of them are measurable but others are not. However, one of the way to evaluate the settlement hierarchy is to examine the total number of functions of a settlement and to classify the settlements into a hierarchical order on the basis of number of functions that a settlement has (Wanmali, 1970; Bhat et. al. 1976). Amenities and facilities which have been considered in the present study of the large settlements in the Chota Nagpur region have been given in Table 5.10.

TABLE 5.10

Chota Nagpur : Facilities and Amenities considered to be Central Functions for Large Rural Settlements (Over 2000 Population)

A. EDUCATIONAL FACILITIES

1. Colleges and Technical Institutions
2. High Schools
3. Middle Schools
4. Primary Schools

B. MEDICAL FACILITIES

1. Hospital/Dispensaries
2. Family Welfare Centres
3. Health Centres

C. POSTAL FACILITIES

1. Post Offices with Telephones
2. Post and Telegraph Offices
3. Post Offices only

D. ELECTRICITY

Besides these, total workers, workers engaged in non-agri-

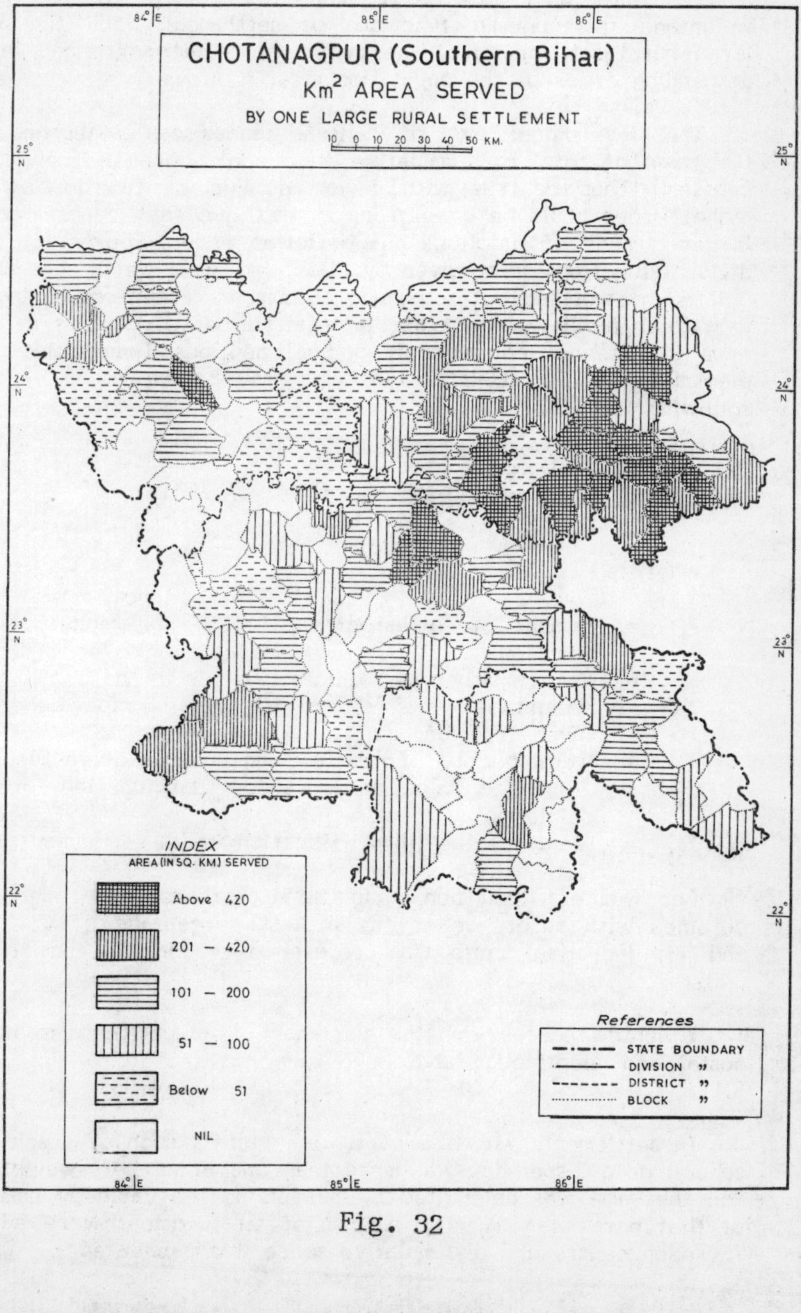
CHOTANAGPUR (Southern Bihar)
Km² AREA SERVED
BY ONE LARGE RURAL SETTLEMENT
10 0 10 20 30 40 50 KM.
84° E
85° E
86° E
25° N
24° N
23° N
22° N
INDEX
AREA (IN SQ. KM) SERVED
Above 420
201 – 420
101 – 200
51 – 100
Below 51
NIL
References
STATE BOUNDARY
DIVISION "
DISTRICT "
BLOCK "

Fig. 32

cultural activities and number of large and medium size industrial units have also been included in order to give due weightage to economic functions of settlements. All the 360 large rural settlements of the region have been arranged in a descending order of the population size.

The hierarchical level of 'central' places was established on the basis of total or cumulative functional score of individual centres. Thus centres with fewer number of functions with higher order could be given more significance than centres with larger number of functions but of lower order. Scores for individual functions were given by allocating them weightages calculated by working out the ratio of number of centres having a particular facility to that of the total number of centres in the area in cases of educational, medical and postal amenities and electricity (Bhat, et. al. 1976) This may be expressed by the following formula:

$$W_i = \frac{N}{F_i} \qquad C_j = \sum_{i=1}^{k} W_i \quad X_{ij}$$

Where:

F_i = number of settlements having the function or sub-function;
N = Total Number of total settlements in the area;
W_i = Weightage or score of ith sub-function under a given function;
k = Total number of sub-function under a given function
C_j = Composite value or score for that function for jth settlement
X_{ij} = Value of the ith sub-function in jth settlement.

For workers, and non-agricultural workers, the ratio was obtained with reference to the highest percentage of workers and for industrial units with reference to highest number of units.

Weighted scores for the variables - educational, medical, postal and electricity have been given in the following Table 5.11.

In settlements where a particular facility such as a primary school, or a dispensary was more than one in number, weightage for the same was calculated by multiplying the value by number of that particular amenity. Scores of all functions were added for each centre and a cumulative score was calculated.

TABLE 5.11

Chota Nagpur : Weighted Scores for Different Amenities (1971)

(Total number of settlements in the Chota Nagpur = 18901)

SERVICE AND FACILITIES		NO. OF SETTLEMENTS HAVING FACILITIES	WEIGHTAGE
A. Educational			
i.	Primary School	7883	2.39
ii.	Middle School	1319	14.32
iii.	High School	306	61.76
iv.	College	50	378.02
B. Medical			
i.	Health Centre*	400	47.25
ii.	Family Welfare Centre	113	167.26
iii.	Hospital/Dispensary	527	35.86
C. Postal			
i.	Post Office	983	19.22
ii.	Post Office with Telephone	129	146.51
iii.	Post Office with Telegraph Facilities	55	343.65
D. Power			
i.	Electricity	1350	14.00

* Health Centre as an input is only a recent phenomenon under planned development. They are relatively few, because the norms laid down in planning do not qualify some Blocks to have even one health centre.

Based on the cumulative scores, all large rural settlements were rearranged in a descending order of values. Scatter and natural breaks in their frequency distribution were identified. Table 5.12 shows the frequency grouping of these settlements.

The spatial distribution of large rural settlements in the region is shown in Fig. 31. The following are the salient features of the spatial distribution and levels of functions of the settlements. (Fig 33).

(a) Distribution of large rural settlements in the region is

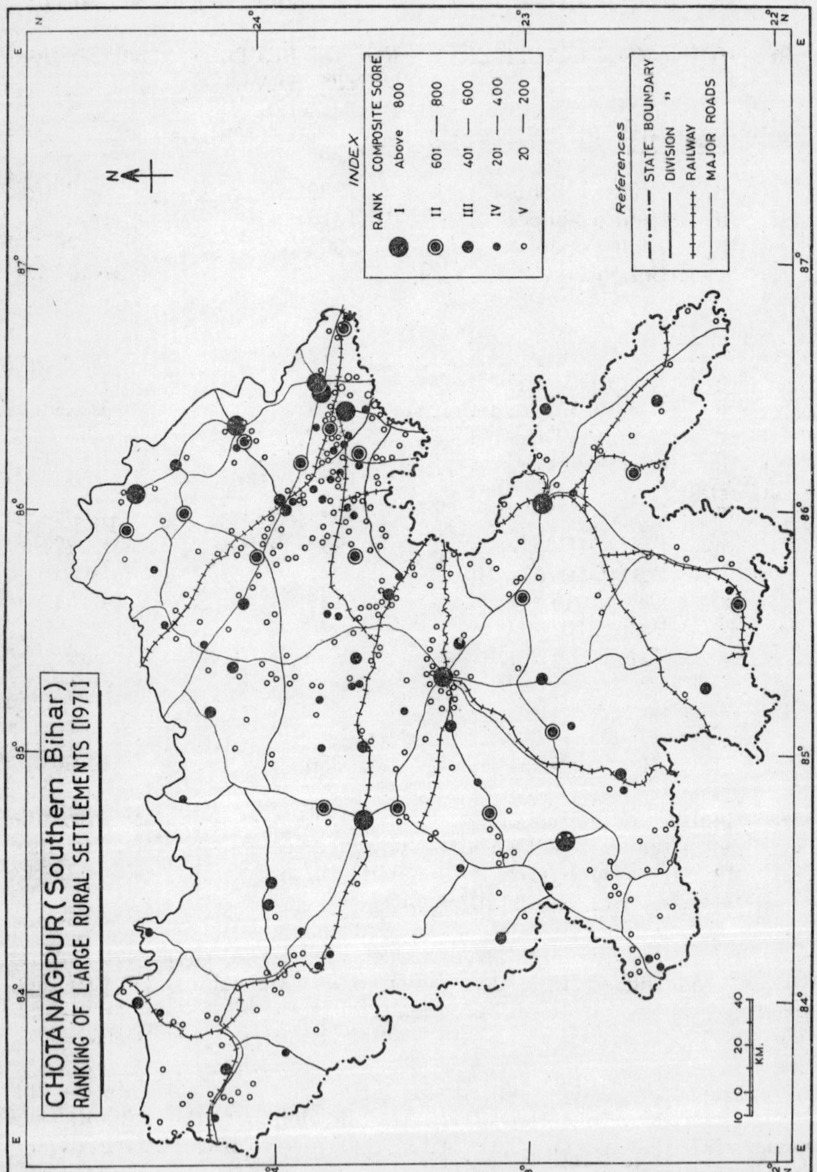
CHOTANAGPUR (Southern Bihar)
RANKING OF LARGE RURAL SETTLEMENTS [1971]
INDEX
RANK COMPOSITE SCORE
I Above 800
II 601 — 800
III 401 — 600
IV 201 — 400
V 20 — 200
References
STATE BOUNDARY
DIVISION "
RAILWAY
MAJOR ROADS
10 0 20 40
KM.
84°
85°
86°
87°
24°
23°
22°
N
E

Fig. 33

TABLE 5.12

Chota Nagpur : Frequency Grouping of Large Settlements According to Functional Scores of Amenities and Other Development Indices

RANK/ORDER	FUNCTIONAL SCORE RANGE	NO. OF SETTLEMENTS		
1	Over 800	9		(Maximum Functional Score is 1288.93)
2	601 - 800	16		
3	401 - 600	20		
4	201 - 400	48		
5	101 - 200	100		(Minimum
6	1 - 100	167	267	Functional Score is 23.99)

very uneven. They show affinity to major transport lines like roads and railways and also a tendency to cluster around major road and rail junctions. Concentration of these settlements is very high in the mining-manufacturing belt of the Damodar basin.

(b) Large number of these settlements (167) have extremely low and almost similar number (148) has very low to low functional scores. Thus out of 360 large rural settlements, 315 are lower order settlements.

(c) Of the remaining 45 settlements, 20 have medium, 16 have high and 9 have very high functional scores. Distribution of these settlements is quite sparse and these occur mostly along transport routes. Settlements with very high functional scores are on the road junctions because of the advantage of its situation in the regional setting.

(d) Districtwise distribution of higher order settlements reveals that of the 9 settlements with very high functional scores, three are in Dhanbad, two in Giridih, two in Ranchi, one each in Palamau and Singhbhum, while Hazaribagh does not have a single settlement with very high score.

(e) Settlements with high functional scores are comparatively more widely distributed and more innumber than previous group having very high scores.

(f) Each successive group of lower order centres has

generally larger number of settlements. This has some implications for evolving a development stratogy using nodality as the basis of functional organisation of formal spaces.

PATTERNS OF FUNCTIONAL ORGANISATION

While nodality is a manifestation of the process of development it is necessary to understand the attributes of the surrounding areas which contribute to and sustain the process of emergence of nodes. To this end economic, demographic and social attributes to development process through their proxy variables* were given weighted scores at the Block level as was done earlier in the case of large rural settlements. All the scores for individual Blocks were added and thus composite scores were obtained for them. These scores were arranged in descending order of values (Appendix I) and break off points were used in grouping the Blocks into different levels of development. (Table 5.13)

TABLE 5.13

Chota Nagpur : Frequency Grouping of Blocks According to Composite Scores of Development

ORDER		COMPOSITE SCORE-RANGE	NO. OF BLOCKS
VH	1	Over 700	2
H	2	401 - 700	14
M	3	301 - 400	42
L	4	201 - 300	72
VL	5	150 - 200	22

It is clear from the above table that a large area (over 62 per cent) of the Blocks in the region have low to very low scores and they are in the districtis of Palamau (21 out of 25 Blocks i.e 88 percent), Hazaribagh (18 out of 24 Blocks i.e. 75 per

----

* Workers as percentage to total population and non agricultural workers as percentage to total workers of the Blocks and industrial units of the Block as percentage to total industrial units of the region were taken in the economic attributes. Percentage of literates to the total population of the Block and the urban population of the Block as percentage to total urban population of the region were taken in the demographic attributes. Number of villages having primary schools, middle schools, high schools and other institutions; health centres, family welfare centres and hospitals/dispensaries; post offices, post offices with telegraph and telephone facilities; and electricty as percentages to total number of all these individual facilities in the region were taken as social attributes.

cent), Singhbhum (25 out of 32 Blocks i.e 78 per cent), Ranchi (17 out of 42 Blocks i.e. 39 per cent) and Giridih (12 out of 18 Blocks, i.e 67 per cent). Dhanbad district is an exception having higher scores. About 28 per cent of the area has medium values on this scale. These are concentrated in Ranchi district. In Palamau, there are four Blocks with higher scores in the midst of areas of low scores. Six Blocks in Singhbhum, 4 Blocks in Giridih and Hazaribagh and 3 in Dhanbad have medium values on the composite score of development and are located mainly in the mining areas. Only 16 Blocks emerge as highly developed (2 with very high scores). Of these 6 Blocks (Nirsa, Baliapur, Baghmara, Chas, Bermo and Peterbar) are located almost contiguously, in the lower Damodar basin. Hazaribagh, Golmuri and Kolebira form 3 isolated patches, of which the first two are located in the middle of the Blocks of low values and the third one is amidst Blocks with medium scores. Patratu - Kanke - Nankum and Kurdeg - Bolba form two separate groups in this category. Except Kurdeg, Bolba and Kolebira, all other Blocks in this category are parts of the mining-manufacturing belts of the region (Fig 34).

If this pattern of development for the Blocks is compared with the distribution of large settlements (rural settlements with 2000 + population and urban settlements) and the pattern of their functional organisation, some clues to the understanding of space relations are obtained. On the lines of the method followed for working out the composite score for large rural settlements and development Blocks, composite scores for urban settlements were also worked out. But social attributes consisting of educational, medical, communication and electricity facilities which were considered to be very important in earlier two cases were left out for the present analysis because all these amenities are present in the urban centres and are, therefore, ubiquitous. Hence, question of testing their centrality does not arise.* These urban centres were organised in a descending order of values and natural breaks were used for grouping them on the basis of differences obtained in the level of values (Appendix II). Five groups were thus identified. For each group, distribution of urban centres by size-class was also marked (Table 5.14).

An analysis of the Table 5.14 reveals that majority of urban centres (approximately 91 per cent) fall in the medium (60 per cent of urban centres) to low and very low (30.6 per cent of urban centres) score ranges. Only 8 urban centres (9.4 per

---

* There are however a number of mining centres - which are small towns and yet they do not act as nodal centres.

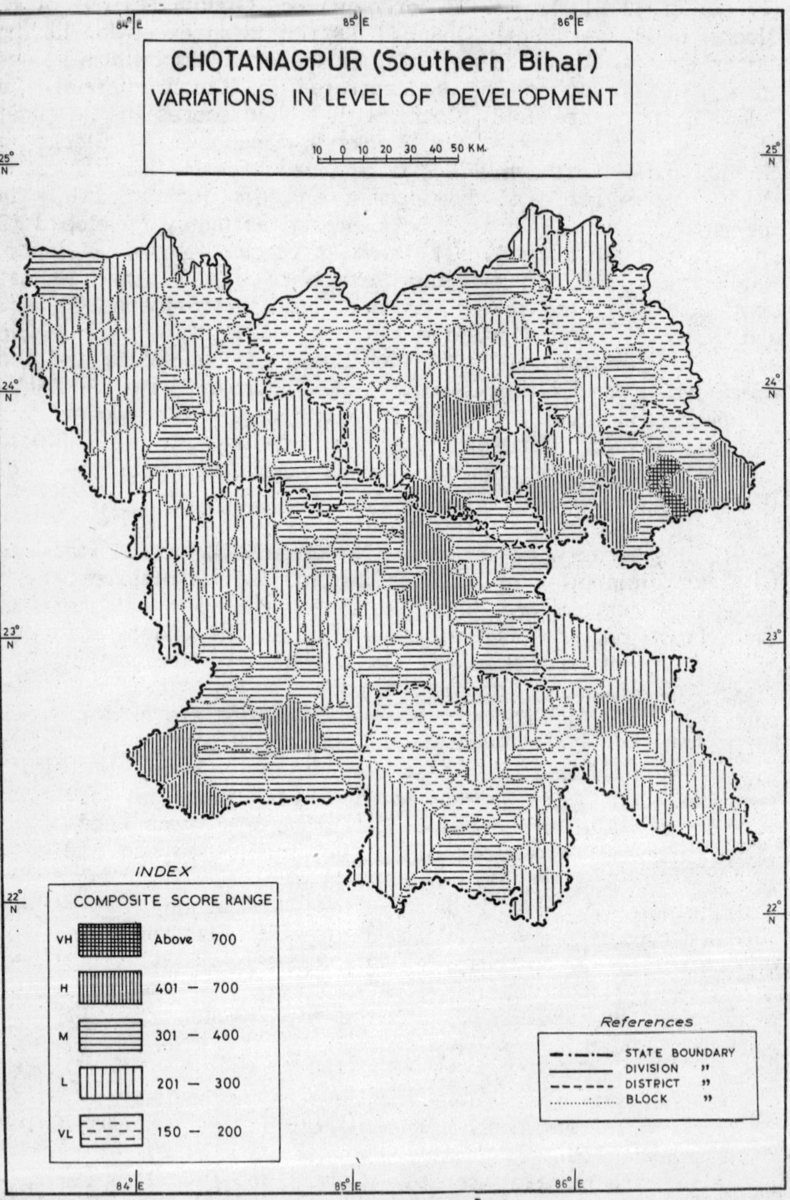

CHOTANAGPUR (Southern Bihar)
VARIATIONS IN LEVEL OF DEVELOPMENT
10 0 10 20 30 40 50 KM.
84° E
85° E
86° E
25° N
24° N
23° N
22° N
INDEX
COMPOSITE SCORE RANGE
VH Above 700
H 401 — 700
M 301 — 400
L 201 — 300
VL 150 — 200
References
STATE BOUNDARY
DIVISION "
DISTRICT "
BLOCK "

Fig. 34

TABLE 5.14

Chota Nagpur : Frequency Distribution of Urban Centres According to Composite Scores

Rank	Order	Composite Score-Range	Number of Urban Centres by Population Size I Over 100,000	II 50,000-99,999	III 20,000-49,999	IV 10,000-19,999	V 5000-9999	VI Less 5000	Total Urban Centres
VH	1	301 - 350	1		1				2
H	2	251 - 300	1	3			2		6
M	3	201 - 250		2	16	17	10	6	51
L	4	151 - 200			1	8	12	1	22
VL	5	130 - 150				3		1	4
Total for Chota Nagpur									85

cent) have a high to very high composite scores. Thus the overall development pattern of urban centres of the region is highly imbalanced. A comparison of the population size of the urban centres with their compsite scores reveal some interesting features of their distribution (Fig. 35).

(a) Of the eight highly developed urban centres, five are cities (2 of class I and 3 of class II categories) and three are towns of class III and V categories. Large urban centres (Jamshedpur and Ranchi in class I type; and Dhanbad, B.S. City and Jagannathnagar in class II type) obviously have higher scores. But Giridih, a class III town and Namkum and Chandrapura - class V towns emerge as of equal or similar importance to large centres because of some highly specialised functions which give them high weightage in development score. For example, Namkum has a number of industrial units and a high percentage of workers which give it a high composite score but the population-size is small due to its limited functions. Similarly, Chandrapura, is high on the development scale because of its highly specialised service function. Giridih which again has a very high value in the composite score due to its very specialised industrial base (mica splitting is the most dominant household industry), has a limited scope of development restricting its population growth also.

(b) In the medium level of development category, there are 51 urban centres. Of these, 2 are in class II, 16 in class III, 17 in class IV, 10 in class V and 6 in class VI categories. Thus 33 urban centres (65 percent) of this group belong to 'quasi-urban' town-group in the size-class of less than 20,000 population. Only 18 urban centres (35 percent) are in the 'effective' town-group, but even in that group, majority (16) of urban centres are in the 20,000-49,999 population size. Many towns in this category are mining and manufacturing centres, without any other important function, and thus have limited growth potential. It can, therefore, be summarised that a large number of urban centres are not only small in size but are also functionally weak nodal centres having little impact on the surrounding region. This observation is further corroborated by low scores of development Blocks in which they are situated.

(c) In the third group of low to very low composite scores, there are 28 urban centres. Almost all these centres (except Gumia which is a town of class III type) are in the 'quasi-urban' town-group of less than 20,000 population size. Majority of these towns are service centres for the agri-

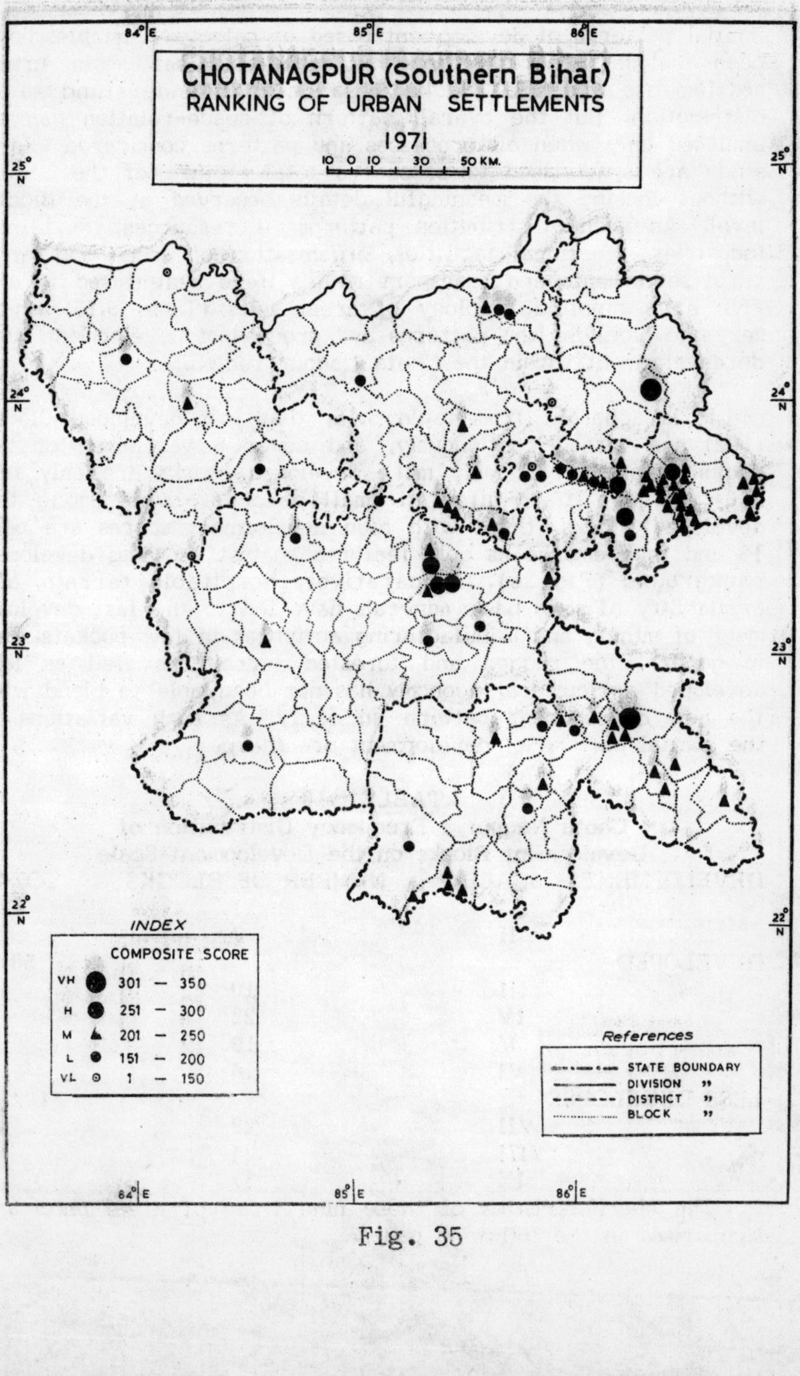
84° E
85° E
86° E
CHOTANAGPUR (Southern Bihar)
RANKING OF URBAN SETTLEMENTS
1971
10 0 10 30 50 KM.
25° N
24° N
23° N
22° N
INDEX
COMPOSITE SCORE
VH 301 — 350
H 251 — 300
M 201 — 250
L 151 — 200
VL 1 — 150
References
STATE BOUNDARY
DIVISION "
DISTRICT "
BLOCK "

Fig. 35

cultural hinterland and their mono-functional character has restricted their growth potentials.

Spatial patterns of development based on selected variables have been analysed separately for the large rural settlemets, urban settlements and the Blocks as a part to understand their distribution. But the overall pattern of space-relation can be analysed only when all processes and patterns considered in the study are synthesised to present a total picture of the region without loosing the meaningful details observed at the Block-level. As such, distribution patterns of resources, land use, industries, functional facilities, organisation of urban and large rural settlements and transport routes were synthesised to arrive at a ninefold typology of areal units (Table 5.15) which serve to highlight the patterns and process of development/ underdevelopment within the Chota Nagpur region.

It is apparent from table 5.15, that less developed Blocks (102) are spread contiguously, and cover a vast area of the region whereas relatively more developed Blocks are only few (50) and are distributed in small patches. Even among the developed Blocks, those with high development scores are only 18 and they emerge as bold features against the less developed background (Fig 36). Comparatively hospitable terrain, and availability of some basic minerals have led to the fast development of mining and manufacturing activities in few pockets. But in general the rugged and forested terrain as well as less developed agricultural economy has not been able to blend with the new development pattern uniformly. As such variations in the spatial pattern of development are sharp.

TABLE 5.15
Chota Nagpur : Frequency Distribution of Development Blocks on the Development Scale

DEVELOPMENT - SCALE		NUMBER OF BLOCKS	TOTAL
	I	11	
	II	7	
DEVELOPED			50
	III	10	
	IV	22	
	V	19	
	VI	14	
LESS DEVELOPED			102
	VII	28	
	VIII	24	
	IX	17	

The characteristics of these nine types of areal units are summarised in the following pages.

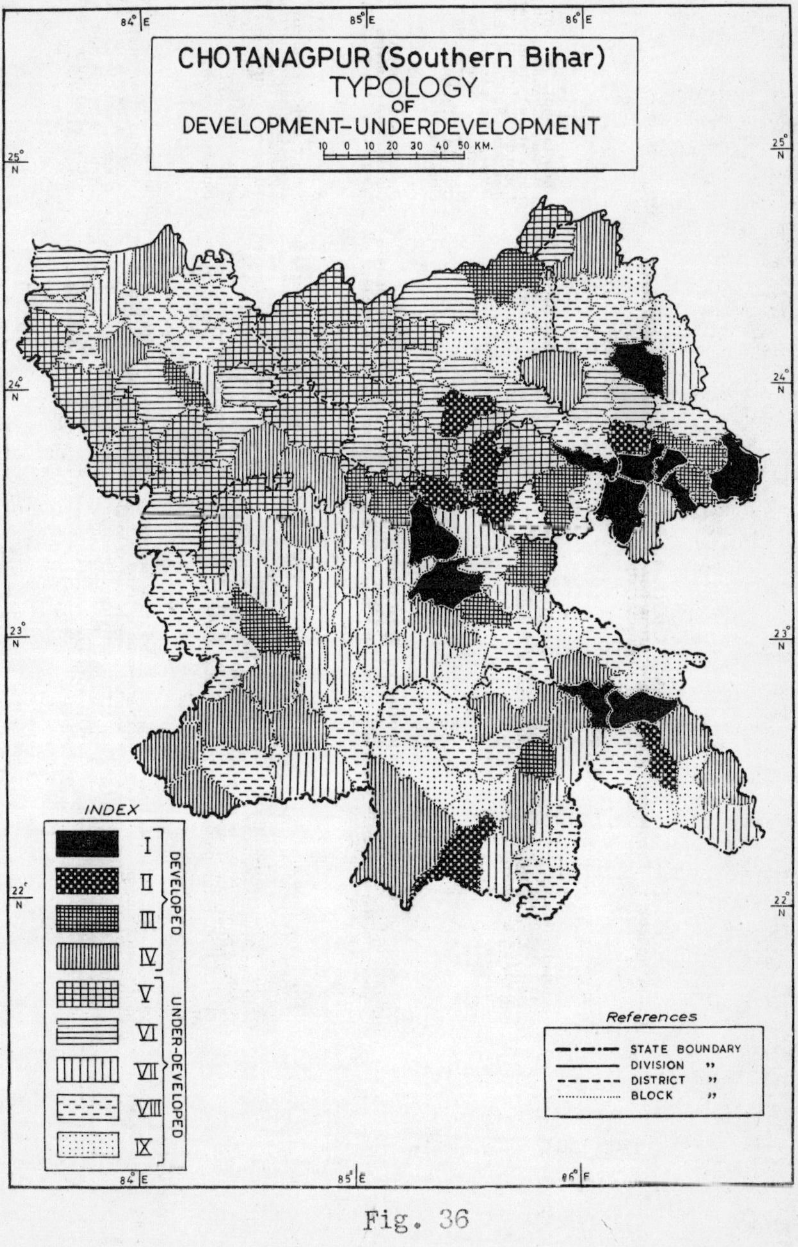
CHOTANAGPUR (Southern Bihar)
TYPOLOGY
OF
DEVELOPMENT-UNDERDEVELOPMENT
10 0 10 20 30 40 50 KM.
84° E
85° E
86° E
25° N
24° N
23° N
22° N
INDEX
I
II
III
IV
V
VI
VII
VIII
IX
DEVELOPED
UNDER-DEVELOPED
References
STATE BOUNDARY
DIVISION ,,
DISTRICT ,,
BLOCK ,,

Fig. 36

TABLE 5.16 (Part one)

Chota Nagpur : Typologies of Developed Areas-based on Physical, Economic and Social Characteristics

TYPOLOGY 1	TYPE I 2	TYPE II 3	TYPE III 4	TYPE IV 5
Name of the Blocks	Dhanbad, Jharia, Nirsa, Chas, Baghmara, Bermo, Giridih, Kanke, Namkum, Adityapur & Golmuri.	Hazaribagh, Patratu Ramgarh, Mandu, Topchanchi, Noamundi & Musabani	Daltonganj, Kodarma, Burmu, Gumla, Bundu, Silli, Chaibasa, Peterbar, Gobindpur(D) and Baliapur.	Hussainabad, Garhwa Latehar, Chandwa, Tisri, Bagodar, Chandankiyari, Lohardaga, Khunti, Palkot, Simdega, Kolebira, Kurdeg, Bolba, Manoharpur, Jhinkpani, Chakradharpur, Kharsawan, Seraikela, Chandil, Ghatsila & Chakulia
Physical Characteristics	Located on different heights but mostly on plain surfaces in the eastern part of the Chota Nagpur region.	Located on Hazaribagh and outer Chota Nagpur plateau with undulating plain surface.	Located on Ranchi and outer Chota Nagpur plateau with mostly plain areas.	Distributed mostly on the Chota Nagpur plateau and margins of Ranchi plateau.
Resource Base	Coal, mica, copper and iron-ore are the most important mineral resources of the region. Agriculture and forest are comparatively less important though they together share more than 40% of geographical area.	Minerals and agriculture are both important resources. Coal, copper and iron-ore are the important minerals. Agriculture and forest together share more than 50% of the geographical area.	Mica and coal are important minerals in some of the Blocks. These Blocks are predominantly dependant on agriculture. Forest is the second main user of land. Net area sown and forest together share 55-80% of geographical area in most of the Blocks.	Forest and agriculture share the major portion (40-80%) of the geographical area in different proportions. Though important minerals are found, only a few are being exploited at present.
Industries	Mining & manufacturing are important economic activities. Most of the large & medium size industrial units (263 out of 288 units) are located within this region.	Mining is the most important economic activity. Manufacturing is the second important activity. Twenty-four large & medium industrial units are located within this region.	52 large & medium industrial units are located in this region. Majority of them are coal & mica based (35 units). Rest of them are forest based, cement, aluminium & engineering industries.	19 industrial units of large & medium size, mostly based on forest and a few on mica, metallic and non-metallic minerals and agriculture, are located within this region.

Population Characteristics	Density of population is high to extremely high, i.e., more than 600 persons per sq. km. in 6 Blocks and between 300 and 440 in the remaining Blocks. Sch. Caste and sch. tribe population is low to very low. Literacy is high to very high i.e. usually more than 30%. Nearly half to two-thirds of workers are engaged in nonagricultural activities.	Density is usually high in the Blocks in the north because of comparatively better terrain. Sch. Caste & Sch. Tribe population is low to very high in the northern Blocks whereas moderate to high in the southern part. Literacy is usually moderate i.e. 21-30% Industrial & service employment together share nearly 50% of the working population.	Density varies from very low to high but in most of the Blocks it is between 200 and 440 persons per sq. km. Sch. caste and sch. tribe population in majority of the blocks is less than 50%. Literacy rate is usually less than 20% in majority of the Blocks. More than 50% workers are engaged in agricultural activities.	Density varies from very low to medium. In majority of the Blocks the density is between 101 and 299 persons per sq. km. Sch. caste and sch. tribe population is high to very high in majority of the blocks. Literacy is generally low in a large no. of Blocks i.e. less than 20%. Agricultural employment is more than 80% in 14 Blocks whereas in the rest it is between 60 and 80%. Proportion of industrial & service employment varies but they are not more than 18 & 22% respectively in any Block.
Settlements	Proportion of large rural settlements is high to very high, i.e. 4 - 76 %. Proportion of urban population is very high (more than 40%). More than 50% towns of the Chota Nagpur region are located within this typology i.e. 42 towns.	Proportion of large rural settlements is usually high i.e. 5-14%. Percentage of urban population is usually between 20 and 50%. 14 towns are located within this group of Blocks.	Proportion of large rural settlements is low to high i.e. in majority of the Blocks it is less than 5% of total rural settlements. While in the rest it is between 5 and 20 percent. Percentage of urban population varies from 9 to 41. There are 9 towns located within this typology.	Small rural settlements constitute more than 95% of total rural settlements. Only 3 Blocks have little higher % of large rural settlements i.e. 7-18%. Urban population varies between 9 and 20%. Only 4 blocks have 21-70% of urban population. There are 15 urban settlements within this typology.
Infrastructure	Rail & road connections are extremely good. Important road & rail junctions are located within the Blocks of this type.	Transport connections are reasonably good as these Blocks are served by railway & road both.	Transport links are available to all Blocks, though their degree varies much among the Blocks as some are served either by roads or railways while some are served by both.	About 50% of the Blocks have good accessibility as they are served by both road and railway but in the rest, transport links are inadequate.

Social Amenities	Percentage of rural settlements having different kinds of social amenities is quite high.	Distribution of different social amenities of all grades in the Blocks is reasonably good	The quantity & quality of the social amenities provided to the rural settlements are comparatively lesser than the previous 2 groups.	Distribution of social facilities is highly uneven. Some of the Blocks of Ranchi, despite low literacy rate and non-agr. workers, have high number of social facilities. But the rest of the Blocks have comparatively few facilities and in lesser number.
Composite scores for large rural, urban settlements and Blocks	Large rural & urban settlements located within the Blocks of this typology as well as the Blocks reveal comparatively higher level of development based on composite scores than other parts of the region.		Majority of large rural settlements of these Blocks are at a very low level of development whereas most of the urban settlements have medium values. Blocks of this unit in general reveal medium level of development.	Majority of the large rural settlements in the Blocks of this group have composite scores of less than 400. They are at a very low to low levels of development. Even majority of urban settlements have low composite scores. But much variations are observed at Block level as they reveal very low to high levels of development.
Remarks	Being located in the mining and manufacturing belt of the region, supplemented with good transport links with other parts, these Blocks show signs of fast development.	Blocks of this typology are located in the mining belt adjoining highly developed Blocks. This is an example of the development of an area along the major axis of transport lines.	Located along the transport axis, most of the Blocks of this typology are on the peripheries of already developed Blocks. Few of them like Daltonganj, Chaibasa, Gumla & Kodarma appear as bold features against the background of vast less developed areas of tremendous resource potentiality.	Blocks of this region have potentiality of development as they contain valuable mineral and forest resources. But at present the resources have not been properly developed. As such wide variations may be observed in the process of industrialisation, urbanisation, and nodalisation.

TABLE 5.16 (Part two)

Chota Nagpur : Typologies of Underdeveloped Areas-based on Physical, Economic and Social Characteristics

TYPOLOGY 1	TYPE V 6	TYPE VI 7	TYPE VII 8	TYPE VIII 9	TYPE IX 10
Name of the Blocks	Dhurki, Ranka, Bhandaria, Barwadih, Garu, Manatu, Balumath, Bishunpur, Kisko, Pratappur, Hunterganj, Simaria, Chatra, Itkhori, Keredari, Barkagaon, Churchu, Gumia & Satgawan	Bhawnathpur, Untari, Chainpur(P), Mahuadanr, Manika, Panki, Chauparan, Tandwa, Katkamsandi, Ichak, Bishungarh, Dumri(G), Pirtanr & Gawan	Lesliegranj, Manjhiaon, Gola, Gande, Tantnagar, Gobindpur(s), Bahragora, Jagannathpur, Jaldega, Ghaghra, Senha, Sisai, Verno, Basia, Kamdara, Rania, Torpa, Murhu, Lapung, Karra, Bhandra, Bero, Ratu, Kuru, Chanho, Mandar, Ormanjhi and Sonahatu	Meral, Bishrampur, Hariharganj, Chhatarpur, Patan, Kasmar, Dhanwar, Birni, Jamua, Nawadih, Tundi, Dumri(R), Chainpur(R), Raidih, Thethaitangar, Bano, Angara, Tamar I, Nimdih, Sonua, Khuntpani, Majhgaon, Manjhari, Potka	Deori, Bengabad, Markacho, Jainagar, Barhi, Barkatha, Jaridih, Ichagarh, Erki, Kuchai, Bangaon, Goilkera, Tonto, Kumardungi, Patamda, Dumaria and Dhalbhumgarh
Physical Characteristics	Located mostly on the hilly and rugged terrains in Hazaribagh, Ranchi and outer Chota Nagpur Plateau.	Located adjoining the Blocks of Type V in the same region with little better terrain.	Located mostly on the Ranchi Plateau with undulating plains.	Blocks of this unit are scattered in small patches on margins of the different plateau surfaces in northern, eastern, southern and western parts of the Chota Nagpur.	These Blocks are located on the eastern and southern parts the outer Chota Nagpur plateau with relatively high percentage of barren land.
Resource Base	Coal, mica, limestone and bauxite are some of the known mineral resources of this area, though the region has not yet been properly surveyed. This area is known for its valuable forest resource. More than 50% of the geographical area of the Blocks are covered with forest. Less than 25% of area is under cultivation.	Forest is the main resource. 40-49% of the geographical area is under forest cover. Some of the important known mineral resources are coal, mica, tin, and bauxite. But inhospitable terrain in most parts has restricted the development of mining activity to the comparatively better terrain in the eastern part.	Few mineral resources like bauxite in Ranchi and iron-ore and manganese in Singhbhum are found in the region. It is predominantly an area of agricultural resources as 40-65% of geographical area is under cultivation. Forest land is usually less i.e. less than 20%.	Forest & agriculture have nearly equal share in the landuse as they cover 20-40% and 30-39% of geographical area respectively. Mica in Giridih, bauxite in Ranchi & some iron-ore and manganese in Singhbhum are important minerals of this region.	Mica, iron & tin are some of the important minerals. Due to extensive mining in some areas or rugged terrain, most of the area is neither suitable for cultivation nor is under forest cover. As a result, percentage of land area under barren and non-agriculture uses are quite high and it varies from 15-30%.

Industries	Only 6 medium industrial units are located in this region. Of these 5 are located in Gumia, (2 coal based, 1 forest and 1 non-metallic mineral based) and 1 forest based unit is in Ranka.	Except for 5 mica processing units of medium size in Dumri there is no other important industrial activity in the region.	There are only 3 medium industrial units in the region.	Only 5 mica processing units are located within this typology.	There are only 3 industrial units of medium size in the region.
Population Characteristics	Density of population is quite low as it varies between 40 and 150 persons per sq. km. Sch. caste and sch. tribe population varies from low to very high. Western and southern parts of this region have high to very high concentration whereas central and eastern parts have low concentration. Literacy is low i.e. between 7 and 17%. Ag. employment shares 65-97% of working population. Only 4 Blocks have slightly higher percent of industrial employment i.e. 10-29%.	Density is little more than the region mentioned in Type V and varies from 64 to little over 200 persons per sq. km. Sch. caste and sch. tribe population is highly variable. The western and southern blocks of this group have comparatively higher percentage of S.C/S.T. population than central and northern parts of the region. Literacy is low and is less than 15%. Ag. employment is very high as it is more than 80% in all Blocks. Industrial employment is usually less i.e. less than 5% in 13 Blocks.	Density varies from 101-300 persons per sq. km. Sch. Caste & Sch. Tribe population is usually high and they constitute approximately 50-90% population of the Blocks. Literacy varies from 11 to little over 20%. Occupational pattern reveals the predominance of agricultural workers which shares more than 90% of working population.	Density of population is very low i.e. less than 100 in the Blocks with comparatively more rugged terrain in Ranchi. In other parts it varies from 101-250 persons per sq. km. Sch. caste and sch. tribe population is usually low in the Block of Dhanbad, Giridih and Hazaribagh. Literacy is generally less than 20% in majority of the Blocks. Ag. employment varies from 81-98%. Industry and service are of little importance as they do not share more than 10 & 9% respectively.	Density is usually low to moderate i.e. between 101 and 250 persons per sq. km. Sch. caste and sch. tribe population is low in Hazaribagh and Giridih whereas it is quite high in the Blocks of Ranchi and Singhbhum. Literacy is quite low i.e. less than 20%. Occupational pattern reveals the predominance of agricultural workers which shares more than 85% of working population.
Settlements	Large rural settlements are usually less than 4% of the total rural settlements and in 8 Blocks they are completely absent. Most of the Blocks are rural in character. There are 4 urban centres in the typology, one of which is in Chatra & 3 are in Gumia. Percentage of urban population varies between 23 and 43 in Chatra and Gumia, respectively.	Proportion of large rural settlements is quite low and it does not exceed 6.5% any where. There is only one small town in Mahuadanr. Urban population is just 7 percent of the total population of the Block.	Large rural settlements are completely absent in 12 Blocks. In the rest, they share 0.5-7% of the total settlements. All Blocks are completely rural.	9 Blocks with comparatively rugged and barren terrain do not have any large rural settlement. In rest of the Blocks depending upon the nature of terrain and type of economic activity, percentage of rural settlements varies from 0.7-15. All these Blocks are completely rural.	There is no large rural settlement in 6 Blocks located in Ranchi and Singhbhum. In rest of the Blocks, its percentage varies from 0.38 to 12. There is no urban settlement in this region.

Infrastructure	Most of the Blocks have poor accessibility as 5 Blocks have no transport connections and a majority of them are served only partially.	Most of the Blocks are accessible either by road or railway or both.	Accessibility is reasonably good in the Blocks of Ranchi plateau and a few more Blocks located on the main trunk routes in Palamau, Hazaribagh & Singhbhum. But some of the blocks in northern & southern extremes of the Chota Nagpur plateau, away from the main trunk routes are completely inaccessible.	All blocks are accessible by road, railways or both except two Blocks in Singhbhum. But the degree of accessibility is highly variable.	4 Blocks in Singhbhum are totally inaccessible as they are not connected with rail or road. Rest of the Blocks are accessible in varying degrees either by road or railway or both.
Social Amenities	Distribution of social amenities is highly uneven. Many of the Blocks are devoid of any high grade amenity like high schools, family welfare centres, hospitals and the like. Even primary schools are comparatively few and the highest percentage is only 66.	Social amenities are distributed unevenly and the highest percentage of rural settlements having primary schools is only 60%. Other higher grade facilities are even less.	Distribution of social amenities reveals that a large number of Blocks do not have many facilities like high schools, colleges, family welfare centres, hospitals, telephones, telegraph offices, and electricity.	Distribution of social amenities reveals the absence of a number of amenities in many Blocks. Only primary, middle and high schools and post offices are available in all Blocks.	Many social amenities are totally absent in quite a large number of Blocks. Only primary schools, middle schools and post offices are available to all Blocks though their percentages vary widely.
Composite scores for large rural, urban settlements and Blocks	Large rural settlements of this typology usually reveal low to very low scores. Urban settlements are in the lower range of composite scores. Blocks of this typology reveal low level of development.		Except for 4 large rural settlements located on the Ranchi plateau having medium to high composite scores, all others have low values. But Blocks have high scores in general, which clearly indicates that most of the amenities are rather uniformly distributed among settlements irrespective of their sizes.	7 Blocks have atleast one large rural settlement with medium to high composite scores, though most of the Blocks show signs of low development.	

SIX

Summary and Conclusions

The foregoing study has focussed attention on the regional structure, process and patterns of development in Chota Nagpur (Bihar). The region displays persistently all the characteristics of underdevelopment despite its rich natural resource base, particularly forest and minerals. As such the main objective of the study was to examine the region at the micro-level so that potentialities and problems could be identified at the lowest possible level (Block-level in this case) with the hope that typologies thus identified in this process might be useful in formulating a spatial development strategy for micro-level planning. Themes of investigation, therefore, have ranged through many facets of regional development of Chota Nagpur which are inter-related.

The study introduced the concept of regional development and its various theories, review of regional development studies in India in general and Chota Nagpur in particular, salient features of Chota Nagpur and the design of the research work undertaken. Review of studies on Chota Nagpur region brings out the paucity of indepth study of the region as a whole in a spatial context which alone can reveal the process and patterns contributing to low levels of development. In most studies carried out from an all-India and state angles, the obvious conclusion has been that Chota Nagpur region with all the investment in basic and heavy industries is still very low in the levels of development and that the "islands" of economic development created around these new centres of economic growth have not brought about any significant spread effect on the surrounding region. On the contrary, very often the felt expressions of the local inhabitants have shown concern for cultural and environmental degradation. This process of underdevelopment, as the findings of the present study would show, has its roots in both intra-regional and inter-regional processes of development that are at work in this part of the country.

An analysis of the resource base - natural and human

suggests that the region has marked variations in the nature of topography which ranges from the high, much dissected 'pat' region of north-western Ranchi and Southern Palamau to the low and plain areas of the Damodar and Subarnrekha basins in the east and south-east respectively. A greater part of the rugged and hilly terrain is covered with forests. As such agricultural land is very limited. Being a part of the old Gondwana land, the region possesses a number of important mineral resources, but only those found in the more accessible parts are being exploited. Water resources in most of the western part of the region has not yet been properly assessed, development of which could have provided irrigation and power facilities for agricultural and industrial development.

Because of unfavourable terrain in a large part of the region, population is distributed sparsely and settlements are mostly small and dispersed. The region, therefore, has a low density of population. Proportion of scheduled caste and scheduled tribe population is usually very high. Though economic participation rate is comparable to the state average, it is quite low. All these characteristics are clear indicators of the region's underdevelopment. Thus, inspite of the region's rich resource base, many resources like water, forest and to some extent mineral have not yet been properly tapped in wide areas due to unfavourable rugged terrain. Comprehensive development strategy for the region should be based on the resource inventory prepared in spatial terms highlighting areas and nature of resources to be developed.

Problems of underdevelopment are further accentuated on account of proportionately very high dependence of the people of the region on agriculture as the source of livelihood whereas the percentage of culturable land (39 per cent) is very low. Not only that, very small percentage of this land is cultivated more than once for want of irrigation facilities and scientific know-how for better farming. As such, inspite of agriculture being the predominant economic activity, the agricultural production is quite low. This is a case of subsistence economy wherein the region whose longterm development norm is rooted to forestry, minerals and allied activities has a larger proportion of people engaged in primary activity. Besides agriculture, people in the forested belt in their spare time engage themselves in the collection of forest products like lac, kendu leaves and katha or cutting trees.

The study also analysed the processes and patterns of industrialisation and urbanisation. It revealed a close association of these processes only in few areas. In most of the areas, there have been industrial and urban growth without industrialisation i.e. gradual shift of workers from agriculture to manufacturing activities or urbanisation i.e. proportional increase of urban population in the composition of total population and emergence of areas or locations of industries throughout the region as a process of vertical and horizontal integration of the space economy. In fact, even industrial development has been closely associated with the development of some basic and heavy industries of national importance which were established in the region because of the raw material availability. But serious efforts have not yet been made to develop the human skills and also infrastructure facilities in terms of power, marketing facility and transport lines which is reflected in the absence of light consumer oriented industries in the region. Areas which have developed faster with basic and heavy industry base mostly had skilled labour from outside. Unless skill is provided to local people and basic infrastructural facilities are developed for the establishment of medium and small scale industries based on local resources which might fill in the gap between the two extremes of econmy - highly developed modern economy with sophisticated iron and steel technology on one hand and undeveloped tribal economy marked with gathering of forest products and subsistence agriculture on the other, a balanced development of the region cannot take place.

With regard to the distribution pattern of nine major industry groups, metal based and engineering are comparatively more important, though they vary significantly in their distribution pattern. Whereas metal based industries are scattered, engineering industries are concentrated mostly in and around important urban centres. In the chemical and non- metallic mineral based industry groups, coke-oven plants and mica processing units share higher percentage of the total units in respective groups. Thus the emerging pattern reveals dominance of raw-material oriented industries over market-oriented industries, agglomeration of diversified industrial units in large urban centres due to advantages of agglomeration economy and nodality and concentration of simple processing and manufacturing units of the same kind in small settlements located in particular mineral belts because of their dependence on the minerals of those areas.

Like industrial growth, urban growth has been rapid though concentrated more in the eastern part of the region. As a result, the region as a whole is more urbanised (19 per cent urban population) than Bihar (10 per cent urban population). But the real urbanisation in terms of significant change in the rural-urban ratio has been witnessed only in few areas, especially where industrial concentration has been high and non-agricultural activities have transformed the rural character to urban character. Three such distinct areas (Dhanbad-Jharia, Kanke-Namkum and Adityapur-Golmuri) emerge in the eastern part of the region with distinguishing features like large number of industrial units, high urban population, large number of urban centres, high literacy rate, high economic participation rate and higher percentage of non-agricultural workers. Rest of the region, particularly western part has only a few urban settlements, mostly 'rural in character' which have emerged primarily as service centres. Here again the process of urbanisation being the cause of the location of major industires does not bring about integrated development as is implied in the principle of functional organisation and emergence of a system of nodal centres which are by and large urban centres or at least large sized nodal villages.

An analysis of the settlement structure, nodality and patterns of their spatial organisation clearly reflects the influence of different factors such as topography, accessibility and economic activity. Large parts of the region do not have a single large settlement with more than 2000 population. Thus Chota Nagpur region has very high percentage (98) of rural settlements of less than 2000 population. This factor coupled with rugged terrain is disadvantageous for the emergence of nodal centres in the natural process of functional-spatial organisation and reinforces the dichotomy between rural-agricultural and urban-industrial structures of the economy.

On this assumption, an attempt has been made in this study to assess the nature of existing as well as potential nodal centres by giving weightages to all the large rural (360) and urban settlements (85) for demographic, economic and social attributes of development; adding all scores to work out the composite index of development and finally grouping them in five classes ranging from very high to very low levels. It appeared from the analysis that large number of settlements (both rural and urban) are of low to very low levels of development distributed in the northern, western and southern parts of the region. Higher order settlements, on the other hand, are only few and most of them are located in eastern part of the region. A similar analysis of the attributes of 152 Development Blocks revealed that Blocks with higher order settlements show high levels of development and vice-versa.

Thus it can be summarised that inaccessible, rugged and forested areas are not only devoid of signs of development but have inherent limitations by having scattered population in small rural settlements which do not attract any of the facilities and amenities though some of them could emerge as the nodal centres. In such a situation the dichotomy between developed and underdeveloped areas becomes sharper than before.

TYPOLOGY OF DEVELOPMENT/UNDER DEVELOPMENT

Against this background of the regional structure and spatial patterns and variations an attempt is made to synthesise the emerging patterns and processes of development/underdevelopment which serve to highlight the weaknesses of the development process within the region that are partly responsible for the overall level of underdevelopment of the Chota Nagpur region. The nine-fold classification of 152 Development Blocks (Table 5.16) is attempted with the following principles underlying the process of development/underdevelopment.

1. If the Development Block as an areal unit has a higher composite score of development and has within it large urban-industrial centres and villages with higher values of composite score it stands out as the highly developed area.

2. If the composite score of the Block is high mainly due to the existence of the urban-industrial centres, it is evident that the latter is 'footloose' in so far as its integration even with areas close to it. The social and economic distance between the centres of growth and the surrounding areas in such cases in maintained at different scales of areas within the region. This is true of the urban-industrial centres within the Blocks like Musabani, Noamundi, Hazaribagh, Patratu, Ramgarh, Mandu and Topchanchi.

3. If the composite score of Development Blocks is medium because these areal units have interaction only with the small towns (of medium score) or large villages (with low to very low composite score) it is presumed that such areas are weak in the process of organisation of the economy around these centres. Situation is again considered another important factor which can either strengthen or render the process of spatial organisation stagnant under the shadow of the large urban-industrial centres to which these settlements and areas are connected by inter- regional transport routes.

4. If the Development Blocks have low to very low score the rural and urban settlements too are of low level in composite score. These areas are considered to be just in the initial stage of organisation of the space economy i.e lower than the category of Blocks mentioned in 3 above.

5. If there are Development Blocks with low to very low score and they are largely devoid of any large rural settlement or even a small town these are considered to be least developed or virtually 'untouched' in the sense of organisation of economy.

The accompanying map (Fig 36) and Tabular analysis of the attributes of development/underdevelopment bring out the following patterns in the spatial arrangement and grouping of development Blocks by High and Low levels of development of varied degrees.

1. Areas of relatively high level of development (I to IV as given in Table 5.16) are few and scattered. These are characterised by less rugged terrain, higher percentage of cultivated land and/or concentration of forest and mineral based industries. In terms of demographic and socio-cultural attributes the population density is relatively high, scheduled caste and scheduled tribe population is low and literacy is high. Thus out of 152 Development Blocks only 50 Blocks belong to this category within which only 11 Blocks stand out as 'islands' of development surrounded by the remaining ones and these are mostly along the transport axis linking the major foci of development. These are located mostly in the east-central and southern half of the region. Further distinction is possible in the case of 'Development Blocks' wherein mining has brought with it the necessary infrastructure and associated activities, e.g. Dhanbad, Jharia, and Giridih.

2. In contrast are the less developed Blocks (102 out of 152 Blocks; V to IX as given in Table 5.16) which are contiguous particularly in the northern area of forested hills marked by low population density, low percentage of cultivated land, inaccessibility, small rural settlements, high percentage of scheduled castes and scheduled tribe population and low level of literacy. While the explanation for very low level of development in the northern forested area is relatively simple the contiguous area of low level of development in the centre is attributed to the negative impact of the developed pockets in their proximity. In some less developed areas the percentage of tribal population is not as high as one would expect. One would be tempted to conclude that part of tribal population would have moved out to the nearby urban centres. This aspect requires local enquiry and is beyond the scope of the present survey.

How far eduation could have its impact on the region is evident in the south-western part where the Christian Missionaries have raised the literacy level and the region's situation along the routes connecting the urban-industrial centres have brought about trickling down effect of the benefits of socio-economic change.

Besides these typologies of development/underdevelopment within the region, the emerging space relations with the rest of India serve to reinforce the hypothesis that the region whose economy is organised around nodes external to them tends to remain underdeveloped. As is evident from the spatial patterns of location, linkages and typologies of development, the urban-industrial activity in Chota Nagpur is linked with Calcutta and the industrial belt of West Bengal. Moreover, the state of Bihar itself has inherited a pattern of development in which the three latitudinal belts - the terai, the central alluvial plain and the Chota Nagpur region have very little economic interactions. These aspects of the development strategy are complementary to the intra-regional development strategy for the Chota Nagpur region. However, the Chota Nagpur region is a 'relatively developed region' of the South-eastern Resource Region which comprises of Chota Nagpur region, eastern Madhya Pradesh, western part of Orissa and West Bengal. It would be a challenging exercise in spatial analysis contributing to development planning in which the backward linkages of the basic and heavy industries rooted to minerals and forests of this region have to be provided the forward linkages to the activities of this region and the rest of India as a policy in the formation of economic regions.

It is hoped that the study through a systematic analysis of the secondary data from smaller areal units like the Development Block and rural and urban settlements as locational components has enriched the knowledge regarding the region; and an understanding of the spatial patterns and processes that are at work serve even partially to explain the process contributing to low levels of development. It should also be added that a multi- disciplinary approach may perhaps throw more light on the dynamics of development of this region.

References

Ahmed, E, (1965), **Bihar: A Physical, Economic and Regional Geography,** Ranchi University, Ranchi.

Alagh, Y.K. (1972), **Regional Aspects of Indian Industrialisation,** University of Bombay Publications, Economics Series No.21, University of Bombay.

Allen, K. and T. Hermansen, (1968), **Regional Policy in EFTA: An Examination of the Growth Centre Idea,** EFTA, Secretariat, Geneva

Barkin, D. (1972), "Regional Socio-Economic Development", **International Social Development Review,** No. 4.

Berry, B.J.L. and W.L. Garrison, (1958a): Recent Developments of Central Place Theory, **Papers and Proceedings of the Regional Science Association,** 4, pp. 107-20.

Berry, B.J.L. and W.L.Garrison (1958b), The Functional Bases of the Central Place Hierarchy, **Economic Geography,** 34, pp. 145-54.

Berry, B.J.L.and T.D. Hankins (1963), A **Bibliographic Guide to the Economic Regions of the United States,** Department of Geography, Research Paper No.87, University of Chicago, Chicago

Berry, B.J.L. (1966), **Essays on Commodity Flows and the Spatial Structure of the Indian Economy,** Department of Geography, Research Paper No.111, University of Chicago, Chicago.

Berry, B.J.L. (1967), **Geography of Market Centres and Retail Distribution,** Prentice Hall, Inc. Englewood Cliffs, New Jersey.

Bhat, L.S. and A.T.A. Learmonth (1958), Recent Contributions to the Economic Geography of India: Some Current Preoccupation, **Economic Geography,** July, 44, (3), pp 189-209.

Bhat, L.S. (1962), **Some Aspects of Regional Planning in India,** Indian Statistical Institute, New Delhi, Ph.D.Thesis.

Bhat, L.S. and R.B. Mathur, (1967), Cement Industy - A Case study in National and Regional Perspectives, **Bombay Geographical Magazine,** November

Bhat, L.S. et. al. (1976), **Micro-Level Planning: A case Study of Karnal Area, Haryana, India,** K.B. Publications, New Delhi.

Boudeville, J.R. (1966), **Problems of Regional Economic Planning,** University Press, Edinburgh.

Bose, A. (1970), **Urbanization in India: An Inventory of Source Materials** Academic Books Ltd. New Delhi.

Bose, A. (1978), **India's Urbanization 1901-2001**, 2nd edition, Tata McGraw Hill, New Delhi.

Britton, J.N.H. (1967), **Regional Analysis and Economic Geography**, G. Bell & Sons Ltd., London.

Brown, A.J., et. al. (1968), Regional Problems and Regional Policy, **Economic Review**, 46, November, pp. 42-51.

Brush, J.E. and H.E. Bracey (1955), Rural Services Centres in South Western Wisconsin and Southern England, **Geographical Review**, 45, pp. 550-69.

Carruther, W.I. (1962), Service Centres in Greater London, **Town Planning Review**, 33, pp. 5-31.

Carter, H (1965), **The Towns of Wales: A Study in Urban Geography**, Cardiff.

Chakraborty, S.K. (1972), **Geology and Coal Reservas of North Karanpura Coalfield**, Vol.1.

Chandrashekhar, C.S. and K.V. Sundaram, (1969), "The Role of Growth Foci in Regional Development Strategy" in **Proceedings of Symosium on Regional Planning**, 21st International Geogrphical Congress, New Delhi.

Chatterjee, S.P. (1940), Place of Geography in National Planning, **Presidential Address**, Geography and Geology Section, Indian Science Congress.

Christaller, W. (1933), **Die Zantralen Orte in Suddeutschland**: Translated by Barkin, C.W. **Central Places in Southern Germany**, Englewood Cliffs, New Jersey, 1966.

Clark, C. (1951), **Conditions of Economic Progress**, London.

Dacey, M.F. (1966), Industrial Location and Economic Potential, **Lloyds Bank Review** October, No.82, pp. 1-17.

Deshpande, C.D. (1948), Administrative Geography and Planning Regions, Chapter XIV in **Western India - A Regional Geography**, Students' Own Book Depot, Dharwar.

Deshpande, C.D. et. al. (1979), **South Kolaba - A Study in Settlement Hierarchy and Rural - Urban Interaction**, Report of a research project sponsored by ICSSR, New Delhi, Department of Geography, Bombay University, Bombay.

Dickinson, R.E. (1934), The Metropolitan Cities of the United States, **Geographical Review**, 24.

Dunn, J.A. (1942), The Economic Geology and Mineral Resources of Bihar Province, **Memoirs of Geological Survey of India**. Vol. 78, pp. 6-14.

Durand, J.D. and C.A. Pelaez (1965), Components of Population change in Latin America, Proceedings of the 60th Anniversary Conference of the Milbank Memorial Fund, New York, April 5-7, edited Clyde, V. Kiser, **Milbank Memorial Fund Quarterly**, 43, No. 4 - Part 2 (Oct 1965)pp. 166 - 96.

Florence, P.S. (1953), **The Logic of British and American**

Industry, London.
Friedmann, J.R. (1966), **Regional Development Policy: A Case Study of Venezuela,** MIT Press, Cambridge.
Friedmann, J.R. (1969). **A General Theory of Polarized Development,** School of Architecture and Urban Planning, U.C.L.A., Los Angles.
Gidadhubli, R.G. (1966), **Planning of the Development and Location of Iron and Steel Industry in India,** Moscow.
Gidadhubli, R.G. (1967), Application of Linear Programming Techniques in Rational Regional Location of Steel Industry in India - Methodological Approach, **First Seminar of Indian Regional Science Association.** I.I.T. Kharagpur.
Gidadhubli, R.G. (1968 a), Location - cum - Transportation Plan for Iron and Steel Industry in India, **Indian Journal of Regional Science,** I.I.T., Kharagpur 1 (1).
Gidadhubli, R.G. (1968 b), Economic Regions and Industrial Location, **Papers of the 21st International Geographical Congress,** New Delhi.
Glasson, J. (1974), **An Introduction to Regional Planning,** London
Government of India (1954), **The Rivers of Central India,** Vol.3, New Delhi
Greenhut, M.L. (1956), **Plant Location in Theory and Practice,** University of North Carolina Press.
Grover, D. and L. Huszar (1964). **The Application of Central Place Theory in the Regional Planning of a Developing country,** Town and Country Planning School, Exeter.
Hansen, N.M. (1967), Development Pole Theory in Regional Context, **Kyklos.** 20, pp 709-25
Harris, C.D. (1954), The Market as a factor in the localization of industry in the United States, **Annals of Association of American Geographers,** 44.
Hemming, M.F.W. (1963), The Regional Problem, **Economic Review,** 25, August, pp. 40-57.
Hermansen, T. (1972), **Development Poles and Development Centres in National and Regional Development, Elements of a Theoretical Framework** in Kuklinski A. (Ed.), Growth Poles and Growth Centres in Regional Planning, Mouton.
Hirschman, A.O. (1961), **The Strategy of Economic Development** Yale University Press, New Haven
Hoover, E.M. (1948), **The Location of Economic Activity,** McGraw Hill, New York.
Hoselitz, B.F. (1953), The Role of Cities in the Economic Growth of underdeveloped countries, **Journal of the Political Economy,** 61
Hoyle, B.S. (1974), **Spatial Aspects of Development,** John Wiley & Sons Ltd., London.
Hoyt. H. (1939), **The Structure and Growth of Residential Neighbourhoods in American Cities,** Washington.

Irrigation Commission, Government of Bihar (1975), **Report on Water Resources of Bihar,** Patna.

Isard, W. and R.E. Kuenne (1953), "The Impact of Steel upon the Greater New York - Philadelphia industrial region: A study in agglomeration projection", **Review of Economics and Statistics.** 35, pp. 289-301.

Isard, W. (1956), **Location and Space Economy,** John Wiley and Sons, New York.

Isard, W. (1975), **Introduction to Regional Science,** Prentice Hall, Inc., Englewood Cliffs, New Jersey.

Jackson, G. (1970), Regional Policy and Planning in Israel, Oxford Polytechnic, O.P.

Jefferson, M. (1939), The Law of Primate City, **The Geographical Review,** 29, No. 2, pp. 226-32.

Johnson, E.A.J. (1970), **The Organisation of Space in Developing Countries** Harward University Press, Cambridge.

Johnson, E.A.J. (1972), "The Integration of Agrarian, Commercial, and Industrial Activities in Functional Economic Areas" in **Market Towns and Spatial Development,** National Council of Applied Economic Research, New Delhi.

Joint Committee for Diagnostic Survey of the Damodar Valley Region, (1968), **Damodar Valley Survey Reports and the Planning Atlas of the Damodar Valley Region,** Calcutta.

Kuklinski, A (1970), Regional Development, Regional Policies and Regional Planning, **Regional Studies,** 4(3).

Lakdawala, D.T., Y.K. Alagh and A.Sarma (1974), **Regional Variations in Industrial Development,** Monograph Series 2, Sardar Patel Institute of Economic and Social Research, Ahmedabad.

Learmonth, A.T.A. and L.S. Bhat (1961), **Mysore State, Vol. I, Atlas of Resources,** Indian Statistical Institute.

Leser, C.E.V. (1951), **Some Aspects of the Industrial Structure of Scotland,** University of Glasgow.

Losch, A. (1940), **Die vaumliche Ordnung der Wirtschaft**: Translated by Woglom, W.H., **The Economics of Location,** Yale, 1954.

Lukermann, F. (1966), Empirical Expressions of Nodality and Hierarchy in a Circulation Manifold, **East Lakes Geographer,** II, pp. 17 44, Reprinted in Brian J.L. Berry and F.E. Horton, Geographic Perspectives on Urban systems, Prentice Hall Inc, New Jersey, 1970.

March, J.G. nd M.A. Simon (1958), **Organisations,** New York.

McCarty, H.H., J.C. Hook and D.S. Knos (1956), **The Measurement of Association in Industrial Geography,** State University of Iowa, Department of Geography, Report I.

Mountjoy, A.B. (1966), **Industrialisation and Underdeveloped Countries,** London.

Ministry of Mines and Fuels, Government of India, (1963 a), **Report of the Committee on Assessment of Resources,** Vol. 1

Jharia Coalfields.

Ministry of Mines and Fuels, Government of India (1963 b), **Report of the Committee on Assessment of Resources,** Vol. 2, Raniganj Coalfields.

Ministry of Mines and Fuels, Government of India (1963 c), **Report of the Committee on Assessment of Resources,** Vol. 3, East Bokaro Coalfields.

Ministry of Mines and Fuels, Government of India (1972 a), **Report of the Committee on Assessment of Resources,** Vol. 4, West Bokaro Coalfields.

Ministry of Mines and Fuels, Government of India (1972 b), **Report of the Committee on Assessment of Resources,** Vol. 5, Ramgarh Coalfields.

Mishra, R.P. (Ed.) (1969), **Regional Planning,** Prasaranga, The University of Mysore.

Mishra, R.P. et. al. (Eds.) (1978), **Regional Planning and National Development,** Vikas, New Delhi.

Mishra, R.P. and K.V. Sundaram (1980), **Multi level Planning and Integrated Rural Development in India,** Heritage Publishers, New Delhi.

Mitra, A. (1965), Levels of Regional Development in India, **Census of India, 1961, Vo. I, pt. I-A (i) and (ii),** New Delhi.

Mitra, S. and D.K. Singh (1971), Indexes of Population Concentration and Temporal Redistribution in the Brahmaputra Valley, **Geographic Review of India,** 33, (1).

Myrdal, G. (1957), **Economic Theory and Underdeveloped Regions,** Duckwarth.

National Council of Applied Economic Research (1962), **Reports of Techno-Economic Survey of States and Selected Regions,** New Delhi.

Pal M.N. (1963), **An Introduction to Regional Planning,** Indian Statistical Institute, Regional Survey Unit, New Delhi.

Pal M.N. and C. Subramanian, (1965), Regional Disparities in the Levels of Development in India, Paper contributed to the **Fifth Indian Economic Conference,** December, Delhi.

Pandeya, P. (1970), **Impact of Industrialisation on Urban Growth** Central Book Depot, Allahabad.

Patankar, P. (1968), **Planning for Micro Regions and the Plan of Infrastrucutre in Wardha,** Mimeo, Wardha

Perloff, H.S. et. al. (1960), **Regions, Resources and Economic Growth,** Resources for the Future, Inc., The John Hopkins Press, Baltimore.

Perroux, F. (1955) La notion de pole de croissance, **Economic Appliquee,** 7, pp. 307-20

Planning Commission, Government of India, (1965), **Resource Development Regions and Divisions of India,** New Delhi.

Planning Commission, Government of India, (1969), **Commodity Transport Studies and Regional Transport,** New Delhi.

Prasad, A. (1969), **Chotanagpur: A Study in Rural Settlements** D. Litt. Thesis, Ranchi University, Ranchi

Pred. A. (1967), Behaviour and Location: Fundation for a Geographic and Dynamic Location Theory, Part I, **Lund Studies in Geography**, Series B, Human Geography, 27

Rao, V.L.S.P. and L.S. Bhat (1960), **Regional Planning in the Mysore State - The Need for Readjustment of District Boundaries**, Indian Statistical Institute, New Delh.

Rao, V.L.S.P. (1964 a), **Regional Aspects of Small and Medium Sized Towns of Telangana**, R.P.C. Project, Planning Commision, Osmania University, Hyderabad.

Rao, V.L.S.P. (1964 b), **The Towns of Mysore State** (A Sample Survey), Indian Statistical Institute and Asia Publishing House, New Delhi

Rao, V.L.S.P. (1969), **Growth - Promoting and Growth - Retarding Factors in Development - Muzaffarnagar District: A Case Study**, R.P.C. Project, Delhi University

Richardson, H.W. (1969), **Regional Economics**, Weidenfeld and Nicolson, London

Rostow, W.W. (1960), **The Stages of Economic Growth**, MIT Press, Cambridge.

Roy, A.K. and S.Sinha (1968), **Ground Water Resources of Bihar with Special Reference to the Problems of Planning and Development of Irrigational Purposes.** Report of the Geological Survey of India.

Roy, P. and B.R. Patil (1977), **Manual for Block Level Planning**, Longmans, New Delhi.

Sengupta, P. and G. Sdasyuk, (1968), Economic Regionalisation of India. Problems and Approaches, **Census of India, 1961. Monograph Series.** 1 (8) New Delhi.

Sharma, N. (1977), **Strategies for Development of Medium Size Towns in Bihar: A Study in Development Technology**, Ph.D. Thesis, Bhagalpur University, Bhagalpur.

Simon, H.A. (1955), On a Class of Skew Distribution Function, **Biometrika** Vl.II, pp. 425-40.

Singh, J. (1964), **Transport Geography of South Bihar**, B.H.U. Press, Varanasi.

Sinha, R.P. (1969), **Industrial Landscapes of the Highlands of Chotanagpur** Ph. D. Thesis, Bhagalpur University, Bhagalpur

Sinha, V.N.P. (1973), **The Chotanagpur Plateau: A Study in Settlement Geography**, Ph. D. Thesis, Patna University, Patna

Slater, P.B. (1977), A Hierarchical Regionalisation of Indian States Based on 1961 Inter-State Migration, **Geographical Review of India**, March 39(1).

Smailes, A.E. (1944). The Urban Hierarchy in England and Wales, **Geography,**, 29, pp. 41-51.

Smailes, A.E. and G. Hartley (1961), Shopping Centres in the Greater London Area, **Institute of British Geographers,**

Transaction and Papers, 29, pp. 201-13

Smith, D.M. (1966) A Theoretical Framework for Geographical Studies of Industrial Location, **Economic Geography**, 42(2).

Smith, R.D.P. (1968), The Changing Urban Hierarchy, **Regional Studies**, 2(1), pp 1-19

Stilwell, F.J.B. (1969), Regional Growth and Structural Adaptation, **Urban Studies** 6, June, pp 162-78.

Sundaram, K.V. (1977), **Urban and Regional Planning in India**, Vikas, New Delhi.

Thompson, W.R. (1957), The coefficient of Location: An Appraisal, **Southern Economic Journal**, 23, January

Thorpe, D. and T.C. Rhodes (1966), The Shopping Centres of the Tyneside Urban Region and Large - Scale Grocery, **Economic Geography**, pp 52-73.

Town and Country Planning Organisation, Government of India, (1968), **Planning Regions of India**, (Mimeo), New Delhi

Town and Country Planning Organisation, Government of India (1970), **Regional Development Plan for South East Resource Region**, New Delhi.

Ullman, E. and C.D. Harris (1945), The Nature of Cities, **Annals of the American Academy of Political and Social Science**, CCXLII, pp 7-17

Wanmali, S. (1970), **Regional Planning for Social Facilities**, National Institute of Community Development, Hyderabad

Weber, A. (1909), **Uber den Standort der Industrien**: Translated by Friedrich, C.J., Alfred Webers Theory of the Location of Industries, Chicago, 1929.

Zipf, G.K. (1941), **National Unity and Disunity**, Principia Press, Bloomington, Indiana

Zipf, G.K. (1949), **Human Behavior and the Principle of Least Effort**, Addison - Wesley, Cambridge, Masachusetts.

APPENDIX - I

Chota Nagpur : Weighted Scores for Demographic, Social and Economic Attributes to Development for Blocks, 1971

Blocks	Educational	Health	Communication	Electricity	Literacy	Urbanisation	Working Population	Non-agricultural Workers	Industrialisation	Composite Scores
1	2	3	4	5	6	7	8	9	10	11
Jharia	347.30	200.00	174.90	100.00	72.63	100.00	78.85	100.00	5.41	1179.09
Dhanbad	75.00	81.20	171.40	45.00	78.78	91.42	78.65	95.17	8.27	724.89
Bermo	63.40	59.40	81.10	35.30	63.01	85.96	66.22	90.21	1.00	565.60
Baghmara	87.20	80.10	122.60	38.30	47.90	15.45	77.86	78.82	0.46	548.69
Golmuri	68.10	36.30	61.20	7.10	100.00	94.84	63.89	93.75	8.66	533.84
Nirsa	88.50	66.70	119.80	28.00	52.49	29.60	72.41	64.35	1.47	523.32
Kanke	104.00	53.30	73.90	27.90	84.23	66.72	60.47	28.38	12.91	511.81
Kurdeg	191.50	56.00	100.00	-	35.47	-	85.46	40.10	-	508.53
Baliapur	140.50	74.30	123.30	26.20	35.51	-	62.29	36.72	0.15	498.97
Bolba	186.30	115.90	57.70	-	32.63	-	66.31	31.12	-	489.96
Kolebira	164.70	66.30	117.90	-	43.02	-	64.00	30.03	-	485.95
Peterbar	113.20	46.50	164.30	21.90	31.50	-	70.85	30.30	-	478.55
Patratu	58.70	128.00	21.00	9.90	49.57	56.69	75.69	68.33	1.93	469.81
Chas	142.70	24.10	44.80	11.90	50.96	52.32	79.33	52.25	1.70	460.06
Hazaribagh	81.10	37.80	37.30	36.20	67.44	51.37	54.82	56.67	5.87	428.57
Namkum	76.20	53.20	41.00	19.20	73.93	55.28	67.87	31.85	2.24	420.77
Daltonganj	88.60	28.30	37.10	23.90	65.77	43.03	60.93	45.64	4.17	397.44
Chaibasa	102.80	35.20	32.80	1.40	66.90	52.32	71.05	40.51	3.94	395.29
Ramgarh	111.30	38.70	54.40	12.80	41.06	29.98	64.24	38.64	3.40	394.52
Burmu	98.40	58.60	65.00	12.80	31.11	13.50	77.07	36.17	0.08	392.73
Kuru	108.20	52.30	73.10	9.20	38.14	-	75.27	35.32	-	391.53
Jhinkpani	117.70	62.10	45.70	8.20	32.39	14.10	82.60	21.19	0.08	384.06
Chandan Kiyari	130.00	44.60	69.80	6.40	35.29	-	63.39	28.38	-	377.86
Kodama	62.60	15.10	33.80	6.70	44.56	42.92	61.54	50.59	5.95	374.26
Topchanchi	81.80	42.00	66.20	27.80	51.39	-	60.97	37.86	0.15	368.17
Lohardaga	123.30	23.40	34.80	9.30	49.31	36.06	61.63	28.92	0.08	366.80

1	2	3	4	5	6	7	8	9	10	11
Ormanjhi	74.80	38.60	101.60	7.80	24.49	–	81.18	38.09	0.08	366.64
Thethaitançar	132.50	41.40	57.10	1.60	35.81	–	65.69	30.83	–	364.93
Simdega	132.80	22.20	48.70	–	45.58	18.41	63.56	29.83	0.39	361.47
Giridih	57.40	33.60	53.60	14.50	49.02	29.90	56.91	55.20	10.59	360.72
Mandu	91.50	51.30	35.00	16.50	27.07	9.78	75.86	52.09	0.77	359.87
Jaridih	126.00	49.40	54.70	14.60	29.89	–	63.89	13.25	–	351.73
Musabani	114.20	12.20	18.00	4.80	45.10	49.48	71.23	33.43	0.23	348.67
Bano	125.70	43.20	41.80	–	40.46	–	63.39	29.75	–	344.30
Noamundi	93.80	16.20	18.00	1.60	41.84	44.19	79.16	48.95	0.54	344.28
Raidih	156.40	33.30	38.70	–	35.18	–	62.09	10.92	–	336.59
Jagannathpur	104.90	41.20	63.30	3.50	34.36	–	73.34	15.29	–	335.89
Palkot	111.00	34.20	77.70	–	29.78	–	76.26	6.20	0.08	335.22
Murhu	73.40	42.60	16.60	4.20	70.17	–	87.28	40.96	–	335.21
Bundu	80.20	22.70	65.50	–	35.25	23.86	72.15	33.86	–	333.52
Barwadih	100.00	71.00	30.50	11.50	31.09	–	68.24	20.37	–	332.70
Jaldega	124.10	44.20	52.10	1.30	35.45	–	64.51	9.57	–	331.23
Chandil	107.50	53.70	44.40	8.70	28.01	–	74.48	13.40	0.70	330.89
Torpa	89.30	42.20	52.20	–	40.89	–	70.17	32.93	–	327.69
Mandar	118.90	36.40	28.70	7.2	34.69	–	68.35	32.08	–	326.32
Bhandra	114.00	40.10	29.60	–	27.48	–	77.79	36.51	–	325.48
Ratu	74.40	41.30	45.30	25.60	40.96	–	65.89	30.92	0.08	324.45
Chandwa	76.80	48.30	67.20	15.50	23.90	–	70.83	16.32	–	318.85
Bagodar	88.00	20.10	83.50	7.30	26.57	10.30	65.36	12.42	–	313.55
Bhawnathpur	119.40	32.80	58.40	–	23.17	–	72.37	6.98	–	313.12
Chanho	92.70	30.30	28.50	19.70	31.06	–	74.68	35.04	–	311.98
Tamar I	84.80	23.70	59.00	0.80	26.42	–	79.44	37.28	–	311.44
Silli	98.80	23.60	25.80	4.70	42.54	9.67	71.71	33.65	0.15	310.62
Gobindpur(D)	90.10	37.10	41.30	16.40	35.21	–	70.28	17.32	0.93	308.64
Sonahatu	96.60	50.40	18.70	–	30.24	–	75.66	35.51	–	307.11
Kamdara	117.90	34.90	30.70	–	39.41	–	75.77	7.17	–	305.85
Kasmar	119.80	46.30	34.40	–	32.71	–	62.40	9.94	–	305.55
Gola	87.00	40.80	62.60	8.10	27.88	–	68.37	8.16	–	302.91
Gumla	99.70	18.70	42.70	1.80	37.92	16.80	66.40	16.57	0.15	300.74

1	2	3	4	5	6	7	8	9	10	11
Bero	96.00	30.70	17.60	0.90	33.64	-	82.17	38.56	-	299.57
Adityapur	47.60	24.60	6.00	1.60	55.64	46.87	69.98	44.45	2.55	299.29
Nimdih	124.10	42.20	22.50	1.20	23.14	-	73.84	6.44	-	298.42
Nawadih	112.80	43.90	28.10	8.70	22.95	-	62.42	19.44	-	298.31
Basia	109.70	45.70	22.40	-	41.21	-	69.56	9.20	-	297.77
Churchu	79.90	39.80	32.80	4.50	25.94	-	73.78	35.03	-	291.75
Barhi	78.60	38.00	63.60	16.00	22.82	-	62.42	9.75	0.54	291.73
Bishunpur(R)	104.00	59.40	29.60	1.50	21.76	-	64.13	9.03	-	289.42
Barkagaon	81.30	31.20	61.90	10.00	24.12	-	65.17	9.27	-	282.96
Dhurki	88.10	67.70	28.80	-	13.54	-	78.61	3.21	-	279.96
Chakradharpur	69.20	15.10	6.70	-	53.51	25.12	71.97	36.11	2.01	279.72
Dumri(R)	107.90	26.20	26.60	0.90	53.88	-	54.69	8.86	-	279.03
Meral	84.70	30.70	62.30	2.10	19.29	-	74.43	3.90	-	278.12
Patamda	94.20	19.10	48.20	3.80	26.88	-	78.01	6.44	-	276.63
Angara	95.80	22.30	20.60	2.20	21.93	-	76.34	35.83	-	275.00
Bishrampur	78.80	10.10	39.80	33.30	28.65	-	71.78	7.82	0.15	270.40
Tandwa	76.40	30.60	57.10	8.50	19.70	-	70.50	6.71	-	269.51
Tantnagar	79.00	46.40	24.70	-	29.11	-	82.47	5.71	-	267.39
Mahuadanr	97.00	31.20	24.10	1.00	33.10	6.56	61.70	11.03	-	265.69
Kisko	68.70	33.80	25.10	7.90	23.84	-	72.13	33.85	0.08	265.40
Lapung	101.60	36.80	9.70	-	27.16	-	63.67	29.88	-	264.31
Gawan	43.00	50.70	44.40	13.20	26.01	-	69.45	16.48	-	263.24
Chainpur(R)	81.00	24.30	37.50	1.20	50.06	-	57.79	10.77	-	262.62
Kharsawan	49.50	28.20	38.80	7.20	40.61	10.01	71.47	16.14	-	261.93
Garhwa	71.60	12.60	12.40	19.80	35.75	21.21	70.13	16.36	1.47	261.32
Ghatsila	49.90	21.20	7.90	4.80	47.64	28.45	70.61	28.63	0.46	259.59
Tamar II	73.00	16.20	14.60	-	22.02	-	90.71	42.57	-	259.10
Ichagarh	97.40	31.20	17.20	-	30.95	-	76.06	6.13	-	258.94
Keredari	76.90	32.10	38.60	9.00	19.52	-	66.70	15.55	-	258.37
Manjhari	90.70	39.40	23.60	-	24.01	-	69.80	6.24	-	253.75
Rania	92.80	15.10	16.90	-	35.70	-	63.39	29.75	-	253.64
Manoharpur	84.20	16.10	17.60	0.60	33.08	11.00	66.18	24.15	-	252.91

1	2	3	4	5	6	7	8	9	10	11
Sisai	84.00	40.70	21.70	-	27.81	-	70.00	7.73	-	251.94
Gumia	48.90	13.70	10.10	-	30.20	45.63	65.01	35.88	2.24	251.66
Hussainabad	63.20	13.10	32.40	19.40	33.26	9.26	63.63	16.03	0.93	251.21
Majhgaon	92.00	28.30	12.70	3.40	28.01	-	77.95	8.26	-	250.62
Bishungarh(H)	66.80	25.10	47.50	6.60	17.70	-	78.92	6.61	0.39	249.62
Hariharganj	56.30	33.30	12.40	38.50	27.83	-	65.96	12.63	0.93	247.85
Khunti	47.50	19.60	4.90	2.70	35.45	19.27	79.31	37.22	0.08	246.03
Bhandaria	88.60	34.60	15.40	-	23.75	-	75.20	7.22	-	244.77
Kumardungi	88.70	30.20	18.00	6.00	21.71	-	70.88	8.93	-	244.42
Potka	73.80	36.10	14.00	1.40	32.73	-	72.13	13.76	-	243.92
Manika	87.20	33.10	10.90	1.80	20.78	-	80.45	6.13	-	240.36
Verno	66.70	28.80	48.30	-	22.21	-	67.12	5.99	-	239.12
Karra	51.50	14.50	45.60	-	28.57	-	67.16	31.52	-	238.85
Garu	67.20	44.30	16.50	-	23.47	-	75.62	10.71	-	237.80
Katkamsandi	72.10	20.10	24.30	17.10	25.51	-	64.97	12.69	0.15	236.92
Senha	72.30	14.20	14.20	1.90	25.71	-	72.74	34.14	-	235.19
Ghaghra	75.50	25.20	35.10	-	22.32	-	71.49	5.44	-	235.05
Tisri	49.40	20.00	35.40	10.60	27.03	-	66.42	24.96	0.62	234.43
Lesliegan]	55.00	11.20	48.60	10.40	30.87	-	71.38	6.36	0.15	233.96
Patan	68.80	24.10	22.50	11.30	27.40	-	71.60	6.82	-	232.52
Satgawan	58.80	34.60	10.90	19.60	30.82	-	69.43	8.00	-	232.15
Dumri (H)	60.50	11.50	44.80	12.30	23.49	-	62.99	13.21	0.46	229.25
Ranka	80.60	14.70	27.00	-	19.29	-	78.63	5.54	0.23	225.99
Dhalbhumgarh	51.80	43.90	6.10	2.20	29.15	-	76.30	15.68	-	225.13
Hunterganj	49.10	19.10	32.50	23.90	21.15	-	71.16	8.20	-	225.11
Bahragora	61.80	15.50	19.10	1.00	43.34	-	73.20	10.57	-	223.52
Ichak	64.00	25.10	23.10	12.70	27.11	-	60.22	10.57	-	222.98
Kuchai	72.40	35.50	15.40	-	19.15	-	71.21	9.04	-	222.70
Balumath	80.50	18.10	24.30	0.60	17.07	-	75.88	5.75	-	222.20
Khuntpani	71.10	13.60	3.40	1.80	23.82	-	100.00	7.51	-	221.23
Panki	62.10	23.10	32.00	0.60	25.34	-	72.13	5.63	-	220.90
Majhiaon	61.80	20.20	27.00	0.70	30.06	-	71.12	6.95	-	217.83

1	2	3	4	5	6	7	8	9	10	11
Chainpur (P)	67.30	18.60	18.70	4.30	24.10	-	74.19	8.83	0.15	216.17
Latehar	61.70	12.60	9.70	4.50	28.13	17.64	67.52	12.16	1.08	215.03
Untari	57.90	20.20	22.00	8.80	25.75	-	71.25	8.51	-	214.41
Chakulia	48.80	13.60	11.60	0.40	38.35	9.09	79.05	12.88	0.46	214.23
Dumaria	77.20	16.60	4.10	-	17.48	-	81.73	10.74	-	207.85
Barkatha	63.20	35.10	19.90	2.60	15.31	-	60.11	6.10	-	202.32
Jainagar	48.70	15.10	33.80	6.70	25.94	-	57.37	13.75	0.39	201.75
Seraikela	43.30	10.50	8.40	1.70	40.93	13.45	71.14	23.26	0.23	199.46
Sonua	53.00	12.10	13.10	5.20	29.31	-	72.02	14.52	-	199.15
Bengabad	50.90	11.60	28.10	6.90	23.54	-	68.99	8.26	-	198.29
Gobindpur(S)	53.60	22.60	7.50	-	28.05	-	81.04	5.30	0.08	198.17
Tundi	49.00	29.10	19.20	-	24.45	-	65.74	7.66	-	195.15
Chatra	30.60	13.60	4.50	0.80	30.91	24.05	72.35	13.33	0.23	190.37
Jamua	47.70	18.00	18.30	6.00	28.50	-	61.48	8.50	-	188.48
Chauparan	48.50	20.10	18.50	14.80	19.24	-	57.65	8.46	0.46	187.71
Birni	59.70	21.00	14.20	3.60	21.99	-	60.03	5.67	0.46	186.65
Goilkela	49.70	15.50	4.50	0.60	22.19	-	84.45	7.24	0.08	184.26
Markacho	48.10	25.70	19.10	6.60	18.44	-	58.69	7.54	-	184.17
Tonto	64.20	12.10	4.50	-	16.51	-	74.85	6.12	-	178.28
Chhatarpur	48.60	10.10	28.80	0.50	18.00	-	67.25	4.68	-	177.93
Pirtanr	41.80	23.70	13.90	0.50	19.07	-	71.47	7.46	-	177.90
Simaria	43.80	10.50	24.00	4.20	15.99	-	71.95	4.53	-	174.97
Itkhori	38.70	9.10	33.90	2.60	21.15	-	63.69	5.77	-	174.91
Manatu	44.80	12.10	13.90	-	25.19	-	72.76	5.03	-	173.78
Dhanwar	40.80	11.10	23.10	2.20	25.77	-	58.93	8.67	0.23	170.80
Pratappur	38.70	18.10	12.10	0.40	17.94	-	75.55	7.06	-	169.85
Deori	39.60	13.10	20.00	2.70	22.82	-	62.55	4.57	-	165.34
Gande	46.40	13.60	4.50	2.30	19.50	-	69.43	6.40	-	162.13
Bangaon	40.80	15.60	4.50	1.20	25.58	-	62.71	9.28	-	159.69

APPENDIX - II

Chota Nagpur : Weighted Scores for the Demographic, Social and Economic Attributes to Development for Urban Centres, 1971

Urban Centres	Literacy	Workers	Nonagricultural Workers	Industries	Total
1	2	3	4	5	6
Jamshedpur	95.6	51.3	99.0	100.0	345.9
Giridih	84.3	42.5	91.7	100.0	318.5
Dhanbad	95.9	56.9	94.7	44.9	292.1
Ranchi	95.7	46.1	92.6	46.9	281.3
B.S.City	59.8	79.6	78.3	46.9	264.6
Namkum	92.5	81.2	80.6	6.1	259.8
Jagannathnagar	90.3	55.0	93.8	14.3	253.4
Chandrapura	90.6	61.2	97.5	2.0	251.3
Sindri	84.5	51.8	90.0	22.4	248.7
Sini	90.6	53.9	96.1	2.0	242.6
Adityapur	73.5	56.5	70.0	40.8	240.8
Doranda	100.00	43.0	95.7	2.0	240.7
Jharia	79.4	54.9	97.8	8.2	240.3
Angarpathar	39.7	100.0	99.8	-	239.5
Kumardhubi	76.3	57.9	99.1	6.1	239.4
Maithon	91.7	50.9	94.1	2.0	238.7
Jhumri Tilaiya	61.6	51.0	78.8	44.9	236.3
Daltonganj	93.4	44.4	91.5	6.1	235.4
Kiriburu	68.4	67.4	99.0	-	234.8
Jugsalai	86.6	49.0	98.3	-	233.9
Chakradharpur	91.5	47.7	92.5	2.0	233.7
Pathardih	56.0	65.6	98.3	10.2	230.1
Jamadoba	56.0	69.5	99.8	4.1	229.4
Kanke	97.2	40.8	90.5	-	228.5
Hazaribagh	86.8	39.5	87.8	14.3	228.4
Chaibasa	91.7	49.2	87.4	-	228.3
Katras	81.7	51.5	94.5	-	227.7
Kerkend	50.2	76.9	98.9	-	226.0
Tisra	42.5	83.4	99.3	-	225.2
Patratu	75.4	64.8	83.6	6.1	223.8
Gomoh	88.5	48.0	84.9	2.0	223.4
Bera	42.9	86.2	94.1	-	223.2
Loyabad	50.0	74.1	98.9	-	223.0
Jorapokhar	58.7	65.6	98.6	-	222.9
Chaitudih	49.4	76.4	97.0	-	222.8
Bhagatdih	50.2	72.9	99.2	-	222.3
Chirkunda	67.6	49.4	97.0	8.2	222.2
Barughutu	60.8	65.1	96.3	-	222.2

1	2	3	4	5	6
Bokaro	83.4	48.0	89.3	-	220.7
Sijua	54.0	63.5	96.7	6.1	220.3
Saunda	53.7	70.1	96.0	-	219.8
Barajamda	58.1	68.5	90.3	-	216.9
Noamundi	66.9	60.8	87.5	-	215.2
Bhowrah	52.2	63.6	96.9	2.0	214.7
Muri	78.9	45.6	86.5	2.0	213.0
Chakulia	79.0	52.8	76.8	4.1	212.7
Bagbera	64.9	52.6	94.7	-	212.2
Ghatsila	77.8	48.1	82.8	2.0	210.7
Jadugora	64.7	69.3	74.7	2.0	210.7
Kenduadih	43.6	74.3	90.0	-	207.9
Bhuli	61.4	57.7	88.3	-	207.4
Jaridih Bazar	56.2	56.1	95.0	-	207.3
Panchet	76.1	50.8	79.6	-	206.5
Barkakana	72.1	48.5	83.0	2.0	205.6
Ramgarh	68.1	56.1	78.0	2.0	204.2
Gua	52.5	51.3	100.0	-	203.8
Kalimati	59.3	52.6	91.1	-	203.0
Musabani	60.2	53.8	87.9	-	201.9
Gumla	87.5	41.5	72.1	-	201.1
Sirka	43.2	63.1	94.3	-	200.6
Bermo	51.3	47.6	97.0	4.1	200.0
Tenudam	46.9	63.9	82.4	4.1	197.3
Lohardaga	73.7	41.7	81.5	-	196.9
Seraikela	90.3	47.6	59.0	-	196.9
Kargali	37.4	61.2	98.1	-	196.7
Chas	61.1	54.5	73.9	2.0	191.5
Dumarkunda	41.1	61.9	85.7	-	188.7
Manoharpur	64.0	53.8	70.6	-	188.4
Gumia	55.3	51.3	75.4	6.1	188.1
Khelari	48.1	55.9	79.7	2.0	185.7
Khunti	80.5	45.5	57.0	-	183.0
Garhwa	61.4	50.0	66.6	4.1	182.1
Kodarma	64.4	45.7	59.4	10.2	179.7
Kharsawan	75.8	46.7	51.4	-	173.9
Jhinkpani	57.0	63.3	51.1	2.0	173.4
Simdega	76.1	45.6	48.1	-	169.7
Dugda	55.5	51.5	60.7	2.0	169.7
Chatra	58.4	45.6	55.2	-	159.2
Bundu	58.2	54.6	46.2	-	159.0
Domchanch	51.4	43.2	54.2	4.1	152.9
Latehar	58.4	58.7	35.0	-	152.1
Netarhat	60.0	54.0	35.5	-	149.5
Saram	38.9	44.3	59.4	-	142.6
Hussainabad	43.6	41.7	48.2	2.0	135.0
Barki Sariya	49.7	50.1	31.0	-	130.8

Index